FROM THE DEBT CRISIS TO SUSTAINABLE DEVELOPMENT

Also by Gianni Vaggi

THE ECONOMICS OF FRANÇOIS QUESNAY

From the Debt Crisis to Sustainable Development

Changing Perspectives on North-South Relations

Edited by

Gianni Vaggi

Associate Professor of the History of Economic Thought
University of Pavia, Italy

St. Martin's Press

First published in Great Britain 1993 by
THE MACMILLAN PRESS LTD
Houndmills, Basingstoke, Hampshire RG21 2XS
and London
Companies and representatives
throughout the world

A catalogue record for this book is available
from the British Library.

ISBN 0-333-56038-8

Printed in Great Britain by
Antony Rowe Ltd, Chippenham, Wiltshire

First published in the United States of America 1993 by
Scholarly and Reference Division,
ST. MARTIN'S PRESS, INC.,
175 Fifth Avenue,
New York, N.Y. 10010

ISBN 0-312-08542-7

Library of Congress Cataloging-in-Publication Data
From the debt crisis to sustainable development: changing perspectives on north–south relations/edited by Gianni Vaggi.
p. c.m.
Includes index.
ISBN 0-312-08542-7
1. Debts, External—Developing countries. 2. Economic development. 3. International economic relations. I. Vaggi, Gianni.
HJ8899.F76 1993
336.3'435'091724—dc20 92-10978
CIP

To Franca

Contents

List of Tables

List of Figures

Preface

In March 1990, scholars from different parts of the world met at the University of Pavia for a conference entitled 'Beyond the Affluent Society: North–South Relationships, Development Policies and the Role of International Organizations'. This book is not simply the proceedings of this conference as, while some papers were presented at the conference, other have been thoroughly revised and new ones have been added. The conference stimulated interests, friendship and research work by the scholars involved and this book grew out of these interactions.

I would like to thank the scholars who were at the conference but who could not contribute to the book owing to their many commitments: Professor Mario Draghi, Director General of the Italian Treasury Ministry, formerly Executive Director of the World Bank; Professor Sebastiano Fadda of the University of Sassari; Mr Roger Lawrence, Director and Co-ordinator of Resources for Development Programmes at UNCTAD, Geneva; Professor Alberto Majocchi, of the University of Pavia; Professor Olagoke Olabisi, of King Fahd University and formerly Managing Director of UNILAG CONSULT at Lagos University.

The conference was organized with the financial support of the Administrative Council and of the Institute for University Studies (ISU) of the University of Pavia and I am deeply grateful to these two institutions. I am particularly grateful to the Vice-Chancellor of the University of Pavia, Professor Roberto Schmid, both for his encouragement and for having opened the conference.

Without the help of Marta Aloi and Alessandro Fabbri the conference would not have taken place. It was their idea to use the financial grant assigned by the university to the student group they represented, the *Comitato per il Diritto allo Studio*, to organize the conference. Moreover they provided invaluable help to solve all the organizational problems.

Some of the authors are at present involved in a joint research project on development economics for the Italian Ministry of the University and of Scientific Research (MURST). Financial support from the above Ministry and from the Consiglio Nazionale delle Ricerche is also gratefully acknowledged.

I would like to remember Paolo Beonio Brocchieri, former Director of the Cesare Bonacossa Centre for the Study of Non-European Peoples of the University of Pavia, who died prematurely in April 1991. This book owes a lot to his example as a scholar and as a man.

The book springs from a students' initiative and among the contributors there are some young researchers, a sure indication that social and economic relationships may be greatly improved in 'our global village'.

GIANNI VAGGI

Notes on the Contributors

Giorgio Barba Navaretti is a research student at the Centro Studi Luca d'Agliano, Turin, and St. Antony's College, Oxford.

Carlo Bernini Carri is Associate Professor of Agriculture and Economic Development at the University of Pavia.

Amit Bhaduri is Professor of Economics at the Indian Institute of Management, Calcutta.

Youssef Boutros-Ghali is Associate Professor of Economics at the University of Cairo and Economic Adviser to the Prime Minister of Egypt.

Giovanni Andrea Cornia is Director of the Economic and Social Policy Research Programme for UNICEF–ICDC, Florence.

Francesco Daveri is a research assistant at the University of Brescia.

Giovanni Goria was formerly Prime Minister of Italy and President of the Political Committee of the European Parliament.

Peter M. Keller is Assistant Director of the International Monetary Fund, Paris.

Luigi Marcuccio is a research student at Bocconi University, Milan.

Marco Missaglia is a research student at the University of Pavia.

Guido Montani is Professor of Economic Development at the University of Pavia and Director of the Altiero Spinelli Institute of Federalist Studies.

Massimo Ricottilli is Associate Professor of Economic Development at the University of Bologna.

Jaime Ros is Professor of Economics at the University of Notre Dame, USA.

Gianni Vaggi is Associate Professor of History of Economic Thought, University of Pavia.

Introduction

Gianni Vaggi

1 THE ISSUES

The debt crisis and the problem of long-term development epitomize much of this story and of the problems which have characterized North–South relationships during the last 15 years. The 1980s were characterized by the emergence of a debt and growth crisis whose dimensions were largely unprecedented, owing both to the size of the debt stock and to the number of countries involved, mainly but not entirely in Latin America. The crisis is not yet over and it has already lasted far too long. Was this problem the result of sovereign debt and of the repayment difficulties which have characterized the international financial markets since 1982? Luckily there are also reasons for optimism; in some developing countries, mainly in East Asia, the economic conditions now look much better than they were a few years ago. How was it possible, as in the case of some Asian countries, to avoid the debt trap? These are some of the questions on which the book seeks to throw some light.

However, to analyse the debt problem in isolation would be of little interest in itself and indeed could lead to false conclusions. Although the debt crisis has clearly marked the past decade, the central issue is still that of economic and humane development for that 85 per cent of world population who live in what are still classified as low- and middle-income countries. The events of the 1980s, and the debt crisis in particular, must be interpreted within the context of what is a likely or possible development pattern for the future. Much has been said and written during the last ten years about the macroeconomic stabilization for 'ill' economies. Much too often the historical and analytical relationships between short-term policies and long-term growth possibilities have not been clearly specified. The same medicine has been used for quite different patients and the responsiveness to the treatment has been assumed to be fairly standardized. All this calls for a reflection on economic theory, as well as on the economic policy of development.

Debts and development may thus be regarded as the two poles of a contraposition which is certainly one of the main economic events of the latter part of the twentieth century and can be used as a key to understand some of the major problems which today face developing countries as well as development economics. Therefore it is not only a contraposition between pessimistic and optimistic experiences, between the 'bad' part of the story, debt, and the 'good' one, economic development; development theory too has a lot to learn from these experiences.

Some of the historical and theoretical features of the two 'poles' are worth remembering:

(a) From 1982 to 1989, the Organization for Economic Co-operation and Development (OECD) and East Asia experienced a period of economic growth, while gross domestic product (GDP) per capita was declining in two continents, Latin America and Africa, and in the Middle East, a phenomenon which affected 1.3 billion people.
(b) Financial instability in many third-world countries was accompanied by major imbalances in the real economy, but the relationships between the two aspects are not always clear.
(c) International agencies such as the World Bank and the International Monetary Fund (IMF) have recommended and imposed short-term adjustment policies of macroeconomic stabilization, but the practical results of these policies have not really been satisfactory. Furthermore the practical and theoretical relationships between short-term stabilization and long-term growth are not completely clear.
(d) A highly fashionable contraposition is that between the countries whose economy is 'outward'-oriented and those countries which implement 'inward'-oriented growth policies.
(e) Unsound domestic policies, fiscal and monetary, are often opposed to external macroeconomic shocks as the major cause of slow economic growth.
(f) The most crucial and perhaps most dramatic problem is that of whether or not the pace of economic liberalization is synchronized with that of political liberalization and democracy.

2 THE BOOK

The book does not try to answer all the above issues completely, but it presents a new perspective for some of them, particularly as it focuses on the analytical and historical relationships between short-term policies and long-term development. Too often priority has *de facto* been given to short-term adjustment, which has been regarded as a necessary and sufficient condition to achieve sustainable development. Doubts are also now beginning to emerge timidly among official institutions.

We have returned to the point where the problem of long-term development must be faced again; or rather we should investigate the causes of the wealth of nations in today's interdependent world. However, long-term sustainable development is not an illusion and must not be analysed *per se*, as if it were a self-contained shell. Development is the top priority, and it should also include some more accurate definition of what we mean by it, but the 1980s have shown how deeply interlinked are all economies, and how strong the influence of financial instruments and macroeconomic policies can be on long-term growth.

The message is clear: short-term measures and macroeconomic policies are not the universal panacea, but equally cannot be ignored and must be part of a long-term development strategy, which can only be effective if it includes new economic relationships between rich and poor countries.

The book is also addressed to a non-specialist audience; thus all the contributors have tried to provide critical information, by facing directly the debatable and open issues which are now on the agenda of North–South relationships. Four major topics characterize the four parts of the book: intersectoral development theories; the debt crisis; structural adjustment policies; and the link between economic development and democracy and a new economic order.

In Part I Bhaduri reminds us of the different opinions concerning the relationships between more and less productive sectors and trade orientation in development theory, a theme which is also taken up by Ricottilli, who emphasizes the role of technical progress and of vertical integration for the success of an outward-oriented strategy. The role of agriculture in the process of development is analysed by Bernini Carri, while Marcuccio sheds some doubts on the traditional view according to which agriculture must necessarily give ground to industrial activities during economic growth.

Part II opens with a brief story of the debt crisis of the 1980s and of the main solutions proposed, which should help the reader who is not familiar with debt 'jargon'. Ros examines the domestic and international reasons for the disappointing growth performance of many less developed countries (LDCs) in the 1980s. Chapter 7 analyses some 'theories' of debt sustainability and hints at the possibility of avoiding repayment crises in the future.

In Part III Keller examines the role of the two Bretton Woods institutions in creating an enabling environment for economic growth, while Cornia is sceptical about the consistency of structural adjustment policies for long-term development and for the welfare of the population in Africa. The theoretical background of specific macroeconomic adjustment policies is examined by Daveri and Missaglia, while Barba Navaretti investigates the possibilities of development offered by foreign investement.

Part IV reminds us that development and welfare are not purely technical problems, but are deeply influenced by the present international political setting. Boutros-Ghali shows that it will be difficult to establish a constructive North–South dialogue unless the debt problem is removed. For Goria the elimination of trade protectionism by the industrialized countries against southern products is one of the cornerstones of a new international economic order. Montani analyses the impact of the political changes in Eastern Europe on multipolar relationships and on the growth persepectives of the LDCs. The concluding chapter summarizes some of the conditions which should be satisfied in order for there to be some hope that the debt crisis is now an event of the past and that the way is open for development in the future.

Part I

Industry versus Agriculture: The Economic Theory of Sectors and Development

1 Orthodox Development Theories and their Application to Less Developed Countries

Amit Bhaduri

The ultimate concern of economic development is the improvement of the quality of life. Increasing per capita income or output is merely a poor quantitative proxy for this process. Nevertheless without substantial increases in per capita income almost no progress can be made in a poor developing country towards improving the quality of life.

Per capita output or income can be statistically decomposed into three basic components (see Appendix): (1) the *participation ratio*, that is, the ratio of active to total population; (2) the *occupational structure*, that is, the distribution of the active labour force by the major segments of the economy, which is typically divided into three sectors: primary or agricultural sector, secondary or industrial sector and tertiary or the trade and service sector; and (3) output per worker, that is, *labour productivity* in individual sectors. It needs to be emphasized that the decomposition of per capita output into these three components is no more than an accounting identity, leaving no scope for disagreement about these three possible sources of economic growth from the supply side.

These three components of growth and their interaction provide a framework for discussing the performance of a less developed economy. In so far as the participation ratio is concerned there are important social as well as economic barriers which hinder higher participation and manifest themselves as open and disguised unemployment. Probably the most important economic problem here is the nature of property or ownership rights in land in the agricultural sector. A skewed pattern of land ownership would typically present a picture where, at one end of the spectrum, there are households with much more land than they can cultivate intensively with existing technology. At the other end of the spectrum there are households who are nearly or completely landless and have no obvious way of using effectively even their household labour.

For reasons which are beyond the scope of the present discussion, the land-lease and the rural labour market function inadequately. The result is the often discussed phenomenon of under-employment or disguised unemployment in the agricultural sector. However, in most instances economic factors alone do not explain fully the low participation ratio. Social factors discouraging the participation of women in the workforce in certain cultures, social barriers of caste, hierarchical division between manual and mental work and so on can also be important explanatory variables. Therefore, the first question which we need to ask is how the proportion of economically active population can be increased to raise per capita income. This is almost tantamount to asking what methods can achieve a higher employment rate in the economy.

Although it is not very fashionable these days to point to the achievements of the centrally planned economies, dispassionate economic analysis requires that we learn from their historical experiences. A somewhat common experience of China and Vietnam in Asia, of Poland and Hungary in East Europe and of Cuba in Latin America is that, during the first phase of their developmental process after the revolution, the main source of increasing output came from an almost spectacular increase in the participation ratio. This is often described as the 'extensive growth phase' where previously unemployed labour is set to work for construction, land improvement and irrigation through various mechanisms fashioned by agricultural communes and co-operatives. The essence of this extensive growth strategy is to organize employment for the previously unemployed or under-employed through a widespread consumption rationing scheme which enforces redistribution from the already employed to the previously unemployed (Kahn, 1972). Typically in this phase, the previously unemployed population found employment in construction and land development work, for example the irrigation teams in the agricultural communes and co-operatives. Also, highly labour intensive techniques with rudimentary capital equipment were chosen in those lines of activity. The most interesting feature of the process of extensive growth was its ability to combine economic 'efficiency' with 'equity' to a very considerable extent. It was efficient because it used a labour force which would have otherwise remained grossly under-utilized. It also had a strong element of social equity in so far as it redistributed consumption in favour of a section of the population which would otherwise have been marginalized from the market process because they had no regular income. It needs to be emphasized that, in the under-developed market economies, such a strategy of extensive growth becomes very difficult to pursue. The main economic reason is that the capital gains, say, from land improvement, accrue to the private property holders in land. And without the ability of the state to tax them and capture a large portion of the capital gains (it amounts to the inability of the state to redistribute consumption systematically in favour of the previously unemployed) the process of extensive growth becomes unsustainable over time.

However, the phase of extensive growth cannot last indefinitely. The subsequent economic failure of many of the centrally planned socialist economies also arose largely on this account. In the process of distributing income from the already employed to the unemployed, difficult problems of maintaining economic incentives appeared. Attempts to solve this problem bureaucratically, without corresponding changes in the organization of production, ran into increasing difficulties over time. This tended to reduce the flexibility of the system and led to various rigidities from which these economies could not escape when they needed to change their strategy from extensive to intensive growth.

The second main source of increase in per capita income comes from what we call intersectoral labour transfer. If we look at the historical experience of capitalism during the nineteenth century to about the first two decades of this century, it is unmistakable that the main structural transformation was the transfer of labour from agriculture to industry and (later) to services. It might be mentioned here that econometric work based only on one sector (Solow, 1970) could not capture this phenomenon of intersectoral labour transfer. Consequently, it attributed much of the growth in output from changing occupational structure to a statistically residual category, incorrectly specified as 'technical progress'. The historical process of intersectoral transfer of labour productivity is substantially higher in industry than in agriculture. Even today, on a rough estimate, industry is twice as productive as agriculture when measured in terms of output per worker in the developed market economies; in the developing countries this can be as high as eight times (see Appendix). The difference in labour productivity between the developed and the developing countries is the highest in agriculture – about 15 to 22 times; in contrast the difference is only four to six times in industry. The reason for this is not hard to find. Despite considerable differences in the level of technology, in industry, fundamentally comparable methods of production are often used. However, the gap between traditional agriculture, where, apart from severe under-employment, the small producer tries to cultivate a tiny plot of land in a primitive way with virtually no capital, and cultivation by advanced agricultural technology is simply overwhelming. Consequently, transfer of labour from extremely low productivity agriculture to high productivity industry in a typical developing economy means considerable increase in overall labour productivity. It needs to be emphasized that in almost all developing countries this underlies the basic political compulsion to industrialize. The compelling logic for industrialization comes from the fact that it is one of the most powerful ways to achieve higher overall labour productivity through continuing change in the occupational structure.

However, enough experience has been accumulated to warn us against the attempts to industrialize at an artificially fast pace. There are two central reasons for this. First, without adequate performance by agriculture, enough marketed surplus will not be available to support the growth of industry. This is also why the industrial revolution was preceded by the agrarian revolution (Jones, 1974). Second, the agricultural and the industrial sector are also linked through demand for one another's product, especially if international trade is not so important. In a closed, predominantly agrarian economy, agriculture not only provides marketed surplus to industry, but it also must serve as the most important segment of the home market for industrial goods. An artificially rapid pace of industrialization could therefore, encounter the Keynesian problem of inadequate effective demand without a sufficiently prosperous agriculture. In short, agriculture can be a barrier to industrialization either from the supply side, in terms of insufficient supply of marketed surplus or from the demand side, by failing to provide a large enough home market for industrial goods.

The cost of artificially fast industrialization can also be very high in terms of the violence it may cause to the environment in a poor country which does not have either the means or the international support for protecting the environment. However, the issue is seldom black and white. As we have already argued, a fairly rapid pace of industrialization seems to be essential in most developing countries for increasing labour productivity through intersectoral labour transfer. At the same time the limit to industrialization comes not only from the lack of agricultural growth, but also in terms of the cost it imposes on the environment. The former problem may seem less acute in an open economy provided it has access to a large and steady flow of external finance. But this is a matter to which we shall turn to later.

The third source of increase in per capita output is sectoral labour productivity. This depends on technology as well as on the organization of production, incentive systems and training of the labour forces. There is a growing literature on the factors determining labour productivity which is concerned with the question of incentive and effort, with or without direct supervision (e.g. Efficiency Wage theories and transaction cost literature). Nevertheless, for a poor country one must reckon with at least two additional problems of growth in industrial labour productivity, namely insufficiency of modern capital equipment and inadequate infrastructure, including training facilities.

In the light of what has been said above, one begins to see why the market-oriented development perspective offered by the IMF and the World Bank tends to have serious problems when applied uniformly to most developing countries. First, as has already been mentioned, in the presence of substantially under-utilized labour, an extensive growth strategy may still form an essential element in the early phase of the development process. However, since such a strategy of extensive growth is not easily compatible with the market mechanism, there is inadequate discussion and debate about this problem. Nevertheless, it is hard to see how unutilized manpower on a massive scale can be brought into use without some emphasis on extensive growth. Indeed, there is something strange about so much attention being paid to 'efficient allocation of resources' and the price mechanism while ignoring the blatant inefficiency of massive under-employment. Second, the conventional wisdom behind the IMF–World Bank type of strategy tends to undermine the role of effective demand linked to the home market. The agricultural sector in many developing countries, as we have already indicated, performs the dual role of supplying marketed surplus and, providing a home market for industrial goods. Therefore, without sufficient prosperity and dynamism of the agricultural sector, it is extremely unlikely that industrialization will be sustainable at a satisfactory pace in a closed economy. At first sight it might appear that a higher price for the agricultural sector and a movement in the terms of trade in favour of agriculture would serve both purposes. On the one hand, a higher price of agricultural goods will lead to an expanding home market in rural areas for industrial products. On the other, a higher price of agricultural goods will provide an incentive to the producers for increasing agricultural output. However, one has to be more cautious because neither of these arguments is fully secure. A considerable amount of evidence has been marshalled (for example Schäfer, 1987) to show that the price incentive effect in the agricultural sector is rather ambiguous for several reasons. Following a study of 202 districts in seven Indian states, Schäfer came to the following conclusions:

(a) The impact of infrastructural variables (extent of irrigation, length of roads, regulated markets and so on) on productivity of labour, cultivated area and total production is considerable and statistically significant.
(b) There was no correlation between real agricultural prices and yields (output per hectare).
(c) There was no unambiguous relationship between prices and *total* agricultural production.

At the same time there are two relatively complex reasons why an expansion of the home market for industrial products through higher agricultural prices may not be achieved. First, higher food prices would mean a reduction in demand for industrial products by the industrial workers which must be counterposed against higher farm income (for example Taylor, 1983). Second, a very large number of marginal to landless farmers may be net buyers of food grains in the market. An increase in food price would reduce their demand for industrial goods. The higher food price may also have a serious impact on rural poverty (for example Ghosh, 1989) because the poorest section of the rural population is precisely most vulnerable to higher food prices. The IMF–World Bank type of stabilization policies which often recommends higher agricultural price along with a reduction in food subsidy by the government can turn out to have quite unintended macroeconomic effects. The poorest, most vulnerable section of the rural population may reach such a level of distress as to be pushed out of agriculture with rising food prices. This could result in heavy pressure on urban infrastructure and a self-defeating vicious circle where most of the resources for industrialization are sucked into a black hole for maintaining minimal urban facilities with rising migration into the big cities.

In orthodox development theory, there is also a tendency to underplay the role of the home market in industrialization by suggesting an outward looking strategy of export promotion. It is often implicitly assumed that an adequate access to the international market would more than compensate for sluggish expansion of the domestic market. In the case of many developing countries such an assumption is likely to be flawed. The most important point here is the time required for adjustment to compete successfully in the international market. Economic theory describes it as a problem of the traverse (Hicks, 1973). In this context, a traverse is from an inward-looking economy with inefficient or non-existent industrial structure to an internationally competitive industrial structure. Such a traverse takes a long time. Since 'opening' the economy to international competitiveness also means partly replacing its earlier production structure with superior international competitors, this will almost invariably lead to industrial decline in some sectors. This will create serious problems of demand management during the traverse. A more efficient industrial structure may become virtually impossible to achieve without a steady international inflow of capital over a sustained period of time, perhaps of the order of at least two decades. The very successful export promoters in recent years, such as South Korea, Taiwan, Hong Kong, Singapore (even Japan at an earlier stage) had the common advantage of having access to a sustained inflow of international capital, probably for geopolitical reasons. It would be unwise to assume that many of today's developing countries would be equally fortunate. This does not by any means minimize the spectacularly successful efforts made by these countries in using foreign assistance effectively. But there is need to point out that they had access to foreign capital at a level and over a period of time which most developing countries will not have.

To return to the central point of this chapter, one of the biggest problems of market-oriented development strategies is an error of omission rather than of commission. They overlook the importance of 'extensive growth' strategy which can lead to a rapid expansion in employment through labour intensive development of infrastructure, especially in agriculture. In turn, this expansion in employment can have an impact on extreme poverty by providing income to the poorest and by improving irrigation and drainage facilities on land to strengthen the livelihood of the marginal population in agriculture. Since this is also the most vulnerable section of the population which would migrate to the cities in times of economic distress, the strengthening of its economic position seems an essential element in the development strategy of agrarian economies. It is not by accident that two of the most original social thinkers of Asia in this century – Gandhi and Mao – came to very similar conclusions on this point, starting from polar opposites of the political spectrum. They both emphasized the need to take industry to rural areas and thereby strengthen the livelihood of the poorer section of the rural population. Without some strategy for expanding non-farm income in the rural areas many of today's developing countries may find industrialization along conventional lines an impossible task. Without economic initiative by the state based on a strategy of extensive growth, this seems difficult to achieve and the simple-minded market 'solutions' provide no credible alternative in some of the poorest, populous economies.

APPENDIX

Let, N = total population and L = active population. If X = total output (GDP), then by definition per capita income,

$$Y \equiv X/N \equiv (X/L)(L/N) \tag{A.1}$$

where, $(L/N) = r$ = participation ratio.
Further,

$$\begin{aligned}(X/L) &\equiv (X_a/L_a)(L_a/L) + (X_i/L_i)(L_i/L) + (X_s/L_s)(L_s/L)\\ &\equiv x_a w_a + x_i w_i + x_s w_s\end{aligned} \tag{A.2}$$

where, subscripts a, i and s stand for agriculture, industry and services respectively and, w_j $(j = a, i, s)$ are the statistical weights of labour force engaged in a sector. Hence, $w_a + w_i + w_s = 1$. Combining (A.1) and (A.2), we obtain

$$y = r \sum x_j w_j, \qquad j = a, i, s \tag{A.3}$$

and, x_j = sectoral labour activity.

Since data are relatively easily available for composition of GDP by sectors and by occupational distribution for developed and developing countries, the sectoral pattern of labour productivities mentioned in the text can be easily calculated from the formula,

$$(X_a/X)(L/L_a) = x_a/x$$

where x = overall labour productivity (X/L).

The difference in overall labour productivity between the developed and the developing countries is taken as 15:1 (the *World Development Report*, 1988, finds GDP per capita difference between developed and developing countries to be 21:1 and as high as 48:1 when only the 'low-income developing countries' are considered).

The figures mentioned in the text are computed according to the procedure indicated above. They are illustrative figures relating to the year 1980.

REFERENCES

GHOSH, A. K. (1989) 'Rural poverty and relative prices in India', *Cambridge Journal of Economics*, vol. 13, pp. 307–31.

HICKS, J.R. (1973) *Capital and Time*, Oxford: Clarendon Press.

JONES, E. L. (1974) *Agriculture and the Industrial Revolution*, Oxford: Basil Blackwell.

KAHN, R. (1972) 'The challenge of development', in *Selected Essays in Employment and Growth*, Cambridge: Cambridge University Press.

SCHÄFER, HANS-BERND (1987) 'Farm prices and agricultural production in developing countries', *Intereconomics*, May/June, pp. 129–36.

SOLOW, R. M. (1970) *Growth Theory: An Exposition*, Oxford: Oxford University Press, chs 1–3.

TAYLOR, L. (1983) *Structuralist Macroeconomics*, New York: Basic Books, ch. 3.

WORLD BANK (1980–9) *World Development Report*, Washington DC (various issues).

2 Perspectives on Development

Massimo Ricottilli

1 THE SETTING

The focus of economic theory often shifts, which is quite understandable, given the problems which beset the world economy. This is a fact which holds true even more so for development economics. This field of theory has lately received renewed attention after undergoing a period of relative neglect. As is widely known, the failure of international trade to sustain demand after the great crash of 1929 directed enquiry towards exploring ways and methods of inward-oriented growth. After this the golden period of international expansion in the 1960s and the good, indeed in a few cases the exceptional, performance of some LDCs in terms of exports seemed to warrant the view that export orientation and outward policy stances were those most conducive to growth and development. The critical state of the world economy after the oil shocks and the process of inflation and monetary instability which followed suit brought to attention the difficulties of both short-term and long-term adjustment. The latter was compounded by a rapidly rising outstanding debt.

The emphasis provided by the economic environment was and still is influenced by the scientific, all too often marred by the ideological, climate which prevailed at any given point in time. Thus, as long as social reformism was the inspiring standard of scientific reflexion, theories stressed the interplay of social classes and issues of distribution and real growth. The emergence and wide acceptance of neoclassical orthodoxy shifted theoretical interests towards the functioning of markets and maximizing behaviour, and hence towards exchange rather than production. Mainstream economics concentrated its aim, and the efforts of scores of graduate students, on problems of choice, efficiency and intertemporal allocation within the broad assumption of methodological individualism. Problems of backwardness and development became special cases to relegate to the least challenging sections of the profession. Quite fortunately not all adhered to this view and to its implicit research programme. The purpose of this chapter is to highlight some issues that have emerged which are of basic importance both for theoretical debate and for policy making.

True to tradition, an overall view of relevant theoretical issues may be had by taking a glance at the development situation as it appears at the present moment. By means of sweeping generalizations it is possible to draw the following development scenario (World Bank, 1990).

(1) Let us begin with South Asia and the Far East. This area, which includes the well known case of the so called gang of four, has witnessed substantial growth. While performance has been quite exceptional in a few countries, there are clear signs that self-sustaining and rapid growth is spreading to other countries in the area, viz. Thailand, Malaysia and, with the help of oil, Indonesia. In spite of recent difficulties, India and China do show signs that per capita income growth is gaining momentum. Only war-ridden countries in the South East appear to be in the grips of stagnation and rising poverty.

(2) A rather different picture emerges when we turn to Latin America. Most of the southern part of the American continent is prey to decadence and stagnation. Even Brazil which in the past had shown a record of rapid growth has not been able to spread the progress of industrialization over its large territory to anything even remotely resembling an evenly distributed pattern, or to bring benefits for social classes which are capable of narrowing down patent and grossly unjust inequality. In Latin America, the purpose of analytical enquiry is best served by a theory of decadence rather than a theory of development as it is normally understood in the profession's mainstream. Argentina, in spite of the fact that its per capita income had ranked among the world's highest until the interwar period, is now witnessing de-industrialization and steeply falling standards of living. It is, in fact, now considered a developing country. Furthermore, the Andean countries have not only failed to generate a meaningful measure of development but run the risk of a disintegrating statehood under the blows of drug trafficking, unbridled criminality and widespread corruption.

(3) An even worse reality affects Sub-Saharan Africa. Here development seems to be almost completely absent. Income per head has actually declined in some years; many countries are in danger of seeing part of their farming lands eroded away by desertification while

poverty is rising and depriving a large part of the population, expecially vulnerable groups, of access to basic necessities such as health, schooling and active social participation. In countries lying in the Sahelian belt drought and famine have struck, with dismal effects on an already extremely low income per head. In most parts of Africa demographic growth has outpaced whatever modest gain in productivity had been achieved in the past.

(4) This bird's eye view of the development situation should perhaps take into account Eastern Europe's process of transition. Although in many ways fully-fledged industrial countries, almost all share at least some of the developing countries' problems. Low productivity, inefficiency and difficulties in sustaining a rapid rate of growth actually make them similar to middle-income LDCs. Yet the crucial problem is here that of pushing towards the frontier of efficiency and competition an outmoded, often obsolete industrial structure. Providing these countries with appropriate microeconomic incentives, a suitable macroeconomic framework and viable monetary arrangements is, of course, an extraordinary challenge.

While this very impressionistic portrait of development does not provide any strong evidence favouring any specific theoretical approach or for that matter any clear development pattern, it does give hints of basic problems. In the following pages I shall raise the following issues:

(1) Both failure and success stories beg the question of appropriate patterns of industrialization. It is in fact quite apparent that fast GDP growth is strongly correlated with the growth of a manufacturing industry as well as with exports of manufacturers. The latter part of this statement implies due consideration of international specialization.

(2) A closely related issue is the time-honoured workhorse of development economics: how open should developing countries be? In the economist's jargon, should policies be inward-looking or outward-oriented?

(3) Quickening the pace of development may require foreign borrowing and therefore indebtedness. LDCs' debt, however, has caused considerable concern and some have argued that it may have jeopardized the stability of the international monetary system. This raises the issue both of an appropriate course towards a deepening industrialization capable of sustaining external debt and of the financial and institutional arrangements to provide development efforts with adequate support. The issue of appropriate institutions

in turn raises the question of how to approach imbalances, especially structural ones.

2 THE NEED TO INDUSTRIALIZE

If there is anything that both failures and success indicate, it is that the key for boosting income per head lies with industrialization. The latter can generally be described as the process thanks to which the share of industry in GDP steadily rises together with its share of employment. This implies large shifts in the latter's pattern, normally away from agriculture and other traditional activities, migrations and far-reaching, often dramatic, social reorganization occurring as a consequence. There is of course, scarcely any debate over the strong relation which links the growth of industry, especially of a manufacturing kind, to the growth of productivity (Sen, 1983). The question over which considerable controversy arose in the past and still rages today concerns the means and more specifically the policies to achieve this and the pattern according to which it is to evolve. This question remains relevant today, given that almost an entire continent seems to be cut off from development while other parts of the world experience either sluggish growth or, in some cases, decay. For instance, how can Sub-Saharan Africa grow? Is industrialization appropriate in this economic environment? In this case, but more generally in the paradigmatic one of a typical under-developed economy, the starting-point, if a start is to occur, is characterized by the near absence of physical capital, which should always be understood as a set of specific means of production, and quite often, but not always, by a relative abundance of unskilled labour. A clear and unambiguous understanding of this statement is therefore in order.

A relative abundance of unskilled labour must be viewed in the context of an economy which, on account of its state of relative backwardness, is still locked in the grips of extensive growth. Economic activity bearing such a characteristic usually is, and historically certainly was, aimed at simply subsistence production, thus concerning an agriculture based, low productivity economy. It may, however, concern also an economy in which industry has gained substantial weight but in which productivity growth is slow and haphazard: a situation in which the same mode of production is constantly replicated. Evidence has invariably shown and theory, especially of the classical strain, has convincingly explained that this state entails decreasing returns due to falling fertility and/or to exhaustion of fundamental natural sources. Thus, given a rate of consumption per head which cannot be significantly lowered, the rate of surplus which the economy yields is not sufficient to generate enough physical capital to be invested to keep a rising population employed according to constantly efficient technical standards. Historically, societies caught in the narrowing prongs of an ever-rising population and diminishing returns have reacted by readjusting the methods of production to accommodate an increasing workforce. Simplifying somewhat the unavoidably intricate pattern of social reorganization, it can be said that the same output is produced by ever larger numbers of workers, a state of affairs which has suggested theories of excess labour supply and development viewed as occurring with an almost perfectly elastic labour supply schedule. Yet, at any particular point in time, labour is in some sense employed, albeit in marginal undertakings or in lowly, productive, menial tasks. It is therefore not necessarily readily available even though incentives of appropriate magnitude may trigger an exodus from traditional occupations.

Provided this process has not gone as far as to cause a Malthusian crisis provoking distressful expulsions from traditional occupations or forcing people to seek their fortune and employment elsewhere, situations which have indeed occurred in history and still could happen today, the workforce can be fully employed in the specific sense outlined above. Physical capital needed in production is being used and reproduced whilst available new capital, investment, is being allotted to increase output in subsequent periods. The only sense in which there is capital shortage in such an economy is that capital is not capable, as was mentioned above, of sustaining employment at an invariant level of productivity. Apart from this, and notwithstanding diminishing returns, capital is a commodity which in equilibrium is produced in the quantities and proportions required to keep the economy growing. Note, finally, that subsistence consumption cannot be held constant indefinitely: excess labour can continuously be employed and yet paid the same subsistence wage only if redistribution occurs away from other sources of incomes: historically this has meant away from rents.

Does such an economy possess alternative ways of producing whatever it does produce? To put it in a different way, are alternative techniques available? The question is purely academic since, had such techniques been known, they would appear to have been discarded long ago according to socially accepted criteria. Presumably, if the economy were governed by a capitalist mode of production (but this is not likely to be the case) that one which affords the highest profit rate under the ruling subsistence wage would be chosen, or, if governed by a collective rule of some kind, the one which yields the highest growth rate. More to the point, in the context of an economy worried by demographic pressure, and given a rate of growth which is consistent with that of population, the technique which affords the highest per capita consumption would be chosen. Whichever the case, the chosen technique would have then been reshaped to accommodate rising numbers of people joining the labour force and its technical competitors would have been long since set aside and, as far as the functioning of the economy is concerned, forgotten. It is in this framework that the question of how an economy such as the one described might start off on a development path must be asked and, if possible, answered. To give a final touch to this picture of a paradigmatic under-developed economy, it is helpful analytically to think of it as being a vertically integrated sector, even if technically fairly primitive, the final output of which is a subsistence bundle of goods; to produce the latter the economy is provided with intermediate goods and capital goods sectors which enter it either directly or indirectly. It is also helpful to assume that this economy is entirely self-contained; there is no outside world with which to trade or which may provide some kind of aid.

In these circumstances, it is all too evident that development can occur only if improvements are introduced into the productive structure of the economy: improvements, that is, which enable it to increase its rate of surplus, to keep consumption per head, which would have otherwise declined, constant and to increase investment to keep pace with population growth. Alternatively, consumption per head, already critically low, could be allowed to rise. The social mechanism through which this could actually be achieved is not unique: capitalism has certainly accomplished structural change on an unprecedented scale, but so too have planned economies, no matter how well they have performed *vis à vis* capitalist ones. The same holds true for some of today's developing economies.

The key lies, therefore, with technical progress. Progress however, implies deep and far-reaching social transformations (Landes, 1969). But how can a country or an economy such as the one which is being discussed, acquire the necessary knowledge and the skills required to implement technical improvements? And what is the nature of such knowledge? Economic theory, let it be said clearly, has not contributed much to answer this question. There are however some notable exceptions. These are the theories which more or less explicitly refer to the neo-Smithian or neo-Schumpeterian tradition. The process of technological improvement is quite complex even in a relatively unsophisticated system. To answer the question, it is therefore convenient to discuss technical progress in quite a general way.

3 THE ROLE OF TECHNICAL PROGRESS

There are two components of technical progress which must be emphasized (Freeman, 1986). The first of such components is exogenous. By this term it is meant that some of its determinants, but not all, as will be argued later, are independent of economic activity as such. Instead they concern social, political as well as institutional factors which are conductive to scientific and technological achievements and to its application in the economic sphere. Inventions are the consequence of scientific capabilities which depend, broadly speaking, on methodological attitudes but also on institutional arrangements which provide support and status for researchers and systematic ways to pass on knowledge. The likelihood of innovations resulting from basic inventions, however, depends also on the existence of attitudes which aim at exploiting them economically and again on institutions which are ready to promote them in terms of actual applications. Historically, state action by means of public expenditure and policies addressed at supporting schools, academies and universities and also by the realization of public works and industries which embodied newly acquired knowledge have played a crucial role in sustaining technical progress. This twofold dimension of state action in furthering and giving scope to scientific enquiry is characteristic of fully developed economies and yet not only has it proved to be decisive in their historical development but it is also quite relevant to developing economies today. Turning to our hypothetical fully closed economy, the fact that whether or not it possesses the institutional and scientific characteristics broadly outlined above is a matter of historical occurrence. In terms of policy, it clearly is of great importance that the knowledge that such institutional and political set-ups manage to produce should be at least potentially absorbable by the existing economy, in other words be adapted and relevant to the productive structure as it is at any given moment in time (at the very beginning a low productivity, subsistence agricultural economy). This simple point is to be kept in mind when considering an open economy which trades in goods with, but also acquires knowledge from, the rest of the world, especially industrialized countries.

The economic significance of these exogenous determinants of technical progress is quite straightforward on account of their productivity-augmenting property. Their impact, however, goes beyond this. As Schumpeter has argued, in a capitalist context the clustering of innovations within a given but fairly short period of time provides a domain of profit opportunities which an entrepreneurial class may exploit through innovative investment. Innovators reap the benefit of higher than normal profit rates which then wanes as a band-wagon effect boosts supply and lowers prices. The likely effect of this initial thrust given to economic activity is to provoke an upswing which is strengthened by endogenous forces (to be discussed below) and followed by a downswing as profits are squeezed by rising costs and lower prices. This time pattern may take the form of a long wave. The implication of this line of thought for development is that when and if inventions, which may have taken a long time to acquire an applicable form, produce a cluster of potential innovations relatively to the existing technical set-up, they may engender a social and economic change conducive to sustained growth.

The importance of exogenous technical progress must be emphasized but a second aspect, which may be called endogenous, plays an equally important role. The term endogenous signifies in this context technical advancement which depends on, or is strictly linked to, economic activity. In order to discuss its determinants it is appropriate to clarify what is to be understood by technique of production for the purpose at hand. Quite simply, it is convenient to designate by this term the combination of means of production, that is of capital goods embodying a specific technical knowledge, the know-how and skills which are closely related to it with the set of rules and organization giving rise to sequences which are normally called 'routines' (Nelson and Winter, 1982). Such a technique implies a well defined production specialization and is the result of past innovative choices. Innovative possibilities, in turn, stem from and are largely constrained by its characteristics. In general terms, the combination of embodied technical knowledge and routines sets in motion two broad processes: the first is a process of learning concerned with how to produce a specific output, normally called learning-by-doing, while the second focuses on the use of means of production, a process known as learning-by-using. The general characteristic of both processes is that their intensity is greater the more sustained in time the economic activity is. This is so given the fact that the former occurs in consequence of experience gained as output increases and the latter as expertise is acquired in manning and operating new equipment and thus as investment increases.

In both cases the result is not merely an improvement in skills and know-how but also the amelioration of processes of production as well as of the needed capital goods. It is now a well established fact that learning processes lead to solutions of problems posed by the operation of existing techniques. There are additional problems when a new technique is adopted, normally in the form of new capital goods, new norms, different or new intermediate goods or simply when a new product is produced unless it is an entirely new production process perfectly operative and perfectly consistent in all its parts and elements and implemented as such. These can create all sorts of bottlenecks as well as problems of compatibility with old or currently available parts of existing plant. But these indicate further avenues of technical improvement. Research, even of an informal kind, is carried out on its technological features, looking for ways to improve production guided by focusing devices (Rosenberg, 1982). The latter are not merely the bottlenecks referred to above but also the relative prices of production ingredients, scarcities, and available skills. Learning makes this search possible even if it is not its sole component. Research and development of various degrees of sophistication are ways in which to generate better products and, what is more, better means of production. Normally they are carried out around extant techniques: it is a process which is often referred to as 'localized search' (Atkinson and Stiglitz, 1969). In order to support it, expenditure is necessary even if not in a formalized manner. The capacity to sustain it depends on the ability to pay and is based on expected future payoff. Either current or future effective demand is what determines both, given a cost and wage structure. In any case, a linkage is established with economic activity; it becomes an endogenous variable.

Even these very synthetic remarks allow us to draw an immediate conclusion: endogenous technical progress builds upon the existing technical structure which each innovation modifies providing scope for new localized search and learning. Every time an innovation is implemented new capital goods and routines appear and therefore new bottlenecks, new problems and, in the last analysis, new technical opportunities. This brings about the next round of innovations which, again, are localized around existing techniques. This process carries on if the link between effective demand and innovative activity is sufficiently strong. If this is so, a technological trajectory is enacted. The strength of such a link is of paramount importance. To this effect, the existence of a capital goods industry which has attained a degree of specialization and autonomy is fundamental. The reason lies with the fact that this industry's output embodies to a large extent results which come from innovative effort. Improvement and modifications are mainly tasks which are carried out in this context. In a sufficiently competitive framework, but also in a planned one in which incentives are provided, realizing industry's output implies stimulating a flow of demand to keep capacity engaged and the profit or financial outlook satisfactory. In a closed economy context, this flow of demand takes the shape of gross investment. While the latter responds in the short run to aggregate demand, in the long run it is the expected profit rate, or more generally the rate of return, which determines it. It is on this rate that technical progress has its impact by allowing costs to fall and new products to appear: new market opportunities and obsolescence therefore stimulate the rate of investment. By these means a linkage is established. It is quite evident however, that the producers' innovative efforts require that they are seen as being opportunities for users. Thus the user–producer relationship takes on fundamental relevance. Industrial economics has dealt at length with these issues and it is to this literature that we should turn for further analysis.

Seen from this viewpoint, technical progress can be considered as a prime determinant of long-term effective demand. But this provides a feed-back for technical progress since, through the sale of output, it warrants past investment both in capacity and in innovative efforts, it enhances the capacity to produce innovations on account of strengthened ability to pay for and to finance research and, finally, it keeps up learning processes of both types. Thus, while innovations stimulate investment, technical progress stimulates innovations: a virtuous circle of productivity growth supported basically by technical progress is established.

The dynamics of such a growth process may be quite intricate on account of the interaction between learning processes and innovative expenditure, of various feed-backs as well as because of obstacles due to demand problems and to the exhaustion of technical opportunities. It is however a continuous factor in time. Thus once new capital goods are installed, new routines are merged with pre-existing ones to form new techniques, the groundwork is set to yield successive innovations as a result of localized research. This gives rise, as mentioned above, to a trajectory. Whether or not other techniques were previously available no longer matters; in fact, the technical set up just abandoned for new means of production and rules of conduct can never be reconsidered for adoption, given the cumulative nature of technical progress. In this sense, technical progress follows a path which is not reversible (Arthur, 1985). To sum up, its basic characteristics are: (1) endogeneity, (2) continuity, (3) irreversibility.

The process which has been described is quite general: it certainly takes place in well developed and technically forward economies but it operates also in relatively simple and unsophisticated ones. Technological complexity, although important for the speed at which the process takes place, is not a binding condition for the existence of a virtuous circle. At the outset of the development process innovation capabilities are necessarily low or barely existent. This is the present situation of many LDCs; their inventions and innovations are still obviously rudimentary. Yet appropriate transfer of technologies can substitute for the former while, even more importantly, imitation, reverse engineering and adaptation can stand in stead of the latter. The basic point is that a self-sustaining process of technical advancement is set in motion. There is, however, nothing automatic about this: it is clearly necessary that an entrepreneurial class or strongly development-oriented and committed authorities with appropriate policies be in existence and able to assume a social and economic primacy.

If technical progress unfolds according to the dynamic principle described, no meaningful ground is left for theoretical constructions which prescribe either a choice of technique or shifts in the production function guided by prices of factors reflecting their relative scarcity. Bottlenecks and shortages do, of course, act as focusing devices but their solution need not be factor-saving in the sense prescribed by orthodox theory. This need not be the case indeed, even if two or more methods were to come up from localized search, each with a different factor intensity. Assume, for example, that two methods were conjured up to solve a technical problem arising from an existing and operative technique, one being directly more labour-intensive than the other. In a context where labour is relatively abundant, albeit as in the sense explained above, and with wages possibly at a subsistence level, neoclassical theory would mandate that the former rather than the latter be chosen. This new technique however generally requires direct or indirect physical capital, means of production which must be, in their turn, produced with whatever technique is currently available. At the new ruling prices, that is to say those which would apply when a new equilibrium is established, the resulting set of techniques defined by the use of all industries concerned, need not be overall any more labour-intensive, once all the directly and indirectly needed processes are taken into account, or the less expensive of the two. Given that prices have to adjust to the new technical environment, it is not the more labour-intensive method but rather the one which is less so, which will have to be chosen (Harcourt, 1972). Furthermore, since any chosen techniques, if choice exists, give rise to specific trajectories, cumulative adoption yields increasing returns. It has convincingly been shown that once a technique has been adopted after a period of time competing, or even initially better ones, will never be eligible. This conclusion highlights irreversibility.

In a long-term perspective, technical progress is the engine of Smithian specialization. As a consequence of innovative efforts new capital goods appear which find applications in the sector of immediate use as well as in others where similar technical principles can be applied. In this sense there are considerable externalities to be benefited from. This also holds quite obviously for radical kinds since new industries must be created; but it equally holds for incremental ones since accumulated innovations along a trajectory will also bring about new goods and processes. In either case, user–producer linkages promote specialization for modified capital goods, for parts of previously undifferentiated production. Thus the growth of the capital goods industry takes place by successive rounds of specialization.

In the ultimate analysis, development is firmly embedded in technical progress and structural change. In the light of ongoing analytical frameworks, some broad policy implications can therefore be derived:

(1) The first and most obvious, but nonetheless of foremost importance, is the deliberate support to be given to a development-oriented social class. This statement is simple but not in the least trivial since social orientations are not necessarily apparent. It can be seen in terms of the potential place such a class is likely to take and the contribution it is likely to make to the dynamics of the virtuous circle described above. Broadly speaking, it is a question of a class ready to invest and innovate in industrial activities even if of a very modest kind.

(2) Institutions can play a fundamental role in spurring technical advance. Of the utmost importance for this effect is an industrial policy aimed at providing deliberate support for sectors in which the dynamics outlined above are likely to materialize.

(3) While protection may prove necessary, it ought to be aimed at creating capital goods industries and thus at strengthening producer–user linkages.

(4) The critical size of the market is of course crucial. It is quite clear that a small Sub-Saharan country can scarcely aspire to create a machine tool sector as it will court sure economic disaster. A regional area establishing a truly common market is possibly the answer.

4 THE PROCESS OF TRANSITION

The appearance of a new technological opportunity in the form of a potential innovation poses structural adjustment problems of considerable magnitude and consequence. This is especially the case with profound technical changes. That is, when technical progress acquires a radical form, entire new industries have to be created while others become obsolete. How is such a new productive environment to rise up in a closed economy context? Normally, the existing vertically integrated sector is functioning, in terms of its capital stock, at full capacity even though the latter may be scant. The new technique, as it results from a process of research, requires nevertheless new means of production, that is, capital goods which, as mentioned above, take time to produce. Capacity cannot, as in putty models, be instantaneously moulded into the new instruments which are needed for innovation. It is as perfectly clear that they have to be produced within the limits of a productive capacity which is currently and entirely taken up by the output of necessary consumption. If the case arises, additional labour forces can be drawn from an excess labour supply, as stated by A. Lewis, and means of production must be shifted away from production of such necessities.

Thus, before the benefits of an increased surplus due to better techniques can be reaped, the standard of living is likely to fall in spite of its being already very low. Whether this is socially acceptable or not is quite clearly a historically open question. It may be noted, however, that this is enough reason to maintain that economies pinned down to a per capita income close to subistence are unable to yield a major structural change towards industrialization. Many development theorists and economic historians have indeed argued that the industrial revolution of western economies and particularly Great Britain's had been made possible by a relatively high level of income per head resulting from a century-old trend.

Traces of an analytical approach to the problems set by this kind of capital shortage can be found in early classical economists such as Ricardo. But it is with Hicks's traverse analysis that it has received proper attention (Hicks, 1973). The model used by him and by some of his followers highlights the efforts required to acquire a capital stock through successive stages in which labour and work-in-progress enter as inputs until the construction period is accomplished. Then and only then can final output appear in the form of consumption or other final goods. When a new technique becomes available the process of production must start anew with labour as the only input whilst available consumption remains tied to the outcome of processes started before the technical option materialized. While very old processes, close to economic extinction, and very new ones, only recently started, may be subject to truncation because of the higher rate of return afforded by the new technology, the consequence on this highly stylized economy differs according to assumptions made on adjustment sequences. If at least part of the consumption is held constant, it can be shown that the divergence of activity levels from those that would have occurred had the economy remained the same would cause initial loss of employment. If, on the other hand, it is the latter which is to be kept constant or growing as it was before, it is consumption which gives way. In either case activity levels are subject to oscillations in relation to the pattern that would have been followed without the adoption. Eventually they converge to a new equilibrium. This may be typified by a higher steady state growth rate. It is interesting to remark, though, that Hayek effects in the shape of negative activity levels cannot be ruled out, at least in theory.

This analytical approach, although of considerable heuristic value, is too abstract to provide sufficient material even for economic abstractions. It is in fact assumed that processes can be initiated by labour alone, a sort of pristine act of production from which the construction phase develops. Each produced stage then enters exclusively into the following one to produce a clear cut sequence in which only labour inputs need appear explicitly. If both assumptions were dropped many of the results which the temporally integrated model can derive would no longer hold. The lesson, however, remains. Indeed, analogous but more powerful results may be obtained when traverse analysis is attempted with a non integrated Leontieff–Sraffa model in which capital takes time to produce and lasts for more than one period of production. None of the binding assumptions of the previous model are required here but it can equally be shown that, if consumption per head is held constant, adopting a new technology implies an oscillating pattern with equilibrium prices causing truncation and warranting the abandonment of obsolete processes. While the actual time pattern depends on assumptions concerning the new technology, losses in activity levels and associated employment are certainly to occur sooner or later along the traverse.

This conclusion is of great relevance for development. It asserts that before the new productive potential is achieved the economy will have to go through losses of employment, or more to the point it will have to generate further excess labour. This time it is not on account of demographic pressures but because of the very process of modernization. Alternatively losses in consumption per head will have to be sustained. Whatever the case, this conclusion sheds a sombre light on endogeneous development possibilities. It is also worth noting that convergence towards a new equilibrium occurs only when certain conditions are satisfied. The problem is of course one of distribution. Part of the current net product must be channelled towards investment which cannot immediately yield an increased flow of goods. Savings must rise accordingly. This is very difficult if not impossible for a subsistence economy or at least it is a heavy burden placed on the population for those economies which have managed to rise above a mere subsistence level.

These results are theoretical and hold in the context of a model in which the net product is shared out between necessary consumption and investment, or in a capitalist framework between wages and profits which are then saved to sustain growth and structural change. This clearly narrows down the options. But, of course, it rarely occurs. Rents normally persist, often the state absorbs a good deal of the social product for no other purpose than supporting armies, large but useless bureaucracies or wasteful expenditure on needless public works. Mustering the part of current capacity which is tied down in this way is not easy. What is usually but also urgently required is a thorough reform of public administrations to allow redistribution through fiscal means as well as policies aimed at supporting productivity growth.

5 OPENING THE ECONOMY

So far the economy has been viewed as a closed and self-sufficient system. It can now be legitimately asked to what extent the analytical approach expounded in previous pages stands to be modified by assuming that links with other countries and economic systems do exist and that, indeed, the typical developing economy faces an industrialized world with per capita income and productivity which are many times higher than that of its own. This question leads us to the second problem raised in the introduction, the question of how open an economy should be, and to the role played by trade.

In the standard neoclassical Heckscher–Ohlin–Samuelson (HOS) model, trade is essential since it is through trade that greater efficiency in resource use and thus greater welfare can be achieved for economies with different factor endowments. It is this difference that fundamentally justifies trade, since on account of it appropriate specialization can be reached. Countries produce in the main and export those goods they are more adapted to produce. It follows that, if the model holds, LDCs being richer in labour than in capital will not only benefit from trading but will have to do so by specializing in relatively labour-intensive commodities. HOS theorems are too well known for us to dwell upon them at any length; a brief reminder will suffice. The gist of the argument lies with the assumed tendency of final goods prices, say consumption goods, to become unique in all countries. In effect, trade, if unhindered by hurdles set by distorting tariffs and by administrative measures meant to regulate import and export flows, should create a single market with the same prices applying everywhere. Once the relative prices of goods are known from demand conditions, costs as defined by techniques picked from identical production functions adjust to them to yield a maximum rate of profits. Note however that the determination of all variables is simultaneous. At any given set of relative prices of final goods a set of relative factor prices must then correspond in order to define the appropriate technique of production and therefore, the relative use of factors. If this is true countries exporting goods whose production requires relatively more of the factor they are most endowed with, and which originally has a relatively lower price than in less endowed country, will make final goods available for the trading partner carrying a lower than autarky price. All partners will thus be able to import goods which are cheaper than in the no-trade case. The domestic price of the export good is, however, higher. But a HOS equilibrium entails higher incomes allowing increased welfare for all. The Rybczynky theorem then tells us that growth is the important thing. If a factor is increased, output will rise for the good which employs relatively more of it; indeed in this case production actually falls for the goods which employ relatively less of a factor not subject to positive variation. From this standpoint the answer to the question as to whether a developing economy should be open to trade is quite obvious. Not only should it be open but barriers should not be raised, especially in terms of measures touching upon prices which would then not be free to reach the desired international equilibrium.

In terms of policy making the HOS framework appeared as a suitable theoretical support for outward-oriented policies, especially export promotion, and as a strong argument belying the inward-looking, import-substituting stance of many LDCs. This it is in stark contrast with the view held by post-war Keynesians, as well as by Marxist and later neo-Ricardians, who held that domestic market growth is essential and preliminary to trade and to be achieved by import substitution under adequate protection. The Great Depression had cast a shadow on the capacity of trade to lead economic development but then the 'golden sixties' seemed to uncover vast new possibilities for trade-oriented LDCs. The outstanding accomplishments of some among them, especially in the Far East, seemed to uphold free trade prescriptions and the principles of at least benevolent government non-involvement. The neoclassical HOS paradigm met with extraordinary success.

This state of affairs did not go unchallenged, both because of theoretical problems and because of the narrowness of the utterly unsuitable underlying hypothesis. From a theoretical point of view problems arise as soon as one stops to consider the meaning of capital as a factor of production. If a view is taken, as is quite obvious, that capital is in fact a set of goods produced by means of other goods with their own equilibrium prices, no measure of this so called factor of production can be made independently of what the pricing system happens to be, given a set of production techniques. As has been mentioned, when trade takes place the price of the final goods varies to ensure higher returns to relatively abundant factors whose price must also vary accordingly. The direction of change should, indeed, be the same. This is not necessarily so, as is shown by a large amount of capital-theoretic literature: techniques which happen to be capital-intensive at a set of equilibrium prices need not be so at another such set. Factor reversal can occur. It follows that no general statement can be made on the relationship between factor endowments and specialization, since the former varies whenever prices vary.

If the standard neoclassical paradigm suffers from criticism levelled basically at its concept of capital and more generally at its view of the production process, an equally biting criticism concerns the adequacy of its assumptions given the realities of modern economies. A good deal of this critical reassessment comes from the ranks of neoclassical theorists themselves (Helpman and Krugman, 1985). The fundamental objection raised deals with the constant returns technology assumed by production functions in the standard case. Evidence clearly dismisses this assumption. Furthermore, trade statistics clearly show that the bulk of gross flows occurs between countries with similar factor endowments, especially in terms of intermediate goods. Thus similarity rather than difference seems to explain the volume of trade which, incidentally, occurs mainly between industrialized countries rather than according to a North–South pattern of manufactures for primary commodities exchange. A considerable part of trade, moreover, involves the same company even if it is spread out geographically. Finally, while very little indication of resource reallocation appears in consequence, it is the productivity of resources which is enhanced by international trade. Quite interestingly, this is explained by resorting to a hypothesis concerning technology which fits available evidence much better, namely that increasing returns to scale are the norm especially in manufacturing sectors. This hypothesis does not necessarily lead to a drastic reformulation of the HOS world: in fact differences in factor endowments still imply a predicted pattern of trade, but it is not the only reason to carry on exchanges. Thus, while comparative advantage still works to allocate different resource endowments, trade also occurs to exploit economies of scale. A basic departure from standard conclusions occurs, however, since the latter are not generally consistent with atomistic, perfect competition.

Theoretical puzzles notwithstanding, what emerges from recent trade literature is that technology and increasing returns matter greatly. If this view is then applied to developing countries, mixed conclusions emerge. LDCs need not confine themselves to trading commodities for which there exists a static comparative advantage but may also engage in developing industries in which economies of scale are easier to reap. This, however, may prove more difficult than expected. The problem is that increasing returns are inherently cumulative. Thus countries which are able to develop a head start in terms of accumulation and growth will lead runner-ups and possibly establish with them a link of dependency. Much evidence has been collected to show that this may indeed be the case: a considerable part of manufacturing industries in LDCs is simply made up of production units of multinational companies linked to headquarters through vertical integration. Where such links do not exist, openness to trade and export-led growth may prove to be highly problematic since technological gaps may well be impossible to fill.

The theories briefly mentioned above in a sense beg the question even if analytical difficulties were to be set aside. The argument unravelled in the previous paragraph may however prove helpful in shedding some light on this issue. Increasing returns occur not simply because the scale of output reaches and goes over a certain quantitative threshold or because it keeps on rising but because technical change occurs in both the form of a radical, mainly exogenous, and of an incremental, mainly endogenous, kind. Increasing returns therefore materialize in consequence of a complex dynamic process in which quantitative growth is as much a consequence as a condition once a virtuous circle is established. But here lies the true problem: if the relationship tying the various factors which explain the motion is sufficiently clear, the same cannot be said of what gets it started. There seems to be scarcely any doubt, however, that it is in industry, especially in the manufacturing sector, that productivity growth is quantitatively and qualitatively more sizable. The experience of those LDCs which have been able to participate in international trade with great success shows that it is through manufactures that this achievement has been possible. In setting up a local industrial base they cannot, however, rely upon the mechanics of relative factor endowment specialization since by definition a labour-intensive agricultural economy can only export agricultural produce. Yet, if productivity growth requires industrial processes and their output is subject to scale effects, then demand of a significant magnitude for such an output must be generated if the economic system in question is to become competitive in world markets. Thus domestic market growth is necessary if the economy is to enter the international market on a sufficiently sound and firm footing.

This conclusion receives stronger support if the problem is viewed in terms of the argument expounded above, centred on technical change. In this sense, competitiveness as revealed by relatively low costs compared to international standards depends crucially on whether an economy is capable of a virtuous circle of productivity growth, thus on whether it has been able to develop the required techniques and, what is more, the processes of learning and search to produce new ones. It is not merely a problem of scale, although the latter certainly depends on accumulated output, but of dynamic capabilities to innovate and at least to keep abreast of a shifting technological frontier. This normally requires a thriving capital goods industry, the very heart of endogenous innovation in productive symbiosis with users' industries, even if the economy in question is a developing one. What is clearly very important is that the economy is enabled to proceed on a trajectory in which new or adapted techniques appear endogenously as solutions to search problems and as a consequence of learning. In the process new routines are derived, new skills developed, and new capabilities are generated. It is such a process which must be strengthened by institutional action and economic policy.

Success stories, and particularly those of now semi-industrialized LDCs, clearly show that manufacturing industries had to be developed by finely aimed import substitution before some sectors could become competitive enough to enter international trade. Experience varies historically and geographically. Surely the often quoted case of South Korea, a widely recognized case of export success, illustrates this point. At least until the beginning of the 1960s, it remained a heavily protected country through tariffs and foreign exchange controls. But more importantly it was, and it remains after external liberalization, a country characterized by tight management of credit flows, of sectoral industrial policies and fiscal incentives. Far from being a champion of unfettered competition and free enterprise, it seems to be an economy closely controlled by oligopolies, trade concerns and a determined state bureaucracy. Quite importantly, many of the firms and sectors to which Korean export success can be attributed thrived as subcontractors of large Japanese enterprises, namely in the case of the automobile industry, shipyards and much of the electronic industry. Before they could come out as strong international competitors and eventually wean themselves away from linkages with mother companies, they built up skills and technical capacity under the umbrella of a more advanced and economically viable system.

It is not the purpose of the present chapter to provide an exhaustive review of export-led economies but both current evidence and historical research firmly indicate that import substitution was clearly a necessary first stage of development strategy. It is, however, an equally well founded argument that protracted and indiscriminate protection may lead to waste and, in fact, to lagging behind technologically. The very thread of the reasoning which emphasizes virtuous circles leads to the conclusion that a competitive environment is conducive to dynamically increasing returns and such an environment is certainly provided by the international market. The compelling element in looking for improvement was held to be, in fact, the necessity to compete for output sale through better equipment, processes and goods. A quasi-monopolistic environment stifles the drive for innovation and renders the user–producer linkage ineffective. Thus the price and cost discipline afforded by international market competition does not so much promote static efficient resource use, as strengthen the productivity virtuous circle which has been described. As was noted above, the growth of a capital goods industry depends on its progress in terms of specialization. This is an ongoing process as long as endogenous innovative efforts occur. The evidence provided by so-called import substitution policies, for instance in many Latin American countries, taking the form of high and lasting protection especially of consumer goods industries, shows that this process was hampered and effectively blocked. This is the case, for instance, with Argentina, where a strong tariff barrier, put in place especially for consumer durables, has led to the setting up of multinational companies' offshoots to produce them with almost no spin-off in terms of forward and backward linkages and with little technological diffusion.

Theory as well as evidence seems to support the view that import substitution, as a period in which domestic market growth is promoted through infant industries, is a necessary step before gradual integration in the international market and therefore export promotion is undertaken. It is this sequence which appears to lie at the root of many export achievements. Protracted protection, on the other hand, in the context of a necessarily limited market, may seal off the economy from pressures stimulating local research efforts producing endogenous technical advances. In this way, export drives are appropriate policy measures only in so far as they strengthen the capabilities of strategic sectors, that is to say those from which diffusion processes spread to generate the virtuous circle of productivity growth described above. Promotion of exports in industries with limited scope for innovation-led growth and with little fall-out on other sectors creates unnecessary cleavages in the economic system, often the phenomena of painful dualism.

Foregoing considerations do not necessarily imply that an as yet under-developed economy should undertake a programme of fast industrialization which is unrelated to its existing economic structure. The development target ought to remain, presumably, the increase of overall productivity in view of a greater income per head. Especially in the case of very low-income countries a rise in product per capita which is well distributed among the various social groups and in any case well spread over the entire population brings about an increase of per capita consumption, especially of agricultural produce. It is the output of this sector, therefore, which must be boosted over and above demographic growth. In order to reach this goal capital deepening is required by implementing techniques which utilize more sophisticated means of production to assist direct labour. It is precisely the production of such capital goods which may start a process of industrialization whose purpose is to provide inputs for agriculture. This process can be viewed in terms of a vertically integrated sector led by agricultural demand generated by rising consumption per head. As long as real incomes increase with productivity, the domestic market is widened and the process is set in motion. Investment would then flow to sustain final demand but would acquire a momentum of its own if and when an endogenous process led by technical progress set in. In this case industrialization occurs in the form of an enlarged agricultural sector whose pace depends entirely on the size of the internal market. Historically, this is not a pattern of development which has often occurred, but there is nothing impossible about it. As with other forms of development several necessary conditions must concur to bring it about: a thorough land reform, a credit system able to provide the required support for investment and thus the monetary means needed by an enlarged and growing production, and an institutional framework setting incentives as well as guidelines.

6 DEVELOPMENT AND FOREIGN BORROWING

Developing countries, almost by definition, are not at the forefront of technological advance. They are, on the contrary, confronted by the conspicuous innovative process of developed countries as well as by a consolidated body of technical knowledge. This fact might be, and indeed has been used, to support the conclusion that the possibility of tapping, albeit at a cost, enormous technological capabilities provides a Schumpeterian domain of opportunities for investment likely to set off a process of fast growth. In this way, this body of already well developed and tried technologies acts as the equivalent of a cluster of innovations which in industrialized countries lays the groundwork for a long-term upswing and eventually a long wave. According to this view, growth induced by technological opportunities with implied learning and imitation effects leads to a catching up process which narrows and ultimately fills the gap between the developed and the developing economies by exploiting such opportunities.

Unfortunately things are not quite so simple. The first reason concerns the problem of adapting foreign technologies to a domestic productive framework. The latter is geared, either out of a spontaneous process or as the outcome of policies but normally out of both, to a pattern of effective demand defining broad economic scopes, the catering for needs and the expression of a social organization and its institutional set-up. Furthermore, the supply side of this economy is above all a system of knowledge, skills and routines which must possess the capability of adopting more advanced and, effectively, foreign techniques. Thus the question of appropriate technologies must be discussed in terms of what is to be produced in view of demand as well as in terms of how ready the existing productive system is to embody new modes of production. In spite of the simplicity of these statements, they are not to be taken for granted given the situation in many developing countries with steel mills, oil refineries, cement factories and even food processing plants running at less than 50 per cent of their capacity, with intractable maintenance and spare parts problems, difficulties in hiring skilled labour and management personnel and poor product quality.

The second problem is strictly related to the one above and it concerns the transfer of technology. The aim of such transfer should be that of promoting a process of autonomous technological improvement. This may, however, be frustrated on account of transfer costs which may indeed be very high. As has been seen, although there are considerable externalities connected with innovation, these are specific to individual companies and transacted on markets which have strong oligopolistic features. In addition, various innovation-hindering arrangements are the norm. Often technologies are transferred with closed market clauses while licences carry tied inputs provisions which effectively ban licensees from developing backward linkages. This is a field in which some research has been done but further work is necessary to find the extent to which diffusion and externalities in receiving countries are actually limited.

There is however, a related macroeconomic problem which must be stressed (Ricottilli and Cantalupi, 1987). The reason for importing technology to a still under-developed economy is precisely to achieve productivity gains which would be impossible to attain without it or would take a long time to develop. Indeed, it may be crucial to obtain suitable technologies at the initial stages of domestic market growth to be able, among other things, to compete internationally at a later stage. Seen in this perspective, technology imports must take place before any meaningful flow of exports can be generated. Abstraction is made here, of course, of special natural resources endowments which may put the country in question immediately in a position to trade. The problems of LDCs as raw material exporters have been thoroughly discussed and debated. The one raised here is in a sense theoretical but can be applied to countries with no potential riches to sell in order to finance a development process. The way this question is put, however, helps to tackle the issue of foreign debt.

It is quite clear that, in the given circumstances, borrowing is necessary, giving rise to an outstanding debt whose magnitude depends on the time profile of the said imports and the repayment schedule. In principle, debt servicing can be met through an adequate flow of exports as soon as the required efficiency level is achieved provided that a suitable period of grace is allowed for. In spite of rising efficiency considerable problems may actually arise on account of the likely inconsistency between the financial terms, namely the rate of interest and the maturity structure set by international financial markets on which a developing economy has no leverage, and production capabilities. To grasp exactly how and why such an inconsistency may arise, it is convenient to turn to a neo-Austrian model which provides the anatomy and structure of an integrated production process. Importing technologies in the context outlined above may, broadly speaking, take either the form of pure knowledge to start the integrated process anew, or that of capital goods and know-how to start the process at a stage nearer the end of the construction period. In both cases the transfer requires borrowing which causes outstanding debt to rise, the sinking of which will weigh on the utilization stage of processes when final output appears to sustain consumption and exports. The latter will have to match the debt service requirement set by loan conditions. Since the output flow is entirely determined by the productive capabilities of the process and initial conditions, it is easily seen that there is an underlying trade-off between consumption per head and, for any given maturity period, the rate of interest. If the latter is set on international markets, it is the former which must carry the burden of adjustment. This difficulty is compounded by the fact that, in spite of the transfer, efficiency standards normally do not match those of the developed economy from which it originates. It is interesting to note that the debt instalment enters negatively into the trade-off between consumption per head and the growth rate. Thus an interest rate–growth rate relation can be envisaged which depends entirely on technical conditions of production and the financial terms of borrowing. This is true in the rather favourable assumption that a market for export does in fact exist and that there are constant terms of trade. Yet even so the internal rate of return afforded by the transfer may not be sufficient to sustain both growth and a constant level of consumption.

Foregoing considerations do not invalidate international lending as a viable means to foster development. On the contrary, it can certainly be said that borrowing and consequently the possibility of getting into debt are crucial in order to take advantage of technological opportunities and thus to quicken the pace of development. Ideally, repayment should be linked to productivity gains which are realized by setting in motion an endogenous process of productivity growth, as is discussed above. In spite of the instalment schedule exhibiting in this case an accelerating pattern, financial conditions would clearly have to adjust to the specific production characteristics of the developing economy, that is to its internal rate of return which is consequently defined. This is an important point. It asserts that there is a close relationship between production possibilities at a given level of consumption per head, and financial terms. The former vary from country to country because of different initial conditions and capacity to acquire and operate technologies; financial terms are the consequence of a financial market which is largely outside the influence of most LDCs. In the context of rising productivity consumption per head can also be called upon to share in the debt burden, adjustment of financial terms to production conditions emerges as a clear policy objective. This is particularly true for economies in which near subsistence levels are still the norm. This objective, however, carries an implicit and obvious condition: it requires that external borrowing be strictly channelled into productivity-enhancing purposes and not used to sustain consumption levels, especially of bureaucratic classes or unproductive public expenditures, as is sometimes the case.

Reconciling local production possibilities with financial market conditions is a task requiring institutional support. Left entirely to market forces, borrowing would either prove impracticable for many LDCs or cause exceedingly high sacrifices in terms of consumption per head. It may also prove to be a threat for financial stability if lending is extended to economies which cannot secure the debt service flows demanded by market conditions. Bretton Woods institutions are, of course, well placed to play a substantial intermediary role. What is required, however, is a long-term approach in which the whole macrostructure of a developing economy is considered as to its initial conditions as well as to the dynamic processes which investment and technological transfers can give rise to. Conditionality can then be fashioned in terms of potential productivity gains.

7 CONCLUDING REMARKS

This brief overview of some development issues is far from being either exhaustive or conclusive. One point is put forcefully, however. Development occurs as a consequence of progress in the technical mode of production which implies deep and far reaching social changes. The chapter argues that long-term and structural transformation depends on the the capability of an economic system to generate a virtuous circle of productivity growth supported by technological progress. The latter's crucial features are continuity, accumulation and irreversibility. This last property is to be understood in terms of currently used techniques: once they have become obsolete on account of improvements either of a radical kind or on an incremental trajectory they will never again be eligible. Irreversibility does not, however, rule out decadence and regress. In spite of backwardness, developing countries' chances of fostering change lie with the dynamics imparted to their economic system by endogenous technical advancement and by the exogenous thrusts of radical innovations.

These statements hold even for very poor and sometimes destitute LDCs. No matter how low their income per head, how thin their capital stock and primitive their techniques, their hope for progress lies with technical transformation. While science and applied technology play a role of the utmost importance in fully developed countries whose economic structure lies on the technical frontier, a radical change of the technical paradigm is not only urgently required in today's developing economies but can also be achieved even with a modest transfer of technology. The latter must take into consideration the existing economic structure in relation to the pattern of current demand and of its likely evolution. Its purpose ought to be that of bringing about a pervasive change across the entire production structure. To achieve this goal an endogenous process of diffusion, adaptation, and original application must take place, even if this is modest compared to advanced standards. The technology to be transferred therefore must be appropriate, in the above sense, to the economic system which is undergoing a structural change. There is no general and sure prescription to be issued. Nevertheless the role of the state stands out as of paramount importance. No change can occur if an existing system is not in some way forced to accommodate it, not by imperative or dictatorial rule, as unfortunately has often been the case, but by the initiative of development-oriented social as well as economic protagonists, aimed at transforming processes of production, behaviours, attitudes and ultimately social relations. It is in this domain that state action can prove decisive in providing incentives, establishing rules and setting guidelines.

If an economy were to seek and pursue transformation entirely autonomously, building step by step the required stock of capital goods and equipment a very painful and socially distressing process of traverse would have to take place. This chapter argues that in such circumstances either employment levels or consumption per head, possibly both, might be required to fall. This process can partly be avoided or at least allayed by importing both the technology and the capital stock embodying it so as to be able to produce earlier the final goods which are needed to raise income per head. This alternative strategy implies borrowing and a rising oustanding debt. The best strategy to cope with its repayment is to synchronize debt servicing to productivity growth. The latter can be accomplished by setting off a virtuous circle supported by technical change. The major hurdle lying in the path of such a growth is the likely inconsistency between interest rates, as determined by financial markets on which a developing country has no leverage, and its internal rate of return. This calls for a very special and development minded exercise of financial intermediation which only international institutions can carry out. The objective is to reconcile financial terms with the production capabilities of a developing economy. The recent and continuing debt crisis and the need to resume lending to foster long-term growth calls for urgent steps to fulfil this task.

The discussion of the nature of technical progress, in the forms it also acquires in a developing context, does not support highly stylized and improbable patterns of international specialization based on relative factor endowments. What matters for economies to be able to stand the rigours of international trade, and also to partake of its benefits, is increasing returns as afforded by the complex dynamics of productivity growth. Both well considered theory and experience tell us that careful policies in order to develop an appropriate industrial structure are indispensable even at the cost of initial protection.

There is, unfortunately, nothing natural or automatic about development. An economist can only point at some very partially understood problems and at some highly stylized facts of a complex and intricate reality: a dismal limitation when what is at stake is the rising from the despair of subsistence, escaping from hunger and illness and quite likely the capacity to maintain even the pale resemblance of peace.

REFERENCES

ARTHUR, W. B. (1985) *Competing Techniques and Lock-in by Historical Events*, Stanford University: CEPR.

ATKINSON, A. B. and J. G. STIGLITZ (1969) 'A New View of Technological Change', *Economic Journal*, vol. 77, no. 3.

DOSI, G., C. FREEMAN, R. NELSON, G. SILVERBERG and L. SOETE (eds) (1988) *Technical Change and Economic Theory*, London: Pinter Publishers.

FREEMAN, C. (ed.) (1986) *Design, Innovation and Long Cycles in Economic Development*, New York: St. Martin's Press.

HARCOURT, G. (1972) *Some Cambridge Controversies in the Theory of Capital*, Cambridge: Cambridge University Press.

HELPMAN, E. and P. KRUGMAN (1985) *Market Structure and Foreign Trade*, Brighton: Wheatsheaf Books.

HICKS, J. (1973) *Capital and Time*, Oxford: Clarendon Press.

LANDES, D. (1969) *Prometheus Unbound*, Cambridge: Cambridge University Press.

NELSON, R. R. and S. G. WINTER (1982) *An Evolutionary Theory of Economic Change*, Cambridge, Mass.: Belknap Press.

RICOTTILLI, M. and M. CANTALUPI (1987) 'A Development Strategy with Foreign Borrowing', *Rapporti scientifici del Dipartimento di Scienze Economiche*, no. 35, Bologna.

ROSENBERG, N. (1982) *Inside the Black Box*, Cambridge: Cambridge University Press.

SEN, A. (1983) 'Development Which Way Now?', *Economic Journal*, vol. 93, no. 372.

WORLD BANK (1990) *World Development Report 1990*, Washington DC.

3 Agriculture and Growth

Carlo Bernini Carri

1 INTRODUCTION

The difference between the agricultural growth performances of the major countries since the 1960s has included the growth of cereal imports to North Africa, the Middle East, Sub-Saharan Africa and Latin America; the change in the status of the heavily populated Asian countries (India, Pakistan, Indonesia, Bangladesh) from being net importers of cereals to being self-sufficient or marginal exporters and the growth of agricultural surpluses in the OECD countries.

The growth of cereal and other agricultural commodity imports in developing countries can be explained by two opposite phenomena. The first is the result of growth of income in countries in early stages of development combined with high demand elasticities for food and other agricultural commodities. Together these factors generate a rapid growth in demand that outpaces even the success achieved in agricultural production. This is the case of many Latin America and Asian countries. On the other hand, increased imports can also be a result of internal production failure in the face of rapid population growth. A growth rate of food and agricultural production that remains well below the population growth rate must be financed through growing commercial imports and foreign aid to meet basic human food needs. This is largely the phenomenon found in Africa (Lele and Mellor, 1988).

Obviously, it is the first type of growth in world trade of cereals and other agricultural commodities which is both sustainable and desirable. Then there is the paradoxical contraposition between the developed world (Europe, USA, Australia and so on), where food surpluses continue to pile up, and the less developed world, where the picture is quite different. We should also add the growing differentiation among LDCs.

In many of the developing countries, food deficits are a recurrent situation. We could look at the food trade for the easiest solution to the world's food problem. Shipping food from more developed 'surplus' countries – like Europe and the USA – to still developing 'deficit' countries – like Africa – might seem to represent the solution to the world's food problem. However this neglects two very important factors. Firstly, hundreds of millions of poor people in the third world now lack the purchasing power to buy more food at virtually any price. These poor people suffer from the disabilities caused by a lack of income and employment opportunities. Thus increased food trade between the developed and the developing countries of the world must be coupled with efforts to raise the purchasing power of low-income people throughout the world. Secondly, in most developing countries accelerated agricultural growth represents the best means to stimulate overall economic growth. In most cases agriculture can play a number of pivotal roles in the development process. Increased agricultural production boosts domestic food supplies at the same time as it stimulates further rounds of employment growth in the service and urban sectors of the economy. Moreover, because of its linkage effects with the rest of the economy, agricultural growth helps to raise the poor's access to food supplies (Mellor, 1976).

2 AGRICULTURAL ROLES FOR DEVELOPMENT

A recent study by Adelman and Morris, focusing on the development experience of 23 countries between 1850 and 1914, has analysed the influence of agricultural development on industrialization. Four different types of development strategy were followed by countries during the nineteenth century. Historically, the role of agriculture and its institutional organization varied with development strategies, initial conditions, and between the early and the later stages of industrialization. But with the achievement of widespread economic growth there were no substitutes for the existence of (1) a substantial agricultural surplus; (2) a widely distributed agricultural surplus; (3) widely diffused incentives to improve agricultural productivity. There was no situation during the nineteenth century in which these conditions were not accompanied by industrialization, or where expansion in primary exportations did not lead to widespread domestic growth (Adelman, 1986).

Research has shown that the means by which agriculture is to be developed is closely related to the functions that it is to perform. Johnston and Mellor (1961) cited four classes of contribution made by agriculture: (1) to meet a rapidly growing demand for agricultural products associated with economic development (essentially a wage goods argument); (2) to increase foreign exchange earnings by expanding agricultural exports; (3) to supply labour to the non-agricultural sector; and (4) to supply capital, particularly for its own growth, for overheads and for secondary industry. There needs to be added at least a fifth role that can be of strategic importance in countries where the rural sector is a large component of the economy: to serve as a market for industrial output. The last role has been particularly emphasized by historical research. Indeed, recent research emphasizes the link between the agricultural revolution and the industrial revolution, the key variable being the interrelation process.[1]

An agricultural development strategy follows these objectives. The most obvious reference is the size of the agricultural sector in relation to the rest of the economy. Particularly in low income LDCs, agriculture may account for at least half of GDP while the share of the labour force located in the sector characteristically exceeds 70 per cent in low-income and 50 per cent in middle-income developing countries.

A homogeneous, traditional agriculture economy can be viewed as a starting point from which development must proceed. Questions therefore need to be asked in relation to how the transformation to a multisectoral, heterogeneous, modern economy can be achieved.

Increased productivity in agriculture has a crucial role to play in ensuring that a surplus of food will be generated. It is important not only to create but also to expand the agricultural surplus. The role of agricultural surplus increase has been traditionally considered together with agriculture in relation to other parts of the economy (agriculture's so-called 'instrumental' role); that is, its part in serving the ends of development by assisting in the growth of other sectors, in particular manufacturing, which has in turn been viewed as a factor of economy-wide development. In this light the agricultural surplus is needed to feed the modern industrial sector labour force. Furthermore, if the withdrawal of labour from agriculture at any point resulted in a reduction of food output by means of a positive marginal product of labour, food would start to become scarce for the modern industrial sector labour force. Productivity increase in agriculture is therefore required if growing food scarcity is to be prevented from turning the terms of trade against the modern industrial sector and thereby slowing or halting its growth as capital profits are eroded (Fei and Ranis, 1975; Jorgenson, 1967; for example).

The agricultural surplus for growth can be divided into two parts. According to Hall (1983), we can establish that a part of the surplus, exchanged for modern sector consumer goods (the 'marketable agricultural surplus') serves the purpose of feeding the modern sector workforce; but it is of at least equal importance to notice that this exchange process also provides a market for modern sector goods. In a closed economy it is the only source of demand for modern sector goods beyond the modern sector itself. The greater the agricultural productivity, the greater will be the agricultural surplus and the greater, therefore, the potential market for modern sector goods. Growth in the agricultural sector thus encourages growth elsewhere, and, to the extent that it is built upon locally created productivity, raises capital equipment and exerts demand upon the producers of investment goods as well as the producers of consumer goods.

Another part of the agricultural surplus generates the basis of capital stock that can be used by the modern sector to start the process of development, via investment and reinvestment, in motion (the 'investable agricultural surplus'). Once again, the greater the agricultural productivity, the more surplus there will be available to finance production in the modern sector (Hall, 1983, pp. 299–300).

In an open economy and in the absence of higher agricultural productivity a developing country may be forced to import food to meet the needs of its non-agricultural labour force as workers move away from food production. There is a serious opportunity cost in terms of goods and materials that could, alternatively, have been imported using the same foreign currencies. Higher agricultural productivity thus permits foreign exchange to be 'saved', or, more accurately, to be used for other productive non-food imports, vital for development. Assuming no domestic food shortages, higher agricultural productivity could increase the surplus by enough to allow food (or other agricultural products) to be exported. This would actually earn the country foreign exchange which would subsequently be used to buy imports. However, the surplus must be transferred and successfully deployed.[2]

Developing countries have, in general, been quite successful in transferring agricultural surplus elsewhere, especially by means of protecting the non-agricultural sector.[3] But protection has often been associated with such inefficiency in the modern sector that the developing potential of transferring the surplus has not been realized. Nonetheless, the dangers inherent in protected import substitution industrialization are now widely appreciated, and together with this advance has gone another, of equal importance for agriculture. Besides this traditional role of the agricultural surplus in connection with other sectors, a growing awareness of agricultural growth for its own sake has been realized since the 1970s.[4]

Indeed, too much emphasis on the instrumental role can lead to the neglect of efforts to develop the agricultural sector for the sake, directly, of its own population. The majority of the population in LDCs still lives in the agricultural sector; it is in this sector that we would expect the comparative advantage of many developing countries to lie; and it is here that poverty in its most intense form can often be found.[5] More recently, much more thought has been devoted, therefore, to raising rural incomes, creating rural employment and reducing inequality both within agriculture and between agriculture and non-agriculture. The achievement of higher levels of productivity is again an objective here, but a simultaneous aim has been to ensure that at least some of the benefits of higher productivity should in this case be felt by rural workers. It is this sort of thinking that has given rise to what is often called 'the Green Revolution'.[6] This is part of the general problem of growth–equity and technological change–social and institutional structure relations. Also, from experience of difficulties associated with the Green Revolution, many commentators have called for land or tenurial reform as a condition for the success of technical changes.[7]

Productivity could be raised simply by adopting more capital-intensive methods. A greater surplus would be generated, but given the evictions and rural unemployment that this approach could bring about, it has not been considered the best approach to the problem when viewed from the perspective of the agricultural sector alone. Land reform by itself can go some way to raising productivity and achieving a more equal distribution of income, but clearly it will achieve both increased yields and output, and improve equality if it is combined with land-augmenting innovations. If applied to appropriate landholding arrangements and with the necessary support of technical advice, credit and marketing services, technological change can not only benefit the entire rural populace but also raise productivity in such a way that should enable agriculture, in addition, to fulfil its instrumental role.

2.1 Growth strategies

The recognition of agricultural roles in the context of the growth process is the basic factor of developmental strategies appropriate for many LDCs. This strategy, the Johnston–Mellor approach, emphasizes consumer goods, employment and trade: these are the major points of departure from alternative strategies (for instance the Feldman–Mahalanobis strategy that can be considered an alternative reference to agricultural in a principal role).[8] There are three important differences. Firstly, it emphasizes consumer goods, both in the agricultural and non-agricultural sectors. Secondly, it emphasizes increased employment with respect both to labour supply and to labour demand. Thirdly, it emphasizes international trade and comparative advantages and hence is not concerned with growth balanced to meet the domestic demand structure as distinct from balance between complementary production processes. Each of these three features has important implications to agriculture's structure and development patterns. Each is complementary to the others. And, each represents a sharp contradiction to the alternative strategy.

The basic prescription for agricultural development under the circumstances of this strategy are the 'expansion of agricultural production based on labour-intensive, capital-saving techniques which rely heavily on technological innovations'. In agricultural development, emphasis was given by Johnston and Mellor to 'non-conventional inputs' in order to complement existing land, labour and capital resources. Explicitly mentioned are the large numbers of trained people needed by institutions for agricultural research, extension, supply or purchased inputs, particularly seed and fertilizer, and other institutional facilities. In the latter context, major emphasis is placed on large expenditure for education (Mellor, 1982). These may now appear as being quite widely accepted and even practical views. In view of this we must ask why this has not been the pattern in much of Africa and why it has not been pushed more vigorously in significant parts of Asia. Furthermore, after a quarter century of upholding these views, what further lacunae can we find in these concepts as they were presented at that time?

Reluctance to pursue this agriculture-based strategy can be explained by three sets of factors. Firstly, there has been explicit rejection of the basic premises with respect to the role of agriculture and consequently there has been a very different set of alternative approaches to agriculture, with important structural implications. Secondly, a number of diversions have occurred, arising from equality and ecological considerations which have been substantially based on ignorance of the context, the process and results of a technology-based development – a point of view which although based on incorrect analysis served to reinforce the conclusions of those starting from very different premises. Thirdly, Johnston and Mellor drew insufficient attention to the requirements of conventional infrastructure and hence to the size of required investment in agriculture and the implications for the structure of both agriculture and industry. Simultaneously the alternative development strategy has suffered from an under-estimation of food requirements, with consequent and unexpected constraints on growth. It is important to sort out these forces because the next few decades are likely to be a period when food demand shifts more rapidly than supply and in which broad participation in growth will be essential for political stability which is itself important for growth and development (Mellor and Johnston, 1984).[9]

If public services are available, the Johnston-Mellor approach leads to a highly competitive small scale sector.[10] If these supporting institutions are lacking, then a large scale agricultural sector will not only result in an even more unbalanced development pattern, but it will fail in at least two of the roles delineated for agriculture. It will be relatively more capital-intensive, because of the diseconomies of scale in labour management, and hence its net contribution of capital to the other sectors will be less. Similarly, because of greater concentration of wealth, the demand stimulus from expenditure will tend to leak out of the country much more than will be the case for smaller farmers (Mellor and Lele, 1973). As has just been said, there are two major lacunae which can be seen in an agriculturally based development strategy which can be found in the early work of Johnston and Mellor. They under-estimate the capital requirements essential for the movement of agriculture and they under-estimate the role of agriculture as a market for non-agricultural capital goods and services and also the key mechanisms for it to play this role.

Since the investment requirements are large, a decision is forced as to the extent to which the development plan is to be based on agriculture, or not at all. If the strategy is to be agriculturally based, a commitment is required in financial allocations and in policy. Closely related to this, Johnston and Mellor pointed out that agriculture's capital contribution came in the form of taxes or low relative agricultural prices. Although they noted agriculture's role as a market, they saw this more as a conflict with the capital contribution and hence a careful balance had to be found. This also resulted in a too restrictive attitude on agricultural prices. By emphasizing the market side more and recognizing the possibility of cost reducing technological change in industry, one can see agriculture as a sector providing a growing demand at constant prices for industrial goods produced at decreasing cost and hence with rising profits. It is the highly elastic demand arising from rising rural incomes that can provide the basis for a high rate of capital formation in the non-agricultural sector. These processes, the interaction with price policy, investment and rural policy, generally need to be elaborated more fully (Mellor, 1982).

The agricultural approach must be part of a global rural strategy. Indeed, for developing countries one of the greatest challenges for the next decades will be to integrate the labour surplus of agriculture and the landless people in rural areas into a growing economy. Policy makers as well as research people are aware that 90 per cent of the absolute poor are living in rural regions and that the absorption capacity of labour-intensive agriculture will be limited. Regarding the rapid expansion of the population in developing countries in the near future, there will be a strong challenge for an effective strategy to offer working places in backward rural regions. The challenge must be met to avoid the acceleration of internal migration from rural areas to over-populated urban agglomerations, which creates great social cost for society as a whole and which can create political unrest (Dams, 1989). In developed as well as in developing countries, there will be a relative decrease of agricultural workers. Nevertheless, owing to the fact that the population in developing countries is increasing, the absolute number of agricultural workers will grow sharply.

No doubt there is great disillusion in regard to the effectiveness of 'the progress of the struggle against poverty and hunger after twenty-five years of development cooperation' (DAC, 1985, p. 272). The catchword of international institutions is very well known: 'The eradication of absolute poverty in rural regions will remain a central area of development cooperation' and progress 'depends upon broadly based development success which in turn requires effective policies and incentive structures which lead to the productive use of all the human and natural resources of each developing country'. However, rural poverty as well as the strategies to overcome it, are very complex.[11]

Technological change in agricultural strategy in this sector of developing countries is critical. What causes technological change and how sources of growth in production change in the course of the development process from the relative dominance of traditional inputs, such as land and labour, to non-traditional, knowledge- and technology-based inputs are questions of particular interest in this decade of structural and sectoral adjustments. Developing countries suffering from macroeconomic difficulties and a debt crisis, especially in Latin America and Africa, have embarked on major programmes of reform backed by balance of payment support from international financial institutions. The major thrust of these recent programmes has been in changing the internal terms of trade in favour of agriculture and, in particular, of export agriculture by the removal of price distortions and by reducing the role of the public sector in marketing arrangements for inputs and outputs. Because of their short-term nature, adjustment programmes do not address issues relating to the role of governments in providing basic public goods – agricultural research and extension, physical infrastructure and education – the various non-price factors fundamental to initiating and sustaining technical change in agriculture. These are areas in which macroeconomic difficulties and related shortages of government revenues and other factors have reduced public investment levels and recurrent expenditure to a minimum (Lele and Mellor, 1988).

In research on growth, a general approach has emerged which stresses the importance of relative prices in determining the rate of aggregate agricultural production mainly through the process of capital accumulation that favourable terms of trade in agriculture cause. It perceives technological and even institutional change as essentially being the embodiment of capital induced by changes in relative prices (Hayami and Ruttan, 1985; Mundlak, 1988). On the other hand, others such as Schultz consider knowledge to be the most powerful engine of production and attribute the dynamics of growth generally to investment in human capital, thus leading to technical change, division of labour, and specialization (Schultz, 1980 and 1986). Others have stressed the limitations of prices in bringing about technical change, citing a number of different reasons, including limits imposed by trends in world market prices conditioned by rapid technical change in more advanced countries (Mellor and Ahmed, 1988). Mellor has also questioned the desirability of using price mechanisms as the principal source of inducement for technical change in view of its adverse income distributional effects (Mellor, 1978).

It is therefore evident that the generation of modern technology and the associated use of increased inputs require substantial investment also in non-traditional types of capital with externalities, such as research and extension facilities, education and other institutions. Rural infrastructure, such as roads, irrigation, drainage systems, communications networks and delivery systems, is necessary to provide farmers with access to markets for modern inputs and for their increased output. All these forms of capital have externalities and require hard investment on a scale which small farmers cannot always mobilize. A great deal of such investment must inevitably be undertaken by the public sector at early stages of development (Lele and Mellor, 1988).[12]

3 AGRICULTURAL GROWTH AND POLICIES

National governments' attempts to control and manage their economies are constrained by the evolution of the international markets which respond to long-term economic forces and to other governments' actions. Because of these interdependencies, public authorities feel the need to co-ordinate their actions; but the absence of a world government or of effective discipline renders such co-ordination very difficult, both for agricultural market interventions and for macroeconomic policies (Petit, 1988).

Technological and ecological interdependencies are also very strong: they also raise major problems of political co-ordination. Taking a global perspective, it has become clear that economy-wide policies in developing countries are major determinants of progress in agriculture. This has been especially evident in Sub-Saharan Africa, the only region in the world where food production has failed to keep pace with population growth.

Specific consequences for agriculture of macroeconomic adjustments are brought about by intersectoral linkages (de Janvry, 1985). Since in most of the developing countries the major part of agriculture is in the traded sector, trade policies must receive special emphasis. Interdependencies among domestic agricultural commodity markets through international linkages have grown in recent decades. This is reflected in the mere fact that international trade represents a growing share of total world production. Trade deficits lead to protectionist pressures. So do major and rapid shifts in comparative advantages brought about by major shifts in exchange rates.

In many developing countries servicing their external debt will require an increase of export earnings. For many of them, particularly in Africa, the prospects for industrial raw material and manufactured goods exports are bleak. This means that agricultural exports must increase. At the same time, rapid demographic growth creates the need to increase domestic food production, even if complete food self-sufficiency cannot be aimed at. In these conditions, managing the balance between export and subsistence crops and keeping total agricultural production growing will represent a difficult challenge in many of these countries (Petit, 1988).

The conditions that less-developed countries face in world markets largely determine the options open to them in formulating their own development strategy. Possible scenarios in international commodity markets, including agricultural products, together with conditions in financial and exchange rate markets, and foreign assistance, mark out the external economic conditions that determine the prospects for LDCs in the next decade.

Pricing and trade policies followed by industrial and developing countries will have a great effect on future growth of rural and (indirectly) urban income, and thus the alleviation of poverty. Trade is what connects national price systems into an international price system, without which we can hardly measure economic rationality. The international price system is the most important information that national price systems process. For agriculture, as for any other highly tradable sector, trade is what makes a national price system work. The problem with agriculture is that world prices are so distorted that it is doubtful whether world markets for many agricultural products deserve to be called markets (Valdés, 1989). Agricultural trade issues are at the centre of the relationship between industrial and developing countries. This is the case for basic foodstuffs, where major growth in agricultural world trade has occurred, and which are increasingly involving LDCs both as importers and exporters. The rate at which many LDCs grow is very much a function of their export earnings, most of which are from agriculture. We have more trade barriers in agriculture now than at the beginning of the Tokyo Rounds in 1973. In no other major sector do we find so much production being sold on world markets at less than domestic prices, to a large extent dictated by the developed countries' domestic farm policies (Valdés, 1989).

Various studies have been made to estimate the impact of a possible liberalization of agricultural trade, that is of a drastic decline in government intervention on agricultural markets. Assuming a positive elasticity of supply, they all point to an increase in world prices of most agricultural commodities. The impact on the welfare of developing countries depends heavily on whether or not the particular country is a net importer or a net exporter of agricultural products. For the former, consumers suffer a loss. Thus there is no doubt that the current situation provides them with at least a term of trade gain. But the most important impact may be the long run effect of low world prices on the development of domestic agriculture. In many developing countries, particularly in Africa, growth of agriculture is a necessary ingredient of any sustainable development strategy. The present situation is not favourable for agricultural growth since imported foodstuffs, supplied to large urban centres benefiting from the subsidy war among developed countries, cost much less than domestic production, penalized in addition by limited transportation facilities. Policy makers, under pressure from urban areas, are tempted to take advantage of this cheap food, thereby sacrificing the potential contribution of agriculture to long-term growth.

The key mechanism by which broad development strategies and macroeconomics policies affect agriculture is the real exchange rate. Agricultural products, besides being generally tradable, are not differentiated much and, as such, the export demand faced by agricultural producers of a given country is usually price-elastic, which means that its export demand is very sensitive to exchange rate variations. An over-valued exchange rate acts as a tax on exports and a subsidy on imports. Tradables are discriminated against in relation to non-tradables. The reverse is true if the exchange rate is under-valued. Of course, these impacts can be amplified or compensated by border measures, as reflected in the concept of an effective rate of protection. Nevertheless, the exchange rate variations tend to lead to changes in relative domestic prices (Petit, 1988; Valdés, 1989).[13] Policies that determine movements in the real exchange rate need to be co-ordinated with sectoral policies if agriculture is to do well and if food security is to be attained.

Adverse movements in the real exchange rate have been serious in Africa and in other countries in South America.[14] However, sectoral policies have also contributed to a serious bias against agriculture. Taking account of both economy-wide policies and of policies on producer taxation and on marketing of agricultural outputs and inputs, agriculture has been systematically discriminated against in developing countries. While 'non-price' measures are also important, experience suggests that incentive policies have been all too often mistaken. Frequently, urban food subsidies policies have been responsible for the low profitability of agriculture. While food subsidy programmes can be made less expensive and better directed to poorer income groups, there can be a trade-off between economic growth and the alleviation of food security problems. This trade-off is particularly serious in low-income countries with unsatisfactory rates of economic growth (Ray, 1986).

While developing countries can do much better in agriculture, the policies undertaken by OECD countries cannot be neglected. These policies have high domestic costs. They also impose costs on developing countries. More liberal trade and domestic policies in both OECD and developing countries are needed. The benefits of such policies will be high, exceeding the annual flow of official development assistance to developing countries. With more liberal trade, many developing countries will be able to increase their agricultural exports, and some of them will emerge as new exporters. The reason for this is that technological progress has been quite rapid in many countries, especially in Asia and South America. Developing countries can now compete in the production of temperate-zone products much more easily than they could two or three decades ago.

In contrast, existing international initiatives have done little. This is especially true in respect to international commodity agreements and special trade preference schemes. Compensatory financing schemes and food aid policies are much better, but they are not fundamental solutions to the problem.

4 AFRICAN AGRICULTURAL GROWTH

Looking at the structure of African economies, agriculture still takes the largest share of the GDP and agricultural population forms the bulk of the national population. Agriculture currently provides 33 per cent of Africa's GDP and 40 per cent of its exports. All this means that Africa is still pre-industrial and, as such, should be more reliant on its agriculture than she has been over the last two decades. A recent World Bank report (World Bank, 1989) underlines the fact that the first generation of African leaders adopted economic strategies that echoed the ideas of famous economists of the day. Industrialization was believed to be the engine of economic growth and the key to transforming traditional economies, partly because the prospects for commodity exports were thought to be poor and partly because of a strong desire to reduce dependence on manufactured imports. Agriculture was relegated to a secondary role of supplying raw materials and providing tax revenues to finance other development. To implement these strategies, African leaders believed that government had to play the dominant role.

During the 1960s agricultural production grew at 2.7 per cent a year, about the same as the population. Thereafter agricultural growth slowed considerably, averaging only 1.4 per cent from 1970 to 1985, half the rate of population growth. This decline was due to many factors, including droughts. But it also reflected the low priority given to farming, a sector in which Africa has a clear comparative advantage, by Africa's post-independence development strategies. Policies kept farm prices low, encouraged labour and capital to flow into cities, promoted cheap imports of food such as wheat and rice, which are preferred by urban consumers, and neglected agricultural research (World Bank, 1989). Africa is a particular victim of the inconsistent versions of the non-agriculture based strategy. With population growing faster than food production, higher commercial food imports and food aid have been necessary, although not sufficient: lack of purchasing power and other distributional factors have meant that hunger has become more widespread.

Agricultural production has gone down in most countries, food deficits have been on the increase and the food import bill has further compounded the debt crisis in Africa. While natural conditions have had their fair share in explaining what has been going on, production relations and the character of the state must be carefully analyzed in trying to diagnose cause factors and in prescribing solutions.

Economic growth in most African countries, over the last 20 years, has been heavily influenced by fortunes in the agricultural sector. From agriculture come the major export crops on which a large number of mineral poor African countries depend for foreign exchange. Agriculture, therefore, has been the backbone of economic development in these countries (Nyong'o, 1988).

> In the course of the last two decades, at a time when the African continent was confronted with a rapid population growth as well as urbanization, the food and agricultural situation in Africa deteriorated very radically: the production and consumption of food per capita fell well below nutritional requirements. (OAU, 1980)

Thus Africa is the only continent which has experienced a decline in per capita food production during the last two decades. Self-sufficient in food production at independence, Africa is today a net food importer. The current agricultural and food crisis in Africa, seen in terms of persistent food deficits, increasing food import and declining food production are but part and parcel of a much more global problem in Africa: the failure of development projects since independence.

Exploiting Africa's land resources offers the best immediate opportunity for raising incomes. Over the longer term and with policies that foster private investment and entrepreneurship, the industrial sector could undoubtedly contribute increasingly to Africa's economic growth. But it is to agriculture that Africa should look for its primary foundation for growth during the coming years. Yields are far below potential. Industrial growth, starting from a much smaller base, could be significantly higher. But neither sector will prosper unless the links between the two are strengthened. In most African countries these links are weak because of poor infrastructure and the failure to gear production to rural needs and to overcome the fragmentation of rural and urban markets. Savings in the agricultural sector provide the basis for capital formation in cities, and surplus earnings in the urban sector are in part channelled back to rural areas.

Agricultural growth stimulates the demand for consumer goods and for agricultural inputs produced by industry, and in turn industrial growth stimulates the demand for food and for inputs into agroprocessing industries (see Nyong'o, 1988). The strategy proposed by the international agencies, such as the World Bank and the IMF, for a plan of action to raise agricultural growth differs significantly from present practice in most countries. Governments still manage agricultural prices, markets, and the supply of farm inputs; use para-state rather than private credit and crop development agencies, emphasize large-scale rather than small-scale irrigation, and provide agricultural research, extension, and animal health services through separate donor-financed area or crop development projects rather than through coherent national programmes. With some notable exceptions little attention is being given to the environment, to land tenure, or to enabling men and women in the rural areas to take full charge of their lives. Agriculture can become the engine of growth only if all this changes. More public investment in agriculture is not the critical factor. The key to success is to make the farm sector more productive through better policies and stronger institutions and most of all, by developing people (World Bank, 1989).

Both the World Bank and the IMF have recently stepped in to prescribe policy options that would make the agricultural sector in Africa perform much better. In essence, both financial institutions are concerned with the fact that the poor performance of African economies makes them poor and unreliable recipients of loans, and hence not very good clients to do business with. If agriculture is to perform better, then state policies must be appropriately tailored to their performance. To date, both bodies argue, price policies, structure of exports, exchange rates and public expenditure patterns have all been ill-conceived and have led to economic distortions; these have all to be adjusted if these economies are to perform better. The concept of structural adjustment generally comes from steps taken to bring domestic economic institutions and policies more into line with world prices, trade patterns and investment opportunities.

Any attempt to improve food production and agricultural productivity in Africa will have to address the following issues: the peasant question, the relationship between agriculture and industry and the role of the state in the economy.

> In the past, these issues have been dealt with under the vague notion of rural development. At other times, they have been looked at in terms of small-scale versus large-scale farming, or commercial versus subsistence agriculture. Where industry is concerned, people are much more concerned about looking into the prospect of agriculture supplying raw materials for industry rather than both agriculture and industry supporting each other. The role of the state is also not simply one of involvement or non-involvement: from Meiji Japan to Stalin's Russia through to the USA, the state has been involved in both agriculture and industry. The difference, of course, is the nature and extent of involvement; there has never been as such, any economy perfectly controlled by market forces (Nyong'o, 1988).

The policy options for the agricultural growth must fit into sustainable development. In the developing countries rapid population growth without management of natural resources is increasingly destroying the vegetation, soils and water supplies which are the basis for agriculture. The regional distribution of populations and of food production shows that most of the world is defeating the Malthusian hypothesis but that Africa is losing the battle. The World Food Programme since 1974 has not succeeded in establishing international food stocks for famine prevention. Improved agricultural technologies have indeed been transferred to developing countries by 30 years of international programmes but implementation has been ineffective. Food production potential is being destroyed by soil erosion; services in agriculture, education and welfare are overwhelmed by present growth rates. The scientific resources devoted to this problem are still totally inadequate (Pereira, 1986).

The outlook for the sustenance of world populations for the next three decades is of over-supply in the high latitudes, of adequate self sufficiency in most of the tropics, but of continuing crises in Africa between the Sahara and the Zambesi River. A detailed study of individual country prospects by FAO indicates that population growth will continue to outrun increases in food production in Africa (Alexandratos, 1988).

4.1 Some implications

Successful pursuit of an agricultural strategy on development requires an active partnership between the developing and the developed world. On the one hand, the developing world must come to recognize the positive role that agriculture can play in its development. It must attempt to stimulate agricultural output by revising their investment, pricing and exchange rate policies. The developed world, in turn, must seek to encourage such policy reappraisals by making available the capital and technical resources necessary to support an agricultural development strategy in the third world. The developed world must also be prepared to provide the food imports that accompany the process of economic growth in the developing world. From the dynamics of such a partnership, the world could conceivably evolve into a place where adequate food is not just a right of all people, but an accepted fact.

The role of Europe with regard to world food problems must be to help the developing countries to grow their own food. Tropical food deficits are not solutions to the problems of the European Community (EC) agricultural surpluses. Disaster relief will continue to be needed, but capital investment, reinforcement of managerial skills by joint enterprises and practical in-situ training, especially in maintenance, should replace the failed policies of academic training.

Now every meeting of policy makers in developed, as well as developing, countries concludes that action is needed to redirect policies and accelerate structural adjustment of agricultural production. The cost of this adjustment would be less if governments acted together. The findings of recent studies in the two aspects (policy reforms in trade and agricultural policy in industrial countries and in general trade and macroeconomic policies in LDCs) conclude that the cost of OECD's agricultural protectionism to LDCs has been large. There is a great deal to be gained by both industrial and developing countries from simultaneous removal of non-tariff barriers on agricultural trade in both groups of countries.

Besides North–South partnership, a strong action for South–South positive integration processes is needed. This is particularly so in order to realize food security, research policies, agricultural and industrial trade increases, technological growth, ecological restorations and so on, overcoming the constraints of integration processes based only on trade liberalization.[15]

The adjustment programmes of international institutions are inadequate for three main reasons: they are not aimed at a long-period development approach that needs structural changes; they aim at the effectiveness of market mechanisms, often under-valuing the non-price determinants of growth; and they have not only pronounced social consequences, but also an ecological impact. Indeed, a strong constraint on the exchange rebalance can lead to unsupportable pressure on natural resources, often the only available capital for LDCs. Africa is looking for a suitable development model, after the failure inherent in the attempt to adapt developed countries' patterns. In many cases, African economies are not yet dualistic structures but prevalently agrarian structures. Agricultural and rural growth are therefore prerequisites for any development model.

NOTES

1. There are two main analytic formulations: the French historical school and Bairoch's works. The first assumes as being strategic the interdependence and the simultaneity of the agricultural and industrial revolution; the second the precondition of the agricultural revolution in the industrial process, at least following the British experience. Both approaches assign a key role to the agricultural surplus, that make possible the establishment of market, which is regarded as the central institution of the growth process (Bairoch, 1963; Leon, 1980; Bernini Carri, 1986).
2. On the question of carrying out intersectoral transfer, it is sometimes assumed that a landlord class, to whom the agricultural surplus goes as rent, sees and grasps the opportunities to invest in modern sector activity. Dixit (1973) has expressed scepticism on this score, pointing out that this view puts an implausibly heavy burden upon the entrepreneurial drive and skills of the landlord group.

   If the institutionally oriented landlord argument is to be discounted, at least four other alternatives might be considered. The first two, the 'Marxist–Leninist' and 'market-oriented' approaches, are analyzed by Owen (1966).

Describing the Marxist–Leninist approach, Owen points to direct state intervention in organizing and operating collective farms as the core of an attempt to maximize surplus. Combined with this is the strategy of requisitioning; that is, relying upon the physical direction of agricultural produce to state procurement agencies to allocate farm output to the non-agricultural sector. This direct, quantity-control approach has to be contrasted with the 'market-oriented' picture. Here agriculture is assumed to be made up of a profusion of price-taking, competitive, family farming units whose productive activity is aimed primarily at permitting them to acquire by exchange the goods and services produced by the non-agricultural sector. To complete the picture, the non-farm sector is increasingly assumed to be characterized by concentration and monopoly in its markets (Hall, 1983).

3. There is the assumption that technical progress raises productivity in both sectors. The asymmetry in market forms, however, results in the benefits of progress passing disproportionately into the hands of the non-agricultural sector. In the farm sector, it is supposed, the pressure of competitive conditions hastens the diffusion (or spread) of new techniques, shifting the sectoral supply curve outwards and resulting in an increased market supply of food at a lower market price. On the other hand, it is argued that farmers as consumers are denied compensating gains from technical progress in the modern sector because, as producers, they have the monopoly power to lay more prolonged claim to the benefits of their higher productivity. Another form of this argument is when the modern sector is protected by tariff and quota. One effect of this will be to turn the terms of trade against agriculture. This can be viewed as raising modern sector real incomes and, assuming a positive (and preferably rising) marginal trend to save, this should increase resources available for investment – the appearance of the 'investible surplus'. While protection of industry is, of course, equivalent to taxing agriculture, governments finally may simply resort to direct taxation of farm incomes to mobilize the surplus for modern sector use (Hall, 1983).
4. For a reference to the historical change in agriculture growth and the development process, see for instance Staatz and Eicher (1984).
5. For a reference on this point, for example see World Bank (1990).
6. Note first of all that productivity can in principle be raised, with higher incomes for all, by exploiting what may be called the 'extensive margin of cultivation'. Here a population of a given size can be envisaged, raising productivity by putting an increasingly large area of land under cultivation by moving into formerly unfarmed territory. The land–labour ratio rises and, in addition, we would expect the ratio of output to labour to rise. This is not the margin with which we are concerned with here, although it could be important in the more sparsely populated LDCs, especially in Africa. Exploiting the 'intensive margin' is achieving higher output per man from a given stock of land by working it harder or 'better'.

   We could think of three ways in which exploiting the intensive margin may serve developmental ends, although in practice the strategies may well be used in combination. Rearrangement of land holdings may achieve a distribution of land–labour ratios across holdings that raises productivity at the same time as creating new employment. Second, innovations may be used that are, at least initially, labour-displacing and thus, by definition, may raise labour productivity and/or which are most effective on larger holdings. Most mechanized innovations can be classed in this way. Finally, scale-neutral innovations can be used to raise output and productivity, in this case without any apparent threat to employment. These innovations, which are most readily associated with the Green Revolution, include high-yielding crop varieties (HYV), chemical inputs including fertilizers, and special cultivation practices. In contrast with the second type of innovation, these techniques should be equally effective whether on large plots or small (Hall, 1983, p. 303).

7. If a country is aiming at encouraging individual enterprise, reform is likely to have as its objectives the desire to ensure security of tenure and the strengthening of mechanisms to permit rewards to be associated with individual effort. It will often also be necessary to provide instruction about new techniques, access to credit and marketing support. The World Bank reports emphasize the security of tenure question, especially for Africa (World Bank, 1989).
8. This structure originated from Feldman's work on the USSR's investment plan during the first phase of planning, subsequently reconsidered by Domar and reformulated by Mahalanobis for India (II five-year plan). These approaches, based essentially on capital goods production, assume the economic growth rate as a function of capital forming. Given agriculture as a consumer goods industry, the scarce resources for it should increase the present welfare to the detriment of future growth; accordingly it does not play a primary role. For these models capital is the limiting factor, not the marketable surplus of wage-goods and employment (Bernini Carri, 1986).
9. For a reference to forecasts, see for instance Paulino (1986); Alexandratos (1988).
10. Indeed this approach is based on privately operated smallholder agriculture which is technologically dynamic, commercializing rapidly and, because of variation in control of resources and in enterprise, experiencing increased income disparities within the peasant farming sector. Large-scale economies in agricultural labour management are such that it is unlikely that such agriculture will be economically organized into large scale units, whether they are co-operative, collective, state farms or plantations (Mellor, 1982).
11. There are many different approaches to overcome this problem. According to Dams, one of these is the theory of central places in integrated rural development or the importance of fostering rural growth centres as a precondition for regional development. That can only be one element of an efficient strategy for rural development which has the main objective of absorbing surplus labour in backward areas. This important element has to be integrated into the concept as a whole; rural growth centres are an infrastructural component which can create a favourable atmosphere for agricultural and industrial development in rural areas. As a reference see Dams (1989).

12. In fact, according to Mellor, the common feature of the success achieved in Japan and Taiwan is that each country created such an effective set of public goods (Lele and Mellor, 1988).
13. The main factors influencing the exchange rates are those which influence the financial flow between a particular country and the outside world. This link is direct when the value of the currency is free to float. In more general cases where public authorities intervene the influence of financial flows (capital movements) remains very strong because they are taken into account by public authorities in their decisions to devalue or to 'peg' their currencies.
14. For a recent reference, see for instance Sorrentino (1990).
15. For a reference to negative integration as opposed to positive integration and to South–South agricultural trade growth chances, see for instance: Bernini Carri (1990).

REFERENCES

ADELMAN, I. (1986) 'Interactions between Agriculture and Industry during the Nineteenth Century', paper presented at the International Conference on the Agro-Technological System Towards 2000: A European Perspective, Bologna.

ALEXANDRATOS, N. (ed.) (1988) *World Agriculture Toward 2000: An FAO Study*, London: Balhaven Press.

BAIROCH, P. (1963) *Révolution industrielle et sous-développement*, Paris: Sedes.

BERNINI CARRI, C. (1986) 'Offerta Alimentare e Sviluppo Economico: Alcune Considerazioni in Merito all'Attualità del Pensiero Classico', *La Questione Agraria*, no. 21.

BERNINI CARRI, C. (1990) 'Integrazione Sud–Sud: Alcune Considerazioni', *SIDEA, Interdipendenza e Conflitti nelle Relazioni Agricole Internazionali*, Bologna: Il Mulino.

DAC (12985) *Twenty-Five Years of Development Co-operation: A Review*, Paris, OECD.

DAMS, T. J.(1989) 'Rural Development Strategies: Theory and Practice from the Viewpoint of Central-Place Theory, in J. W. Longworth (ed.), *China's Rural Development Miracle*, St. Lucia: University of Queensland Press.

DE JANVRY, A. (1985) 'Integration of Agriculture in the National and World Economy: Implications for Agricultural Poicies in Developing Countries', Working Paper, no. 360, University of California, 1985.

DIXIT, A. (1973) 'Models of Dual Economies', in J. A. Mirrlees and N. Stern (eds), *Models of Economic Growth*, London: MacMillan.

FEI, J. C. H. and G. RANIS (1975) 'A Model of Growth and Employment in the Open Dualistic Economy: the Cases of Korea and Taiwan', *Journal of Development Studies*, no. 11.

HALL P. (1983) *Growth and Development: An Economic Analysis*, Oxford: M. Robertson.

HAYAMI, Y. and V. RUTTAN (1985) *Agriculture Development: An International Perspective*, Baltimore: Johns Hopkins University Press.

JOHNSTON, B. F. and J. W. MELLOR (1961) 'The Role of Agriculture in Economic Development', *American Economic Review*, September 1961.

JORGENSON, D. (1967) 'Surplus Agricultural Labour and the Development of a Dual Economy', *Oxford Economic Papers*, no. 19.

LELE, U. and J. W. MELLOR (1988) 'Agricultural Growth, its Determinants, and its Relationship to World Development: An Overview', paper presented at XX International Conference of Agricultural Economists, Buenos Aires.

LEON, P. (1980) *Storia Economica e Sociale del Mondo. Le Rivoluzioni 1730–1840*, vol. 3, tomo 1, Bari: Laterza.

MELLOR, J. W. (1976) *The New Economics of Growth: A Strategy for India and the Developing World*, Ithaca: Cornell University Press.

MELLOR, J. W. (1978) 'Food Price Policy and Income Distribution in Low Income Countries', *Economic Development and Cutural Change*, no. 1.

MELLOR, J. W. (1982) 'Agricultural Growth. Structure And Patterns', paper presented at III Session of the International Association of Agricultural Economists, Jakarta.

MELLOR, J. W. and B. F. JOHNSTON (1984) 'The World Food Equation: Interrelations Among Development, Employment and Food Consumption', *Journal of Economic Literature*, no. 22.

MELLOR, J. W. and R. AHMED (1988) *Agricultural Price Policy For Developing Countries*, Baltimore: Johns Hopkins University Press.

MELLOR, J. W. and U. LELE (1973) 'Linkages of the New Foodgrain Technologies', *Indian Journal of Agricultural Economics*, no. 1.

MUNDLAK, Y. (1988) 'Capital Accumulation, the Choice of Techniques and Agricultural Output', in Mellor and Ahmed (eds), *Agricultural Price Policy*.

NYONG'O, P. A. (1988) 'The Political Economy of Agriculture in Africa', in XX International Conference of Agricultural Economists, Buenos Aires.

OAU (The Organization of African Unity) (1980) *The Lagos Plan for Action for African Economic Development, 1980–2000*, Addis Ababa: OAU.

OWEN, W. (1966) 'The Double Developmental Squeeze in Agriculture', *American Economic Review*, no. 56.

PAULINO, L. (1986) 'Food in The Third World: Past Trends and Projections to 2000', Research Report no. 52, Washington, International Food Policy Research Institute.

PEREIRA, C. (1986) 'Agricultural Output Growth, Technical Progress and Environment Carrying Capacity: A Historical and Technological Analysis', paper presented at the International Conference on The Agro-Technological System Towards 2000, Bologna.

PETIT, M. (1988) 'Presidential Address', in XX International Conference of Agricultural Economists, Buenos Aires.

RAY, A. (1986) 'Agricultural Policies in Developing Countries: National and International Aspects', paper presented at the International Conference on The Agro-Technological System Towards 2000, Bologna.

SCHULTZ, T. W. (1980) *Investing in People*, Berkeley: University of California Press.

SCHULTZ, T. W. (1986) 'On Investing in Specialized Human Capital to Attain Increasing Returns', paper presented at the Symposium on The

State of Development Economics, Economic Growth Center, Yale University.

SORRENTINO, A. (1990) 'Il Ruolo del Tasso di Cambio nella Valutazione del Protezionismo Agricolo nei PVS', *Rivista di Economia Agraria*, no. 3.

STAATZ, J. M. and C. K. EICHER (1984) 'Agricultural Development Ideas in Historical Perspective', in Eicher C. E. and Staatz J. M. (eds), *Agricultural Development in The Third World*, Baltimore: Johns Hopkins University Press.

WORLD BANK (1989) *Sub-Saharan Africa. From Crisis To Sustainable Growth*, Washington, DC.

WORLD BANK (1990) *Poverty. World Development Report 1990*, Oxford: Oxford University Press.

VALDÉS, A. (1989) 'Impact of Trade and Macroeconomic Policies on Agricultural Growth', in J. W. Longworth (ed.), *China's Rural Development Miracle*, St. Lucia: University of Queensland Press.

4 Peasants and Capitalists in Developing Countries' Agriculture with Particular Reference to India

Luigi Marcuccio[1]

1 INTRODUCTION

From the sixteenth to the nineteenth century, British agriculture was characterized by a process of land concentration, through the enclosures and the eviction of long-term tenants by the feudal landlords. As a consequence large estates, managed by dynamic individuals, willing to invest capital for profit, arose. At the same time, the decline of proto-industrial and handicraft activities, whose products could not compete with similar ones of industrial origin, determined the proletarianization of the rural masses. These processes triggered the capitalistic development in agriculture and industry, firstly by providing cheap labour for both sectors, and secondly by raising agricultural productivity through the use of technologies characterized by economies of scale.

On the basis of this historical experience many social scientists, from orthodox Marxists to liberals to radicals, are still convinced that the destruction of non-capitalistic forms of production in agriculture is inevitable in the course of social change and also highly desirable. Consequently, the undeniable persistence of such forms is seen as a non-structural phenomenon, determined by the insufficient development of the area in which they are present (see Lewis, 1954 and 1958; Rostow, 1960; Feder, 1977–8) or by the capitalistic development itself, so as to be thought the 'other side of the coin' to it (see Frank, 1975; Stavenhagen, 1969; Amin, 1973). Finally, the non-capitalistic forms of production are thought to be backward, compared to progressive capitalistic development.

Contrarily to this idea I would argue, first, that the capitalistic transformation in developing countries, in agriculture as well as in industry, does not necessarily imply, even in the long run, the disappearance of non-capitalistic forms of production in agriculture. Second, I think non-capitalistic farms are not necessarily backward, and structurally incapable of investing in agricultural improvements, though the determinants of their investment decisions are different from the capitalistic ones. Third, the persistence of non-capitalistic forms of production in the primary sector, within a capitalistic framework, is highly desirable, from a static as well as a dynamic point of view, given some features of agriculture and, above all, of the capitalistic development in the primary and the secondary sectors. Fourth, it is my view that, as the peasant families would be worse off if the capitalistic ones did not exist, both enterprises gain from their relationships. Fifth, I think that agricultural capitalistic transformation and 'peasantization', that is the process through which the peasant farm becomes indiscernible from the capitalistic one looking at the yields per acre, are not necessarily mutually incompatible, but often highly correlated phenomena.

2 THE CONCEPT OF THE PEASANT FORM OF PRODUCTION

In this chapter, I will use the terms 'peasants', 'peasant farm', or 'family farm' to indicate an enterprise cultivating some land mainly through family labour, and involved in a wider economic system, in which non-peasants act (see Saul and Woods, 1971). Regarding the first feature of the peasant farm, as a consequence of the identity between the family and the enterprise, the concept of salary has no explicative power, and labour becomes a fixed cost: all the members of the family, apart from their utilization in the agricultural activities, have to be fed, because of an extra-economic obligation. This does not mean, however, that the family farm will employ labour to the point that its marginal productivity becomes equal to zero: the self-demand of labour, as a matter of fact, can be thought of as resulting from a process of utility maximization, through which, at the same time, the levels of production and family income, the factoral demand functions, and the leisure time are determined. Concerning the existence of some relationships between the family farms and other agents, economic or not, these have not necessarily to be of the market type or to imply an exploitation of one part by the other.

It is necessary to point out that referring to the familiar organization of labour (see Chayanov, 1924 and 1925) is not sufficient to define unequivocally the peasant farm, because such a definition, focusing on the internal features of this enterprise, neglects the analysis of its relationships with external agents. On the other hand, stressing the mere existence of such relationships, rather than specifying them, permits us to subsume in this concept a variety of historical experiences, from ancient regime family farms to those operating today in developing as well as developed nations. By this definition, then, it is possible to distinguish the peasant farm from the primitive tribal group, which, by hunting and gathering, do not apply labour in order to get a future utility, and from the capitalistic farm, which relies mainly on hired labour.

In the definition presented above, there is intentionally no reference to some features traditionally ascribed to the peasants, such as the production mainly for self-consumption, the backward technology utilized, the limited or, at least, non-large size of the holding, and the labour intensity of the techniques chosen. Concerning self-consumption, the existence of market-oriented peasant farms, in developed as well as developing nations, clearly shows that, because of the asymmetry between the involvement in the market from the point of view of the outputs and of the inputs, mainly labour, not all the commodities have necessarily to be produced through commodities: in other words, the commercialization of agriculture is not sufficient to eliminate the familiar organization of labour. Concerning the level of technology, it has to be noted that this prejudice comes from the idea that agricultural technology is profitable only if implemented in large estates, because of the economies of scale. The diffusion of green technology in South Asia in the 1970s, on the contrary, indicates that innovations such as the use of high yield varieties, fertilizers, pesticides and so on can be adopted by peasant farms leading to high production increases. As pointed out by Patnaik (1986), then, there is no strict relation between the form and the scale of production. The concept of family farms as small and medium-sized derives from the assumption that the amount of family labour is limited, so as to prevent the cultivation of large holdings by peasant farms. This conception, nevertheless, can be valid only if technology and cropping patterns are fixed: a large estate can be managed with less labour than a small one, if labour-saving techniques, involving mechanization, are implemented, and/or labour-saving crops are cultivated. Regarding the factorial intensity of techniques chosen, finally, it cannot be denied that family farms, because of their inner structure, tend to utilize labour-intensive techniques. The choice of techniques, however, depends on the ratio between the absolute availability of non-marketable inputs, namely labour, and the land cultivated. Consequently, if family labour is insufficient for agricultural activities, the peasant farm chooses between demanding hired labour or increasing the use of capital, adopting similar criteria to the capitalistic one, that is the comparison between the marginal productivities of these factors, divided by their respective marginal costs.

The set of the peasant farms, of the relationships between them and of those between each farm and the 'others' define together the peasant form of production. This concept, however, is different from that of mode of production (see Ellis, 1988), as peasant households are always embedded in a larger society where a particular mode prevails: social reproduction within them obeys the rules of the dominant mode of production, even if peasants have some ability to reproduce independently from that mode.

Finally, in order to show the empirical importance of the concept of the peasant farm, I will analyse briefly the Indian experience. In this country, the percentage subdivision of the agricultural labour force between cultivators and agricultural labourers,[2] from 1951 to 1981, has not varied: the former still represented, in 1982, 62.51 per cent of the total, without substantial variations between backward states, like Bihar and Orissa, and advanced ones, such as Punjab and Haryana. Furthermore, not only has utilization in some states of family labour in percentage terms in total labour use for agricultural activities not declined over the years, but also it is not greater in the backward states than in the advanced ones.[3] On the contrary, it seems to have a fluctuating trend, probably determined by the fact that, if the harvest is abundant, casual labourers are hired, and consequently the percentage share of family labour in the total decreases.

3 CAPITALISTIC PENETRATION IN THE PRIMARY SECTOR

Let us analyse capitalistic penetration in agriculture, distinguishing between two levels, a general and a specific one. First, the development of capitalism in the secondary sector transforms the global environment in which agricultural enterprises act: it determines a multiplication of intersectoral relationships by stimulating all agricultural enterprises to produce for the market, and to use, for production as well as for consumption, commodities of industrial origin. Second, this process triggers the formation of capitalistic farms, as the demand of industrial labour destroys the familiar organization of this factor.

By 'capitalistic farm' I mean an agricultural enterprise using hired labour in order to get a profit, which is mainly reinvested in the economic activity. It has to be pointed out that both conditions have to exist in order to qualify such a farm as capitalistic. First, hired labour can be used only to satisfy the personal needs of the employer, or to produce a surplus which is totally consumed: for example, for centuries in some Indian regions there have been agricultural labourers, hired by the feudal-type landlords in the peak periods of the agricultural year. The use of hired labour, then, *ceteris paribus*, is directly linked to the dimension of the farm, that, as seen above, cannot be taken as a proxy for its inner nature. Second, the propensity to invest, by hiring labour, by purchasing or renting agricultural machineries, by implementing irrigation systems and so on is not peculiar to capitalistic farms, as it also characterizes, given some conditions, the peasant ones.

It is very difficult to give statistical evidence about the existence of capitalistic farms in developing countries. However, Indian experience, for example, shows the rise of an all-India agricultural labour market,[4] based on economic relationships between the employer and the employee: poor peasants have, in the last two decades, been migrating from backward states, like Bihar, to advanced ones, like Punjab and Haryana. Furthermore, from 1971 to 1981,[5] average permanent attached workers per farm have increased from 1.87 to 2.39, and, at the same time, farms reporting permanent attached workers have decreased dramatically in relative terms, from 18.96 per cent to 5.89 per cent; so, while previously many farms used permanent hired labour, in the 1970s there has been a process of polarization between farms utilizing only family labour and casual hired labour and farms using hired labour, both permanent and casual, in bigger and bigger quantities.

The capitalistic transformation in developing countries' primary sector, nevertheless, though undeniable, has led in most cases to the development of backward capitalists (see Patnaik, 1986), usually extracting surplus through semi-feudal as well as capitalistic relationships, and structurally incapable of raising the level of productive forces beyond a certain point, after which their monopoly of power is challenged. It is necessary to stress, however, that this fact has no strict relation with a supposed 'Prussian path' having occurred in these nations, in contrast to a preferable 'American path' (see Lenin, 1908), because both have been happening. Such backwardness rather depends, in my view, on the limited relationships between urban and rural capital and, through the demand of labour, the nature of capitalistic development in the industrial sector. As a matter of fact, in most cases, the growth of capitalistic farms in developing countries has been, and still is, semi-endogenous: it has been triggered by that in the secondary sector, through a multiplication, from both sides, of intersectoral relations; but it has been implemented without the active involvement of the urban capital, which mostly has been refraining from agricultural investments. Consequently, the capitalistic transformation of feudal-type relations within the primary sector has been carried out almost exclusively by people, though coming from the peasantry as well as the landlords and the rural merchants and money lenders' social groups, with a rural background, embedded in the existent social structure, and unwilling to transform it radically.

Finally, the notion of backward capitalism, though it stresses the persistence of feudal-type economic relations within agriculture, is profoundly different from the so-called 'semi-feudalism hypothesis' (see Basu, 1984; Bhaduri, 1983). According to this idea, agriculture in developing countries is characterized by the pre-eminence of semi-feudal production relations, which oppose economic development. Contrarily to this notion, I would argue that backwardness is not determined by a lack of capitalistic transformation, but by its inner nature: consequently, as pointed out by Rudra (1982) with reference to India, no alliance between progressive capitalists and landless labourers against feudal landlords can be implemented, as the former and the latter form a unique social group.

4 WHY PEASANT FARMS PERSIST

There is a lot of evidence about the persistence of family farms in developing countries, even if capitalistic transformation has been occurring. In India, for example, between 1953 and 1982, though land reform was a failure, the distribution of owned and even operated land patterns has not shown any concentration process, and the share of family labour in the total has not decreased.[6]

Let us now enucleate the factors that hinder the complete destruction of peasant farms distinguishing between those inherent in the peculiarity of agriculture and those derivating from the nature and the pace of capitalistic transformation, in both agriculture and industry. Regarding the former, it is necessary to stress the distinction, peculiar to the agricultural activity, between production and labour time. As, because of this discrepancy, there are some periods in which the labour force cannot be employed, the family farm, relying on non-economic ties and flexible in the use of this factor, has a structural advantage compared to the capitalistic one.

This fact, if it can justify the persistence of family farms, is not helpful, however, in explaining why capitalistic farms arise. I think that it is the very nature of capitalistic transformation outside agriculture to shape the features and the pace of capitalistic transformation inside, so as to influence strongly the persistence of family farms. Contrarily to the traditional view (see Lewis, 1954 and 1958), historical experience proves that an unlimited supply of labour is not always sufficient to trigger a capitalistic development: often it is the latter, instead, which determines the degree of proletarianization.

As pointed out by Gerschenkron (1962), late-comer countries cannot simply imitate, in order to develop, the path followed by Great Britain, because of the presence, at the moment of their take-off, of already industrialized nations. In particular, I would stress that in developing countries, contrarily to the 'English path' during the industrial revolution, if land concentration is not necessary for capitalistic development, proletarianization can be even harmful and waste resources.

Concerning land concentration, the agricultural technology available to developing countries, consisting mainly of the adoption of high-yield varieties, the use of bigger quantities of pesticides and fertilizers, and the implementation of irrigation facilities, does not need large estates to be profitable. Consequently, capitalists do not need to dispose of large plots of land to implement these innovations: at the same time, given a certain amount of disposable capital, they prefer to use it for adopting the new technology rather than for buying land.

Going on to the proletarianization issue, let us distinguish between labour demand coming from the industrial and the agricultural sectors. Concerning the first, an analysis of the patterns of industrialization followed by developing countries clearly reveals that, contrarily to the 'English path', it has been concentrated mostly on capital-intensive sectors, characterized also by a positive correlation between sectoral growth and labour productivity (see Kaldor, 1966; Verdoorn, 1949) and, consequently, by a dynamically declining labour demand. Furthermore, it was calculated (see Bairoch, 1963) that, on average, the capital requirements per worker have increased 70 times since the Industrial Revolution: this strongly favours the adoption of labour-saving techniques within each industrial sector. Finally, the pace of demographic increase in developing nations implies that, even if labour demand from the secondary sector grows in absolute terms, its percentage share of the labour force probably will not vary: for example, in India, even if there has been in the last 40 years a not negligible industrialization process, the share of the total labour force employed outside agriculture has been stable at the 30 per cent level.[7] Regarding the agricultural labour demand, the adoption of high-yield varieties and of bigger quantities of pesticides and fertilizers has to be distinguished from mechanization (see Table 4.1). The former, by and large, has the effect of increasing labour demand, though of casual hired labour and family labour more than permanent hired labour; the latter, on the contrary, determine a contraction of labour demand and particularly of hired permanent labour. It is necessary to bear in mind, then, that the two innovations mentioned above are, at least in the long run, correlated, because the multiple cropping, made possible by the first, determines a contraction in the time available for ploughing and reaping and the need to use farm machinery: so, in the long run, the adoption of technology reduces the agricultural labour total demand, and, at the same time, in percentage terms in the total, that of hired permanent labour. Therefore, proletarianization very probably would transform a supposed disguised unemployment in the

Table 4.1 Percentage patterns of employment during different stages of mechanization in sample farms in India, 1971–2

Stages	*Family labour*	*Permanent hired labour*	*Casual hired labour*
Pure bullock farm	56	26	18
Plus tubewell/oil engine	66	11	23
Plus other farm machinery	46	24	30
Plus tractor	25	25	48

Source: A. Parikh (1984).

countryside into an absolute one in the rural and urban areas, into increasing social tensions, and into a reduction of agricultural production (unless it is unrealistically assumed that expelled agricultural workers had zero or negative productivity) without a parallel increase in the industrial one.

Such reflections could make students incline towards a neo-Marxist explanation (see Frank, 1975) for the persistence of family farms. On the contrary, it has to be taken into account that, if some factors stimulate the family farm not to disappear, some others allow it not only to resist the capitalistic forces, but also, as will be seen later, to compete with the capitalistic enterprise. Furthermore, Indian experience in this regard shows that agricultural development is not incompatible with the persistence of such enterprises: in India, though peasant farms represent the majority of agricultural enterprises, agricultural production more than doubled from 1950 to 1986.[8]

5 AN ANALYSIS OF THE RELATIONSHIPS BETWEEN CAPITALISTIC AND FAMILY FARMS

Capitalistic farms and peasant families relate to each other in numerous ways, inside the outputs as well as the inputs markets. First of all, as there is no substantial distinction between these two kinds of enterprises in the choice of cropping patterns, their relations regarding the product market, undoubtedly of market type, are very similar to those between one of the two farms and the industrial sector. Regarding the inputs markets, it is useful to distinguish between those of capital, of agricultural machinery, of land, and of labour, beginning with the first.

Often in agricultural societies the landlord, more or less capitalistically oriented, also lends money, either in exchange for a committment of future labour, or at high interest rates. This phenomenon, being a particular aspect of the so-called 'interlocked (or interlinking) markets hypothesis' (see Bardhan, 1984; Bhadhuri, 1983), has been traditionally considered a major hindrance to agricultural development. The historical experience of Western Europe, however, in which usury played a fundamental role in the accumulation of capital, suggests we should attenuate such a negative judgement. Even if the lender takes a bigger advantage, the borrower, if other sources of agricultural credit are scarce, can have its utility in obtaining capital for agricultural improvements. Rudra (1982) then stressed that not only landlords lend money, as there is usually in the countryside a social group specifically involved in this activity: for example, in mediaeval Europe only landless Jews practised usury, because religious precepts forbade Christians to earn money through lending it.

Concerning the market for agricultural machinery, Shergill (1988) noted that, in India, the number of farms using it is far larger than the owning ones. Through the rising of a market for the leasing of agricultural machinery, the capitalistic farm, which usually has capital to buy it, takes advantage of the existence of peasant families to lease it to them; on the other hand, the latter, which cannot afford to buy the machinery, can use it if it is indispensable for getting high yields.

Going on to the land factor, traditionally two opposite ideas, regarding the identification of the leasor and the leasee, have dominated. According to the first of them, in developing countries it is mostly the landlord who leases some land to backward peasants (see Bhadhuri, 1983; Basu, 1984), as under the European feudal system. On the other hand, scholars like Rudra (1982) advocate, even if with strict reference to India, that it is the small peasant who rents the land he owns to the larger ones and to the landlords. This idea, though resembling the classic one of land concentration and proletarianization as correlated to agricultural capitalistic development, differs from it in one fundamental feature. According to this vision, the peasant, being aware of the imperfections in the hired labour market and the declining trend of the demand for hired labour, prefers not to sell his land, but to rent it. Examining this issue with particular reference to India, one gains the impression that both dynamics occur in rural societies, so that the net effect is often zero: in India, in point of fact, there are no differences between the trends of owned and operated land concentration ratios, from 1951 to 1982.[9] Concerning the first idea, most of the landlords in developing countries have begun, during the last decades, to cultivate personally or to supervise the cultivation of the land they own, looking for a profit; on the other hand, the rented land is leased in by both capitalists and peasants. Regarding the second idea, as pointed out above, the peasants can sustain the competition of capitalistic farms, because of the scale-neutrality of available technology; at the same time, given the features of labour demand in the agricultural and industrial sectors, they do not want to abandon the land, even for a limited period. The decision to lease land in or out actually concerns both peasant families and capitalistic farms, and sometimes even the same enterprise adopts both measures. It depends, first, on land fragmentation, as all farms prefer to lease out the plots which are distant from the main one or from the family residence, in order to lease in some closer ones. Second, this decision is strongly influenced by the interdependence between soil quality and/or existing infrastructures such as irrigation facilities, on one hand, and cropping patterns, on the other. For example, a peasant farm, if it can dispose of abundant family labour, can lease out some rain-fed plots where labour intensive crops cannot be profitably cultivated, in order to lease in irrigated ones. It is to be taken into account, finally, that the relationship between the capitalistic and the peasant farm concerning the land renting market is not a zero-sum game, in the sense that, if one of them increases its operated land, the other diminishes it: in rural societies a considerable amount of land is owned by people living in the countryside, who, for cultural and religious reasons, cannot cultivate it (for example, the brahmins in India), and by persons living in urban areas. In India, for example, non-agricultural families, living in the village or having emigrated, represented, in 1981, 26.58 per cent of all landed families, and they owned 8.74 per cent of cropped land.[10] In conclusion, the renting process, allocating land in a better way, favours both capitalistic and peasant farms.

Finally, let us analyse the relations between them concerning the labour market. In some developing societies landless agricultural households have not, in percentage terms of all agricultural households, increased, but, on the contrary, decreased in the last decades: for example, in India,[11] they passed from 28.86 per cent in 1961–62 to 23.09 per cent in 1971–2 to 11.33 per cent in 1982. Consequently, most of the hired labour employed in the capitalistic farms does not come from the landless, but from the peasant families. By hiring peasants instead of proletarians, given the necessity of casual rather than permanent labour, capitalists get rid of the labourers' feeding burden in the slack periods of the agricultural year; on the other hand, peasants dispose of an additional source of income. It does not mean, of course, that the peasant family does not hire labour in the peak periods of the agricultural year and/or if the ratio between labour force and consumers within it is, in some periods, too low for implementing cultivation on the operated land. On the contrary, as labour is dishomogeneous and/or some members of the family are hired outside as permanent labourers, peasant farms, at the same time, often hire in and out labour (see Bardhan, 1984). In conclusion, the analysis of the relationships between peasant families and capitalistic farms clearly reveals that even if peasants are exploited by agrarian capitalists, they would definitely be worse off if the latter were absent: such an exploitation, therefore, can be considered as 'socially necessary' (see Roemer, 1982).

6 THE SOCIAL OPTIMALITY OF THE COEXISTENCE OF PEASANT AND CAPITALISTIC FARMS: FROM A STATIC TO A DYNAMIC VIEW

In this chapter I will use the term 'socially optimal pattern' to indicate a desirable pattern, from a static as well as a dynamic point of view. Concerning the latter, such a pattern is, at least, compatible with, and often favours industrial as well as agricultural development. Regarding the former, such a pattern determines a 'socially optimal resource allocation', that is, an allocation whose change would determine a reduction in the national income and an undesired increase in the total leasure time of a social group. It is necessary to stress that, if some factors are relatively scarce, such as capital and land, an efficient allocation is also socially optimal: on the contrary, if they are relatively abundant, as with labour in developing countries, an efficient allocation, that is one made on the basis of the equality between marginal productivity and cost, is not socially optimal. It is my opinion that the coexistence of capitalistic and peasant farms, typical of some developing countries, is a socially optimal pattern.

From a static point of view, as stressed by Sen (1964), if peasant families use labour inefficiently, but in a socially optimal way, capitalistic farms utilize efficiently, and at the same time in a socially optimal way, capital and land. The peasant farm, as a matter of fact, because of its inner structure, can use labour apart from the level at which the wage equals the marginal productivity of labour, so that, feeding expenses being equal, a higher level of production can be achieved than in the case in which such a constraint works. In countries such as most developing ones, then, characterized by an abundance of labour compared to capital and land, family farms using labour-intensive techniques ensure a more socially desirable use of this factor; on the other hand, reaping with a scythe rather than with a machine has not necessarily a negative impact on the yields per hectare. Finally, the family farms can use non-marketable inputs, such as the labour of young and old people, and, above all, women. As revealed, however, by the debate on the size of holding and the yield per acre, a peasant solution cannot be completely accepted. As a matter of fact, all the empirical studies on this issue, if they cannot deny the existence of some kind of inverse relationship between these two variables, at least with reference to India in the 1970s, they do not explain why it happens (see Bharadwaj, 1973). According to this relationship, peasant families, supposing they are small and medium-sized, can obtain higher yields per unit of land applying the same amount of inputs as capitalistic farms, or bigger quantities of non-marketable inputs (mainly labour), or bigger quantities of inputs that could be otherwise utilized, like pesticides and fertilizers (see Shergill, 1988), or because the land they own is more fertile (see Sen, 1964). I think that all the last three explanations have to be accepted: as a matter of fact, because of the complementarity between different inputs, the inefficient, but socially optimal, use of labour by family farms leads to an inefficient, and socially sub-optimal, utilization of capital and land by them. The existence of capitalistic farms, therefore, because of their utilization of land and capital deriving from neoclassical laws, determines a more efficient utilization of land and capital within the whole agricultural sector.

Such an analysis, however, is not satisfactory. First, focusing mainly on the agricultural relations, it does not take into account the intersectoral links; second, if it can depict the coexistence of such types of farms, it is useless in explaining the rise of capitalistic ones and, at the same time, of 'peasantization', typical of some developing countries, such as India. It is necessary to note, then, that, as the nature and pace of capitalistic transformation within the primary sector are fundamentally determined by the industrial one, the two issues mentioned above can be subsumed.

Let us analyse, therefore, the social optimality of the coexistence of capitalistic and peasant farms from a dynamic point of view. As stated before, the technology available in agriculture as well as in industry, on the one hand, does not need such processes as proletarianization and land concentration. On the other, the peasant farm can take advantage of the presence of the capitalistic one because of the availability of agricultural machinery to rent, of getting additional sources of income, of technological externalities, so increasing the chances of modernizing itself: the capitalistic farms, as a matter of fact, can with less difficulty bear the risks and the costs of technological innovation that, by spillover effects, also benefit peasant families. Thirdly, the persistence of peasant farms can keep the labour force within agriculture rather than expelling it, so limiting urban migration. As peasant families can crop land whose cultivation is not profitable for capitalistic farms, and capitalistic farms diffuse agricultural innovations, agricultural production can grow at the same pace as the food demand coming from urban areas, and consequently the scissors trend of agricultural prices versus industrial prices is hindered. Finally, the coexistence of capitalistic and peasant farms can conciliate the trade-off, existing at least in the short run, between the necessity of capital accumulation, through income polarization, and that of the expansion of the market for industrial goods, through a more equitable income distribution.

Summing up, in analysing the social optimality of the coexistence of capitalistic and peasant farms in agriculture, we should distinguish between capitalistic agricultural development, on the one hand, and pure agricultural development, that is yields as well as rural masses' purchasing power increases, on the other. These processes are usually thought to be the two sides of the same coin, because, during industrial revolution, they occurred simultaneously. On the contrary, the historical experience of developing countries, like India, during the last 30 years clearly shows that they are different phenomena, as a high growth of agricultural yields and rural consumption have been obtained without such processes as land concentration and proletarianization. As a matter of fact, if agricultural capitalistic transformation depends on the nature and pace of the industrial one, through the industrial labour demand, the industrial take-off depends on the agricultural development, through the rural demand for industrial goods and the supply of agricultural products. Therefore, if on the one hand, because of its inner nature and pace, industrial capitalistic transformation does not need a lot of proletarians, and, on the other, if agricultural production and rural consumption grow more if peasant farms are not squeezed but coexist with capitalistic ones, such a pattern is dynamically optimal.

7 CONCLUSIONS

From the destruction of the feudal-type mode of production and the capitalistic development in the primary and the secondary sectors, capitalistic farms, though backward, have been emerging, and, at the same time, peasant farms, previously operating at a low degree of productivity, have begun to modernize themselves. The coexistence and correlation of such processes, occurring at least in some developing countries, is also socially desirable.

I would stress that much more attention has to be paid to the idea, developed by social scientists such as Laclau (1971), that the modes of production articulate each other within a single economic system. Such a theory could provide useful insights for understanding the fact that, within the capitalist mode of production, non-capitalist forms grow and reproduce, without being ancillary to it. Finally, I think that all the 'constrained' development theories, that is those sharing the common vision that all societies have to pass through similar stages of development, which strongly influenced most of western thought, from Marx (1867) to Parsons (1955) to Rostow (1960), have to undergo a profound revision.

NOTES

1. I would like to express my deep gratitude to Professors Krishna Bharadwaj, Carlo Filippini and Gianni Vaggi for their fundamental contributions. Of course none of them has any responsibility for what is written here.
2. Census of India, 1961, 1971, 1981.
3. S. Bhalla, 'On the Proliferation of Small Farms and Labour Absorption in Indian Agriculture', unpublished manuscript.
4. Census of India, 1981.
5. National Sample Service, *Reports* nn. 215–331.
6. Government of India, 1988.
7. Census of India, 1961, 1971, 1981.
8. Government of India, 1988.
9. National Sample Service, *Report* no. 331.
10. National Sample Service, *Report* no. 338.
11. National Sample Service, *Report* no. 331.

REFERENCES

AMIN, S. (1973) *Le développement inégal. Essai sur les formations sociales du capitalisme périphérique*, Paris: Editions de Minuit.

BAIROCH, P. (1963) *Révolution industrielle et sous-développement*, Paris: Sesdes.

BARDHAN, P. K. (1984) *Land, Labour and Rural Poverty in India*, New York: Columbia University Press.

BASU, K. (1984) *The Less Developed Economy*, Oxford: Basil Blackwell.

BHADURI, A. (1983) *The Economic Structure of Backward Agriculture*, New York: Academic Press.

BHALLA, S. (1988) 'On the Proliferation of Small Farms and Labour Absorption in Indian Agriculture', unpublished manuscript.

BHARADWAJ, K. (1973) *Production Conditions in Indian Agriculture*, Cambridge: Cambridge University Press.

CHAYANOV, A. V. (1924) 'Zur Frage einer Theorie der Nichtkapitalistischen

Wirtschaftssysteme', *Archiv fur Sozialwissenschaft und Sozialpolitik*, Band LI, pp. 577–613.

CHAYANOV, A.V. (1925) *Organizatsiya krest'yanskogo khozyaistva, Iz Rabot Nauchno-Issledovated'skogo Instituta s.-kh. economii*, Mockva: Tsentral'noe tovarichestvo kooperativnogo.

ELLIS, F. (1988) *Peasant Economics*, Cambridge: Cambridge University Press.

FEDER, E. (1977–8) 'Campesinistas y descampesinistas: tres enfoques divergentes (no incompatibles) sobre la destrucción del campesinado', *Comercio Exteriór*, vol. XXVII, no. 12, pp. 1439–46 and vol. XXVIII, no. 1, pp. 42–51.

FRANK, A.G. (1975) *On Capitalistic Underdevelopment*, Bombay: Oxford University Press.

GERSCHENKRON, A. (1962) *Economic Backwardness in Historical Perspective*, Cambridge: Harvard University Press.

GOVERNMENT OF INDIA (1988) *Agricultural Statistics at a Glance*, New Delhi: Ministry of Agriculture.

KALDOR, N. (1966) *Causes of the Slow Rate of Growth in the United Kingdom*, Cambridge: Cambridge University Press.

LACLAU, E. (1971) 'Capitalism and Feudalism in Latin America', *New Left Review*, no. 67, pp. 19–38.

LENIN, V.I. (1908) *Razvitie kapitalizma v Rossii, Izd. 2–e dopoln.*, St. Petersburg: Knigoizdatel'stvo 'Pallada'.

LEWIS, W.A. (1954) 'Development with Unlimited Supply of Labour', *Manchester School of Economic and Social Studies*, vol. XXII, no. 2, pp. 139–91.

LEWIS, W.A. (1958) 'Unlimited Labour: Further Notes', *Manchester School of Economic and Social Studies*, vol. XXVI, no. 1, pp. 1–32.

MARX, K. (1867) *Das Kapital*, Hamburg: Meissner Verlag.

PARIKH, A. (1984) 'Employment and its Determinants in Indian Agriculture', *Asian Economic Review*, vol. XXVI, nn. 1–2, pp. 1–19.

PARSONS, J. (1955) *The Social System*, Glencoe: Free Press.

PATNAIK, U. (1986) *The Agrarian Question and the Development of Capitalism in India*, Delhi: Oxford University Press.

ROEMER, J.E. (1982) *A General Theory of Exploitation and Class*, Cambridge, Mass.: Harvard University Press.

ROSTOW, W.W. (1960) *The Stages of Economic Growth*, London: Cambridge University Press.

RUDRA, A. (1982) *Indian Agricultural Economics. Myths and Realities*, New Delhi: Allied Publishers.

SAUL, J.S. and WOODS, R. (1971) 'African Peasantries', in T. Shanin (ed.), *Peasants and Peasant Societies*, Baltimore: Penguin Books, pp. 103–14.

SEN, A.K. (1964) 'Size of Holding and Productivity', *Economic Weekly*, vol. XVI, nn. 6–7–8, pp. 323–6.

SHERGILL, H.S. (1988) 'New Technology and Farm-Size Productivity Relationship: A Decomposition Analysis', *Asian Economic Review*, vol. XXX, no. 2, pp. 246–57.

STAVENHAGEN, R. (1969) *Les classes sociales dans les sociétés agraires*, Paris: Anthropos.

VERDOORN, P.J. (1949) 'Fattori che regolano lo sviluppo della produttività del lavoro', *L'Industria*, no. 1, pp. 45–53.

Part II
Lessons from the Debt Crisis

5 A Brief Debt Story

Gianni Vaggi

1 INTRODUCTION

This chapter provides a short guide to the problem of LDCs' debt in the 1980s. Various aspects of this question are analysed in other chapters of the book, therefore some non-exhaustive information about the problem may help us to understand both the issues involved and the economic 'jargon' which has arisen from the debt crisis.

The issue of developing countries' debt displays a certain 'irrationality', and peculiarity *vis-à-vis* accepted economic theory. The most intriguing aspect of this question, but also the most worrying, is the time factor, for a variety of reasons. First, these debts were accumulated in the space of very few years in the second half of the 1970s and continued to grow from 1980 to 1982, even though the level of indebtedness had already caused concern. In short, commercial banks did not appreciate the economic dangers of the situation quickly enough. Second, these were short-term loans, which were then hastily transformed into long-term commitments by mutual agreement between creditors and debtors. Third, since the crisis surfaced with Mexico's 1982 moratorium declaration, seven years passed, a period in which the pretence that these debts were totally redeemable was maintained. In reality the impossibility of debt redemption for most debtor countries was already clear in 1982. Finally, in March 1989, the Brady Plan hinted at the possibility of debt cancellation, albeit restricted to a very modest 20 per cent. Fourth, from 1983 onwards debtor countries have made payments to their creditors, above all large commercial banks, in excess of new loans, but this has not significantly improved the situation.

Thus a solution to the debt crisis needs to be found quickly, since prolonging the situation a further 10 to 15 years may cause very strong social and political tensions to escalate in developing countries. At the same time the foreign debt issue of these countries is a symptom of unbalanced North–South trade relations, which are heavily weighted in favour of rich countries, and by itself the cancellation of these debts would not have a decisive effect on the South's development. Some of these issues are examined below with the aim of assessing what rationale, if any, governed the decisions which were made.

2 DEBTS AND THEIR ORIGIN

Since 1989 there have been 15 countries which are regarded as being 'heavily indebted': Argentina, Bolivia, Brazil, Chile, Colombia, Côte d'Ivoire, Ecuador, The Philippines, Yugoslavia, Morocco, Mexico, Nigeria, Peru, Uruguay, and Venezuela. From time to time, the addition of Costa Rica and Jamaica brings the total to 17. However this list does not include some debtor countries, such as South Korea, Egypt, Indonesia and India, which have sizable accumulations of debt, but only those named in the Baker Plan, whose debt is mainly with commercial banks (World Bank, 1989, p. 16).

In 1990 total accumulated debt was around $1220 billion (see World Bank, 1990b, p. 126), this was almost 44 per cent of the overall gross national product (GNP) of indebted LDCs and less than 9 per cent of the GNP of OECD countries. The situation is less serious in Asia than in Africa or Latin America; African countries south of the Sahara had amassed a debt totalling 160 billion dollars by 1990 and would have to forfeit more than one year's worth of GNP and 3.5 years' worth of their exports to pay off their debt. The debts of Sub-Saharan Africa amount to slightly more than 1 per cent of the GNP of OECD countries. The dramatic situation of Sub-Saharan countries is well described by the usual ratios which assess debtor countries' credit-worthiness – that is to say their ability to repay debt. In 1990 some of these ratios for Sub-Saharan Africa were as follows (see World Bank, 1990b, p. 130):

Total debt stocks/GNP	111.9%
Total debt stocks/exports	351.6%
Debt service/GNP	7.8%
Debt service/exports	24.4%

The situation is not much better in other regions such as Latin America, North Africa and the Middle East and some Mediterranean countries. It must be remarked that the situation has improved slightly since 1986, but the above figures clearly show that the debt problem is far from being solved.

In the 1960s and early 1970s many developing countries had higher growth rates than industrialized countries (see World Bank, 1989, p. 7; World Bank, 1987, p. 16). Moreover, the strong surge in oil prices and other raw materials between 1970 and 1974 (World Bank, 1989, p. 11) increased commercial banks' faith in the economies of developing countries. Hence short-term loans were granted without stringent conditions in the belief that they could be repaid in the very short term, on the basis of recent economic performance in developing countries and their export goods price trend throughout the 1970s. It is also relevant that demand for credit in the richer countries stagnated during these years, concurrent with abundant liquidity on international markets. Until 1982 banks under-estimated the riskiness of these loans to less developed countries.

Developing countries' current account deficits increased up to 1982 (World Bank, 1987, p. 17; Nunnenkamp 1986, p. 4) yet they were nevertheless able to pay for these deficits, having access also to private financing from 1975 to 1981 (World Bank, 1987, p. 18). Since 1982 private financing has been drastically reduced. The strong decline in real terms of raw material prices compared to their 1976–7 levels (World Bank, 1989, pp. 9, 11) reduced the 'export unit values' in terms of US dollars of debtor countries – particularly up to 1986 (see World Bank, 1990b, p. 139). Therefore the foreign currency required to repay former debts became more and more scarce for indebted countries. In addition, tight monetary policy and fiscal expansion adopted in the USA from 1980 onwards caused a sharp increase in interest rates on international markets. The real interest rate for LDCs – that is to say the nominal LIBOR deflated by the change in the export price index of developing countries – which was negative in 1980 rocketed to 22 per cent in 1982, and remained consistently above 8 per cent except for 1987 (see World Bank, 1987, p. 19). Nominal interest rates were unilaterally increased by the lending banks. These increases forced debtors to make net transfers abroad earlier than anticipated (so that interest payments and capital repayment were far more than new disbursements); in 1987, 38 billion dollars were transferred out of developing countries (see World Bank, 1989, p. 18).

The increase in interest rates and the drop in export earnings represent unexpected macroeconomic developments that debtor countries hold should not be accounted to them. Latin American countries demand instead that debt should be reduced in proportion to these external factors, namely the difference between interest rates in the 1970s and 1980s, which they attribute to US monetary policy.

Clearly, in addition to external causes, internal factors also encouraged the increase of debt; in particular capital flights are likely to explain a large share of Latin American debt. According to some authors capital flights and the financial transfer due to interest and profit payments abroad explain more than 50 per cent of debt contracted in 1987 (see Parboni, 1987, p. 31). Other domestic causes which led to the inefficient use of foreign loans were a large and often unproductive public sector, corruption, over-investment, slow reaction to the financial crisis, inaccurate trade policies and over-valued exchange rates.

3 EVENTS SINCE THE CRISIS OF 1982

Paradoxically, but not overly so, there exists a problem of credit rather than one of debt. Since 1982 there has been a drastic reduction in private credit to the developing world. Large commercial banks, especially American ones, suspended financing when they realized that it would be difficult or impossible for developing countries to repay the debt. Financing fell from more than 50 billion dollars in 1980 and 1981 to a point where the flow of capital was reversed in 1986 (Guttentag and Herring, 1989, p. 5). When a country does not repay its debt it is no longer considered creditworthy; this fate has befallen many African countries. International financing has concentrated above all on Japan and America, owing to high interest rates in the USA and the anticipated revaluation of the yen.

Developing countries have had to rely solely on official assistance, which has been barely sufficient to pay interest to private creditors. In addition, lending from official institutions was often linked to the adoption of so-called Structural Adjustment Programmes by the receiving countries. Thus loan conditions dictated by the International Monetary Fund and the World Bank often compelled these countries to adopt policies designed to contain demand: reduced public spending, elimination of subsidies on basic necessities, devaluation, foreign trade liberalization, money wage freezes and reduction in the real value of wages. Hence living conditions declined. Of all the measures 'suggested' by the IMF undoubtedly the hardest for populations to bear has been the abolition of subsidies on basic necessities. This factor has provided the fuel for revolts in Yugoslavia, Venezuela and Algeria. For sure in many LDCs recession would have occured even without the implementation of the policies suggested by the IMF, but it is also true that until now these policies have neither restored growth in the poorest countries, nor have they channelled to them substantial private lending.

In the 1980s, developing countries cut back sharply on imports; the most heavily indebted countries with average import growth rates of 5.5 per cent during 1973–80, recorded rates of –6.9 per cent in the period 1980–6 (see World Bank, 1987, p. 26). From 1980 to 1987 in Nigeria the average annual 'growth' rate of imports was –14 per cent (see World Bank, 1989, p. 190). Many debtor countries have not maintained their infrastructures, or renewed fixed capital, and have cut back social spending and the funding of state enterprises (ibid., p. 12). Clearly the drop in developing country import levels signifies a reduction in world trade and harms industrialized countries as well since they forfeit potential markets; the case of OPEC countries is the most widely known.

Average export levels also have decreased, weakening the capacity to repay debt. Nevertheless many developing countries have surpluses on their non-interest current account, and with this surplus they pay part of the interest due (see ibid., pp. 28–9). This is the phenomenon of the 'negative net transfer', which since 1983 has characterized financial flows between North and South. Before 1982, an amount equal to 2 per cent of their GNP was annually transferred *to debtor countries*, but since 1983 a 3 per cent of debtors' GNP has been transferred *to creditors* every year (see ibid., p. 17). This fact, and the prohibitive cost of external financing, have resulted in nil net investment levels (see ibid., p. 13).

4 THE LENDING BANKS

In December 1982 large American banks were heavily involved with lending to developing countries, and some found themselves on the brink of financial disaster. The ratio between exposure and reserves, for the nine most heavily exposed banks, averaged 172.5 per cent (see Guttentag and Herring, 1989, p. 15); for a few banks the ratio exceeded 200 per cent and yet they did not collapse (see Nunnenkamp, p. 102). From 1982 this situation improved significantly; in December 1987 this ratio had become 95 per cent (see Guttentag and Herring, 1989, pp. 19, 24, 34). What happened?

The international financial system, and especially the American one, sought to buy time by pretending that these loans were recoverable.

Banks were unable to write off these loans because this would have resulted in a decrease of the banks' capital, with a further worsening of the ratio of unrepaid credits to capital. This could have provoked a crisis of confidence among shareholders and thereby a fall in stock exchanges. Instead the average maturity of loans was extended, increasing the reserves for unrepaid loans. Reserves have been increased, using a procedure called 'provisioning' to augment 'loan-loss reserve' funds, as in the case of Citicorp which in May 1987 boosted its funds by three billion dollars, as have Chase Manhattan, Manufacturers Hanover, and J. P. Morgan more recently (see Guttentag and Herring, 1989, pp. 2, 27). Such reserves, provided they are not 'allocated' against a specific loan, reduce net profits and hence dividends (see ibid., p. 7); nevertheless unlike 'charge-offs' they are counted as part of the bank's primary capital along with the share value, and thus rather than depleting banks' capitalization levels they increase them. In addition, in the case of Citicorp (and probably other banks), stock markets had already taken these developments into account as they affected shares' prices, as is testified by the fact that market prices have not fallen markedly since 1982. From 1982 until 1987, Citicorp comprehensively reduced the exposure to its four main Latin American debtors from 195 per cent of primary capital down to 54 per cent (see ibid., pp. 32–3). The ratio of reserves to exposure to LDCs of major American banks has continued to improve from 1987 to 1990, and the same is true for commercial banks outside the United States (see ibid., p. 2 and World Bank, 1990b, p. 87).

In conclusion, then, the international financial system and American banks managed to deal with the worst aspects of the crisis in five or six years, and are now in a much more secure state as regards profitability and capitalization (see Sachs, 1990, pp. 20–3).

5 SOME PROPOSED SOLUTIONS

We shall not discuss the details of the many ideas which have been advanced to solve the sovereign debt problem, but we shall try to point out the underlying 'philosophy' of the actions undertaken and of the proposed plans. In August 1982 the announcement of Mexico's repayment moratorium marked the beginning of the crisis. From 1982 until 1984 top priority was given to prevent a collapse of many commercial banks, above all American ones, with very high exposure to LDCs. Therefore the outbreak of the crisis triggered off a process of increasing the repayment period, with banks accepting the conversion of debts from short-term loans to medium- and long-term loans, since debtors continued to pay the interests due, or part of them. It was hoped that indebted countries were experiencing temporary problems of liquidity and that in the space of a few years they might again start to pay back the debt itself. In reality the size of the debt, already about 850 billion dollars by 1982, made total repayment clearly impossible.

By 1985 it became abundantly clear that it was not a short-term financial problem and until 1988 the emphasis shifted to the need to restore economic growth inside debtor countries. The *Baker Plan* – named after the then US Treasury Secretary James Baker – was aimed at restoring the lending process by commercial banks to LDCs, after the credit squeeze following 1982. According to the plan, indebted countries should have continued to receive financing on the basis that they were able to make interest payments. Moreover, countries who wanted to make use of this refinancing plan had to agree to make policy adjustments dictated by the IMF and the World Bank. This was the period of the 'adjustment with growth' approach, which relied on Structural Adjustment Programmes (SAP) as the major instrument for triggering the growth process. The idea was that either by restoring or by imposing an appropriate macroeconomic discipline and the necessary incentives, growth rate rates would go back to their levels of the 1970s. This was a typical 'supply side' approach; the crisis would be overcome provided that domestic resources were efficiently allocated according to the 'right prices' – that is, those prevailing on international markets.

However, it was also clear that, even after many reschedulings, most of the heavily indebted countries were unable to fulfil their obligations to commercial banks and official creditors. Therefore some 'market based' solutions were investigated to ease the burden of repayment. Some of these are briefly summarised below.

Debt–equity swaps were used for 6 per cent of the total debt, except in Chile where 40 per cent of loans were dealt with in this way. The prices at which debts should be converted into property rights of some LDCs' companies were those of the secondary market, which were often 40–50 per cent of nominal values (see Guttentag and Herring, 1989, p. 30), and sometimes as low as 30 per cent. Frequently, creditors and debtors could not agree on what to exchange for debts – in general developing countries feared that by this arrangement they would lose their best enterprises in the most profitable and strategic sectors for development. In short they feared expropriation. It has been calculated that creditor banks could have bought up virtually all the industrial capital stock of debtor countries (see Parboni 1987, p. 30). Citicorp made large use of this expedient in part also because it was able to profit from the fact that it owned banks throughout Latin America.

Exit bonds converted loans into long term bonds, either as government debentures or with direct governmental guarantees. *Buy-back* entailed the repurchasing of loans at secondary market prices. Some governments, such as Argentina, Chile and Yugoslavia, purchased loans privately thereby hoping to maintain good relations with commercial banks, but this strategy did not succeed. All of these initiatives have resulted in the most modest of reductions in net obligations for developing countries (World Bank, 1989, p. 17).

It was only in March 1989, seven years after the outbreak of the crisis, that with the initiative of the US Treasury Secretary Nicholas Brady a strategy of debt relief, and of debt cancellation entered the agenda. The *Brady Plan* contemplated three possibilities from which creditor banks could choose: (1) Reducing the face value of the debt by 20 per cent (although it became 35 per cent for Mexico); (2) Converting loans into public bonds carrying a fixed rate of interest; (3) Providing new financing to LDCs (up to 25 per cent of the bank's loans). All these measures were to be carried out with the support of official financing from the World Bank and the IMF. In this case too, developing countries accepting funds had also to adopt the economic policies suggested by the World Bank and the IMF. As for the Baker Plan the Brady Plan represents an attempt to re-open credit provisioning; the difference is that the Brady Plan accepts that financial mechanisms have failed and that at least a part of the debt needs to be written off (on the successes and the failures of the Brady Plan see Perasso, 1991, pp. 23–31).

Commercial banks have shown no enthusiasm in supporting the fundamental aspect of the Brady Plan: the refinancing of LDCs. A 'tug-of-war' has begun between governments and commercial banks to obtain tax relief on losses. Moreover there is the well-known 'free rider' problem, namely the fact that each bank has an interest in waiting for other banks to provide some debt forgiveness. This should increase the value of remaining debt on the secondary market, thus the bank which has not participated in the cancellation plan could either sell its credit at higher prices, or – in particularly favourable circumstances – could expect the debtor to fulfil the scheduled interest and amortization payments. To overcome this problem commercial banks should co-ordinate their actions, and international agencies should provide some form of 'assistance'.

Creditors reject debt cancellation also because of the problem of 'moral hazard'. Basically debt forgiveness rewards a defaulting debtor; unfulfilled contracts would create a dangerous precedent and would be an unfair solution both for the debtors who repay their debts and for those countries which have refrained from requesting excessive credit.

The Baker and Brady initiatives were mainly concerned with the debt of Latin American countries to commercial banks; the idea was that of providing some debt relief and, above all, new private lending, which could bring fresh currency to debtor countries. However, there was also the problem of official debts, that is to say the unrepaid loans made by government and by official institutions. This was the case for most small and poor countries of Africa, for which it was also clear that they were simply too poor to be able both to repay a reasonable part of their debts and to attract private lenders.

Toronto Terms is the name of a 'menu' of options devised at the June 1988 meeting of the leaders of the seven most industrialized countries (the so called G-7), to reschedule the non-concessional official debt of the low-income African countries (see World Bank, 1990b, p. 27). These countries had service and debt ratios which clearly could only lead to default (see Stymne, 1989, pp. 23, 26a). Here too the creditors were offered three alternatives which were different combinations of longer repayment, interest rates below market rates and cancellation of one third of eligible maturities. In 1990 this menu of options was extended to all the poorest countries, technically all those classified as IDA (International Development Association)-eligible by the World Bank.

6 DEBT FORGIVENESS AND THE NEED FOR AN INTERNATIONAL AGENCY

As early as 1987 some authors maintained that the amount of debt relief needed to find a solution to the debt crisis required the cancellation of a much higher share of the debt stock than that provided in the Brady Plan (see Fischer 1987, p. 169). This opinion received more support towards the end of the 1980s, when it became clear that it was also necessary to increase the debt relief for low-income countries which was provided for by the Toronto Terms.

The *Trinidad Terms* for official debt refers to a proposal made by the then Chancellor of the Exchequer John Major at a meeting of Commonwealth Finance Ministers held at Trinidad on September 1990 (see World Bank, 1990b, p. 95). The Trinidad menu prescribes the increase of maturities and that all the debt stock, and not simply the debt maturing in a certain year, must be rescheduled according to the new scheme. This indication was meant to overcome a serious limitation of the Toronto Terms, according to which it would take many years to reschedule the entire debt along the new lines. Moreover, two thirds of the debt stock had to be cancelled. Hence, the Trinidad menu of possibilities looked very much like an enhancement of the Toronto Terms, both in the sense of increasing the share of debt forgiven and also because of the introduction of new principles, such as that of linking the actual future payments by the debtor country to the growth of its export capacity.

In September 1990 the Netherlands Finance Minister Jan Pronk called for a complete cancellation of bilateral official debts of low-income countries, provided that they implemented sound economic policies (see ibid., p. 95).

In December 1990 the General Assembly of the United Nations voted a report on 'External Debt Crisis and Development' which recommended much longer maturities and the cancellation of a higher share of debt than those provided both in the Brady and the Toronto menu, and that the debt of the poorest countries should be completely cancelled. There were also some important innovations, for instance debt could be paid in local currency and could be used to give rise to trust funds which should finance environmental and social development projects (see United Nations, 1990, pp. 5–6, 27). The report also stressed the need for OECD countries to increase the funds of the Development Assistance Committee (DAC) to be used as official aid to LDCs.

Therefore since 1990 the issue of debt forgiveness has gained momentum among official institutions and political circles. But it must also be remembered that, since 1986 at a conference in São Paulo, the delegates of Latin American countries requested that debts be cancelled in a proportion which should have taken into account both their value on secondary markets, and the difference between interest rate levels when loans were contracted in the 1970s, and the 1980s. In fact the secondary market prices for the debts of highly indebted countries ranged from 0.4 per cent of the face value in Peru to 64 per cent in Chile (see Rogoff, 1990, p. 4).

Debt forgiveness gives rise to many problems, including the obvious one of 'moral hazard' and of 'free riding'. Therefore there is a widespread belief that an international authority should supervise both debt cancellations and new reschedulings in order to ensure that all debtors and creditors should receive fair treatment. This may also imply the creation of an international agency which should take care of the problem. Some authors have argued for the need of a solution similar to the provisions of Chapter 11 of the US Federal Bankruptcy Code (see Cohen, 1989, p. 3). In brief they believe that a supranational institution empowered to arbitrate between creditors and debtors is required, with the objective of ensuring that the greatest possible proportion of loans are repaid by mutual agreement, hence avoiding repudiation of the debt itself.

Peter Kenen has asked for the creation of an International Debt Discount Corporation (IDDC) by the governments of the major industrial countries, which should issue its own long-term bonds to raise the money needed to repay commercial banks (see Kenen 1990, pp. 13–15). Jeffrey Sachs has called for an International Debt Facility (IDF), that is to say an authority lodged in the IMF and the World Bank which should act like a bankruptcy court to settle conditions for cancellations and reschedulings (see Sachs, 1990, pp. 24–5). Sachs suggests some of the conditions of the new reschedulings: they should imply fixed and not variable interest rates, which should be below market levels and the principal remaining after cancellation should have a long maturity – thirty years.

7 THE LESSONS OF THE DEBT CRISIS

Years of debate on the debt issue seem to have eventually produced some widely shared views:

(1) Debt forgiveness is a necessary stage to overcome the debt crisis and to restore the growth prospects in many LDCs. At last both economists and international agencies seem to have abandoned the pretence of believing that, sooner or later, these loans will be entirely repaid. The problem is to find a level of debt reduction which will facilitate repayment. However, it is clear that the reduction must be very high: for the 17 most heavily indebted countries a 50–70 per cent write-off is a realistic scenario; in 1991 these were the figures involved in the debate on debt cancellation for Poland and Egypt. In addition,

different countries require different treatment, for the low-income countries of Africa total cancellation would make sense (see Beltratti, 1989, pp. 10–11, 19). Resource-rich states such as Mexico, Brazil and Indonesia could probably service a slightly higher level of debt.

(2) The case-by-case approach to the debt crisis which has characterized the political and theoretical debates of the 1980s has slowly given room to the belief that general rules, a global view, and some sort of authoritative estimate of the percentage of debt forgiveness are required to overcome the 'debt overhang' problem and to restore the confidence of private lenders.

(3) The solution to the debt crisis can only be brought about by a mixture of market-oriented instruments, such as debt–equity swaps, buy-backs of debt, fiscal incentives for commercial banks and so on, and of plans by international agencies and OECD governments. Moreover, no solution can be easily reached in the short term. Even 100 per cent debt forgiveness might not be a 'solution', because it would not prevent new debt crisis in the future.

(4) Sound domestic policies are necessary to restore growth in LDCs, but for many countries, particularly low-income ones, a substantial increase both in the degree of concessionality of new loans and in the amount of development aid is equally important.

Nowadays these considerations enjoy large support but some warnings about future analysis of the debt problem may be appropriate. The debt problem has often been treated as a disgraceful event which has happened and needs to be solved, but whose story, whose characteristics and whose boundaries are well-defined and in many ways not replicable. This is probably explained by the fact that the large majority of literature has dealt with a specific type of debt, that of Latin American countries with commercial banks. Of course Latin American debt is still the largest and it seems more complicated to deal with private debt than with the official one. Moreover, Latin American countries, and the Philippines, were the first debtors with debt-servicing problems and the crisis was largely originated by their inability to pay interests and principal. This explains why the plans proposed, including both the Baker and the Brady plans, and the other solutions suggested were mainly concerned with the Latin American debt problem.

It was only in 1988, with the Toronto meeting of the so-called G-7, that it clearly emerged that the debt of poor Sub-Saharan African countries needed a very different treatment from that of Latin

America. The appendix to this chapter shows that in the Mediterranean, in Eastern Europe and in South Asia there are economies either with already serious debt problems, or which could face a debt crisis if growth were to slow down in the near future. Even the fast growing countries of Asia might face a debt crisis if the GDP growth rates of the 1990s were to continue to decrease as in 1991 (see *The Economist*, 1991, p. 115), and to remain substantially lower than those of the 1980s. Turkey is another indebted country where the slow down of the growth rates of GNP and of exports might bring back a debt crisis (see Boeri, 1991, pp. 2–3). A few years of real interest rates higher than growth rates plus a deficit – or a decreasing surplus – on current accounts are sufficient to worsen the debt–GDP ratio (see chapter 7, section 2).

To use a metaphor: the debt crisis of the 1980s has often been regarded as a 'stock' problem, which will slowly disappear in the future thanks to a combination of long maturites, low real interest rates and moderate debt cancellations. It would be wiser to consider the debt crisis as a 'flow' problem. New countries might replicate the Latin America 'debt syndrome'; new types of 'debt syndrome' might arise, with different features from those of the Latin American and Sub-Saharan African debt; countries which have overcome the debt crisis of the 1980s might again have solvency problems.

We should also remember that the international financial markets of the 1990s will see a huge demand for financing coming from Eastern Europe, which did not exist on this scale in the 1980s. This fact might put fresh pressure on world saving, with rising real interest rates. The economic events following the reunification of Germany clearly seem to point in this direction (see International Monetary Fund, 1990, pp. 44–7). This will have negative effects on the current accounts of countries still relying a lot on new non concessional loans, such as India and Indonesia (see World Bank, 1990b, p. 3), and of the countries with a large share of debt at variable interest rates.

APPENDIX

Table 5A.1 presents some figures for 27 large debtor countries, these countries satisfy two conditions: (1) they have an overall debt stock larger than 10 billion dollars; (2) their debt/GNP ratio is higher than 15 per cent. Two important debtors are not included in Table 5A.1: China and the Soviet Union, which together account for more than 90 billion dollars, but which do not fulfil condition 2. Greece would fulfil both conditions, but from 1990 it is no longer considered a developing country because of her GNP per capita (see World Bank, 1990b, p. 12). In 1990 Bulgaria seemed to satisfy both conditions (see International Monetary Fund 1991, p. 85), but we have considered the situation existing at the end of 1989, hence debt cancellations such as those from which Egypt and Poland benefited are not included. For each country the first three columns give the total debt stocks (EDT) for the years 1980, 1985, 1989; columns 4–6 give the debt–GNP ratios (EDT/GNP) for the same years (see World Bank, 1990b, vol. 2). Columns 7–9 give the average annual rates of increase of EDT for the periods 1980–5, 1985–9 and 1980–9, which we call d_{80-5}, d_{85-9} and d_{80-9} respectively. The last element is the average annual rate of growth (g) of GDP from 1980 to 1988 (see World Bank, 1990a, pp. 180–1). All debt figures come from the *World Debt Tables 1990–91*, with the exception of the 1980 figure for the debt of Poland, which in fact refers to 1981, and of her 1981–9 growth (see Moct-Most 1991, pp. 124, 130).

Table 5A.1 The debt situation of 27 'large debtors' in the 1980s

	EDT (\$ millions)			*EDT/GNP (per cent)*			*EDT, growth rates (per cent)*			*g*
	1980	*1985*	*1989*	*1980*	*1985*	*1989*	*80/5*	*85/9*	*80/9*	
India	20561	40886	62509	11.9	19.2	23.9	14.7	11.2	13.2	5.2
Pakistan	9941	13362	18509	42.5	43.6	46.9	6.1	8.5	7.2	6.5
Bangladesh	4056	6629	10712	31.7	41.6	52.3	10.3	12.8	11.4	3.7
Indonesia	20944	36670	53111	28	44.4	59.8	11.9	9.7	10.9	5.1
Philippines	17431	26819	28902	49.5	83.5	65.7	9	1.9	5.8	0.1
Thailand	8258	17528	23466	25.9	47.8	34.1	16.2	7.5	12.3	6
Malaysia	6611	20387	18576	28	70.3	51.6	25.3	−2.3	12.2	4.6
Korea	29486	47133	33111	48.7	52.5	15.8	9.8	−8.4	1.3	9.9
Nigeria	8934	19551	32832	9	22.2	119.3	16.9	13.84	15.6	−1.1
Sudan	5163	9127	12965	65.7	143.7	82.9	12.1	9.2	10.8	2.5
Côte d'Ivoire	5848	9746	15412	58.8	154.6	182.2	10.8	12.1	11.4	2.2
Egypt	20384	40218	48799	95	128.1	159	14.6	5	10.2	5.7
Morocco	9678	16409	20851	53.1	135.6	95.9	11.1	6.2	8.9	4.2
Algeria	19377	18374	26067	57.1	33.3	57.6	−1.1	9.1	3.4	3.5
Turkey	19119	26010	41600	34.3	50.5	53.8	6.4	12.5	9	5.3
Portugal	9700	16627	18289	40.4	84.9	41	11.4	2.4	7.3	0.8
Yugoslavia	18486	22278	19651	25.6	48.2	33.5	3.8	−3.1	0.7	1.4
Poland	*26000*	33336	43324	*115*	48.7	68.3	*5.1*	6.8	*5.8*	0.8
Hungary	9756	13955	20605	44.8	70.2	75.8	7.4	10.2	8.7	1.6
Ecuador	5997	8705	11311	53.8	77.5	112.9	7.7	6.8	7.3	2
Colombia	6941	14240	16886	20.9	42	45.8	15.5	4.4	10.4	3.4
Peru	10038	14279	19876	51	89.4	70.2	7.3	8.6	7.9	1.1
Chile	12081	20384	18241	45.2	143.3	78.3	11	−2.7	4.7	1.9
Argentina	27157	50945	64745	48.4	84.2	119.7	13.4	6.2	10.1	−0.2
Venezuela	29330	35332	33144	42.1	59.1	79.9	3.8	−1.6	1.4	0.9
Mexico	57378	96865	95641	30.3	55.2	51.2	11	−0.3	5.8	0.5
Brazil	70957	105526	111290	30.6	48.7	24.1	8.3	1.3	5.1	2.9

Sources: World Bank, *World Debt Tables 1990–1* for the first three columns and Moct-Most (1991) for Poland in 1980; *World Development Report 1990* for column ten. Columns four to nine are elaborations.

In Table 5A.2 the 27 countries are grouped according to the geographic region they belong to (see World Bank, 1990b, p. xxi); for each group we have the value of the debt stock of the countries considered and the percentage it represents of the total debt stock of that geographic group. Therefore we can see that the countries considered account for 82 per cent of the total debt stock of developing countries in 1989. The low percentage of Sub-Saharan Africa reflects the well-known fact that in this area there are many severely indebted low-income countries with a very small overall debt, few billion dollars, but whose EDT/GNP ratios are in some cases higher than 200 per cent. It is now widely felt that the debts of these countries should be almost completely cancelled (see United Nations 1990, pp. 31–2).

Table 5A.2 Total debt stock (EDT) of the 27 'large debtors' and as a percentage of total debt by geographic regions, 1989

	EDT (*$ millions*)	%
Sub-Saharan Africa	61 209	42
East Asia and the Pacific	202 023	98
Europe and the Mediterranean	143 469	99
Latin America and the Caribbean	371 104	88
North Africa and the Middle East	69 650	56
South Asia	91 730	89
Total	939 185	82

Source: World Bank, *World Debt Tables 1990–91.*

Table 5A.3 gives the growth rates of the total debt stock for all countries and for the six geographic groups of the *World Debt Tables* (see World Bank, 1990b, vol. 1, pp. 126–63) for the periods 1980–5, 1985–90 and 1980–90.

Table 5A.3 Average annual growth rates of the debt stock during the 1980s (per cent)

	d_{80-85}	d_{85-90}	d_{80-90}
All countries	11	5.4	8
Sub-Saharan Africa	11.4	10.8	11.1
East Asia and the Pacific	15.3	6	9.8
Europe and the Mediterranean	9.5	5.8	7.6
Latin America and the Caribbean	9.9	1.9	5.7
North Africa and the Middle East	9.3	7.2	8.2
South Asia	12.3	11	11.7

Source: Elaborations on figures of Table 5A.2.

By splitting the period 1980–89 into two sub-periods Table 5A.1 allows us to capture the different dynamics of the debt stock during those years. We can appreciate the debt situation of a country at the beginning of the 1980s and whether the debt grew more rapidly during the first part of the decade or later. We can also compare the growth rate of debt stock with that of the economy. Figure 5A.1 summarizes the behaviour of the different countries with respect to the growth rates of debt stock and to the level of the debt–GNP ratio.

Figure 5A.1 The 27 'large debtors' in the 1980s

d_{80-89}	*EDT/GNP*	$d_{85-9} < d_{80-5}$	$d_{85-9} > d_{80-5}$	
<8%	$\uparrow$ >100%	Ecuador		
		Venezuela	Pakistan	A1
	$\cup$		Algeria Poland	A2
	$\cap$	Brazil Chile Mexico Yugoslavia Portugal Philippines	Peru	A3
	<20%	Korea		
>8%	$\cap$	Malaysia Thailand Sudan Morocco		B1
	$\uparrow$	Colombia India Indonesia	Bangladesh Turkey Hungary	B2
	>100%	Nigeria Egypt Argentina	Côte d'Ivoire	B3

The upper part of the figure includes the countries whose debt stock from 1980 to 1989 increased by less than 8 per cent a year, which is the average annual growth rate of the debt stock of all countries (see Table 5A.3). The countries in this group can be regarded as 'early borrowers'; they borrowed heavily in the second half of the 1970s and entered the 1980s with already high debt–GNP ratios, Yugoslavia had the lowest debt ratio of the group, with 25.6 per cent. In this group we can distinguish three main debt patterns.

A1. This first pattern identifies the countries whose debt ratio has increased during the 1980s even if they borrowed less than during the 1970s. Of the six groups this is the most heterogeneous one: Venezuela suffered from very slow economic growth, Pakistan's debt ratio increased only slightly, while in 1989 Ecuador had a debt ratio higher than 100 per cent. Notice that the Soviet Union would be in this group, in the same part of the chart as Pakistan, if it were not for her still modest debt ratio in 1989 (see Moct-Most, 1991, p. 142; Fischer and Gelb, 1990, Table 1).
A2. The debt ratio has a U shape; these countries improved their debt situation during the first part of the decade, but it deteriorated again after 1985. Algeria is an example of 'out and in' the debt crisis: the debt stock was stable from 1980 to 1985, then it increased, moreover the terms of trade worsened with negative effects on the growth rate of its economy and on the debt ratio.
A3. This is the *Latin American* pattern, where the debt ratio has an inverted U shape, ∩. The debt ratio was already high in 1980 and the situation worsened until the mid-1980s, when it improved; the debt stock either decreased or increased moderately and there was a slight economic growth. Most Latin American debtors are in this group, but it also includes the Philippines, Portugal and Yugoslavia.

In this group there is also South Korea, which is the only large debtor which has been able to repay a substantial share of her debt and to bring the debt ratio below 20 per cent.

In the lower part of Figure 5A.1 we find the countries whose debt stock during the 1980s grew at an annual rate higher than 8 per cent, we can call them the 'late borrowers'. Some of these countries, notably Nigeria and India, entered the decade with very low debt ratios. Then they built up a remarkable debt stock, particularly during the first half of the 1980s. Here too we can identify three main debt patterns.

B1. These countries borrowed heavily during the first part of the 1980s, but here too the debt ratio has an inverted U shape. Thus we can regard this group as a variation of the Latin American pattern, or an *East Asian* pattern, because of the presence of Thailand and Malaysia; notice that only Malaysia managed to reduce her debt stock.
B2. The debt ratio keeps on rising during the whole period, we can regard this as a *South Asian* pattern. This group includes some debtors, such as India, Indonesia and Turkey, whose debt stock is larger than 50 billion dollars; China too would be here, in the same part of the chart as India, if she had a higher debt ratio.
B3. Here there are the most desperate situations; the debt ratio is rising and in 1989 is higher than 100 per cent. This is the *Sub-Saharan* pattern, which characterizes the debt conditions of most low-income countries of Africa; we find also two middle-income countries, Egypt and Argentina.

Groups A3 and B1 include the 12 countries where the debt situation has improved during the 1980s, with a typical inverted U pattern. During the same period the situation of the remaining 15 countries worsened. Figure 5A.1 also shows that eight countries, of which two in South Asia, two in the Mediterranean and two in Eastern Europe borrowed more in the second part of the period than during the early 1980s.

Therefore the debt problem is an evolving, 'flow', phenomenon and not a 'stock' one; in particular it is not limited to the two regions of Latin America and Sub-Saharan Africa, which 'traditionally' had debt-servicing difficulties. As can also be seen from Table 5A.3 during the 1980s there has been heavy borrowing by countries in Asia, in Europe and in the Mediterranean. In particular, South Asia, Eastern Europe and the Mediterranean basin are three regions which, given their debt story and both their short- and long-term economic perfomances, seem to be particularly vulnerable to a slow down of economic growth and hence debt-servicing difficulties might arise.

REFERENCES

BELTRATTI, A. 1989, 'Investments and the value of foreign debt: a vector autoregressive methodology', *Luca d'Agliano Development Studies Working Papers*, no. 9, March.

BOERI, T. 1991, 'Problems in implementing structural reforms in developing countries: the experience of Turkey in the 1980s', *Luca d'Agliano Development Studies Working Papers*, no. 35, February.

COHEN, B. J. (1989) 'Developing-Country Debt: A Middle Way', *Essays in International Finance*, no. 173, Princeton University.

FISCHER, S. (1987) 'Sharing the Burden of the International Debt Crisis', *American Economic Review*, vol. 77, no. 2, May.

FISCHER, S. and GELB, A. (1990) Issues in Socialist Economic Reform, mimeo.

GUTTENTAG, J. M. and R. HERRING (1989) 'Accounting for losses on sovereign debt: implications for new lending', *Essays in International Finance*, no. 172, Princeton University.

INTERNATIONAL MONETARY FUND (1990) *World Economic Outlook*, October.

INTERNATIONAL MONETARY FUND (1991) *IMF Survey*, March 18, Washington.

KENEN, P. B. (1990) 'Organizing Debt Relief: The Need for a New Institution', *Journal of Economic Perspectives*, vol. 4, no. 1, Winter.

MOCT-MOST (1991) *Economic Journal on Eastern Europe and on the Soviet Union*, no. 1.

NUNNENKAMP, P. (1986) *The International Debt Crisis and the Third World*, Brighton: Wheatsheaf Books.

PARBONI, R. (1987) 'Un debito per ricolonizzare il Terzo Mondo, *Politica ed Economia*, no. 7–8.

PERASSO, G. 1991, 'From Baker to Brady: is the end of the debt crisis any closer?', *Luca d'Agliano Development Studies Working Papers*, no. 33, February.

ROGOFF, K. (1990) 'Symposium on New Institutions for Developing Country Debt', *Journal of Economic Perspectives*, vol. 4, no. 1, Winter.

SACHS, J.D. (1990) 'A strategy for efficient debt reduction', *Journal of Economic Perspectives*, vol. 4, no. 1, Winter.

STYMNE, J. (1989) 'Debt Growth and the prospects for Debt Reduction: the Case of Sub-Saharan African Countries', *International Monetary Fund, Working Paper*, WP 89/71, September

THE ECONOMIST 4 MAY 1991.

UNITED NATIONS (1990) *External Debt Crisis and Development*, October.

WORLD BANK (1987) *World Development Report 1987*, Oxford: Oxford University Press.

WORLD BANK (1989) *World Development Report 1989*, Oxford: Oxford University Press.

WORLD BANK (1990a) *World Development Report 1990*, Oxford: Oxford University Press.

WORLD BANK (1990b) *World Debt Tables 1990–91*, 2 vols, Washington.

6 The Development Crisis of the 1980s: A Review of Analytical and Policy Debates

Jaime Ros

1 INTRODUCTION

In the background of current debates on development strategies, of policy discussions between international financial institutions and developing country governments, and of the mutual recriminations between creditor and debtor countries, is the extent to which the massive development crisis of the 1980s has been the result of a major deterioration of the international economic environment for development or, rather, the result of flawed policies in the developing countries themselves leading to macroeconomic instability, misallocation of resources and supply side deficiencies.

This chapter looks at the main hypotheses and the evidence on this issue. Its presentation is organized around two major themes: the comparative economic performance of developing countries in the 1980s and the role of domestic policies and external factors, both in explaining the crisis currently experienced by most of these countries and in potentially changing their development prospects for the future. The chapter begins by examining the main features of the development performance in the third world during the past decade and reviews the debate on the causes of the development crisis. It then considers the implications of this debate for current controversies on the future of macroeconomic and development policies in the South.

2 DEVELOPMENT PERFORMANCE IN THE 1980S

As it is well documented by now, the third world has experienced a more or less sharp and general economic and development crisis in the

1980s.[1] Across Africa, Asia and Latin America, economic growth and, especially, industrial development have slowed down and turned into economic decline in most countries. Economic stagnation and sharply reduced investment rates have been accompanied, in many cases, by huge amounts of capital flowing out of the local economy and towards developed countries. Social spending, and often vital social indicators, have suffered severe and generalized setbacks. Under-employment and open unemployment have been rising in several regions, while a large number of countries have, at the same time, recorded a sharp acceleration of inflation rates. In some of them, this has turned into periodic episodes of high inflation or even hyperinflation. The crisis, however, has affected different countries and regions in different ways and with varying intensity.

3 THE COMPARATIVE PERFORMANCES OF DEVELOPING COUNTRIES

Three main groups of countries should be distinguished when considering the development performance of the South in the 1980s (see Table 6.1). A first group includes China, India and a few other countries in South Asia where, in fact, there has been no economic crisis at all. On the contrary, the pace of economic growth has accelerated in these countries during the 1980s; moderately in South Asia and much more sharply in China which has recorded a GDP growth rate of over 10 per cent on average from 1980 to 1988. It should be noted that these are a few among the 130 or so developing countries in the world while, at the same time, accounting for around half the total population of the South.

A second group includes the semi-industrialized economies of East Asia, that is the old newly industrializing countries (South Korea, Taiwan, Hong Kong and Singapore) as well as the new NICs such as Malaysia and Thailand. With the exception of South Korea, these have suffered a significant slow-down in the pace of economic growth, with their growth rates being cut in some cases by nearly half of what they were in the 1960s and 1970s. Yet because of their very high growth in the past, these countries have maintained respectable rates of growth in the 1980s, of the order of 5 to 7 per cent or even more, as in South Korea. In the East Asian region, the Philippines stands as the major exception to this pattern with a decline in growth performance down to much lower rates than in the past, and falling per capita GDP during the 1980s.

The third group is by far the largest in terms of the number of countries involved and the one for which the expression 'development crisis' fully applies. For there is no doubt that it is the developing countries of Latin America and Sub-Saharan Africa, joined by those of North Africa and the Middle East after the 1986 oil price collapse, which have been the most severely hurt over the past decade. Their reasonably satisfactory growth performance up to 1980 has turned into economic stagnation and plunging per capita incomes since then (or even before, since the mid 1970s, as in Sub-Saharan Africa). Decline and retrogression have undiscriminatingly ravaged the economies of those two regions, with only a few exceptions in Sub-Saharan Africa – rather small countries under very particular circumstances[2] – and hardly any exception in Latin America.[3]

Table 6.1 Growth and inflation performance in the South, 1965–80 and 1980–8

	Average annual growth rate (%) GDP		*Average annual rate of inflation (%)*	
	1965–80	*1980–8*	*1965–80*	*1980–8*
China	6.4	10.3	0.1	4.9
India	3.6	5.2	7.5	7.4
South Asia[a]	3.7	5.1	8.3	7.5
East Asian NICs[b]	8.8	7.9	12.5	4.2
Europe, M. East and N. Africa[c]	5.9	2.9	13.2	25.8
Sub-Saharan Africa	4.8	0.8	12.5	15.5
Latin America and Caribbean	6.0	1.5	29.4	117.4

Notes

(*a*) Includes Bangladesh, Bhutan, India, Myanmar, Nepal, Pakistan and Sri Lanka.

(*b*) Includes Hong Kong, Rep. of Korea, Malaysia, Singapore and Thailand.

(*c*) Includes all the economies of N. Africa and the Middle East plus Afghanistan and eight developing countries of Europe (Cyprus, Greece, Hungary, Malta, Poland, Portugal, Romania and Yugoslavia).

Source: World Bank, *World Development Report 1990*, *World Debt Tables 1989–90*.

Inflation has accelerated almost everywhere in these countries. Seven Sub-Saharan economies have recorded inflation rates over 30 per cent on average in the period 1980–8 (Ghana, Mozambique, Somalia, Sudan, Uganda, Zaire and Zambia), while Latin America has suffered most in this respect. Inflation accelerated above 70 per cent on average in six countries in this region,[4] with some of them going into hyperinflation episodes and the almost complete collapse of their monetary systems (Argentina, Bolivia, Peru and Nicaragua). Capital flight has also been a more or less generalized feature of the decade in those regions, being again particularly acute in Latin America. But the development crisis is undoubtedly most profound and worrying in Sub-Saharan Africa, where wars and drought combined with a population explosion and environmental degradation have aggravated the hardships coming from a low level of economic development and massive poverty.

4 TWO VIEWS ON THE DIVERGING PERFORMANCES IN THE SOUTH

What has caused this massive development crisis and what accounts for the diverging performances of developing countries in the past decade? Answers to these questions have been given from two different perspectives stressing respectively the role of world economic forces and of differences in economic structures (see, in particular, Fishlow 1987, and Singh, 1990) and the role of domestic policy factors and development strategies in the different countries and regions. The latter – present in the writings of a number of academic economists (see Balassa, 1984, Balassa *et al.*, 1986; Sachs, 1985) — underlies the views and policy orientation of the World Bank and the International Monetary Fund.

As Hughes and Singh (1988) and Singh (1990) have argued, the international economic environment of the 1980s adversely affected most or all developing countries through four main channels. The first two were a direct consequence of the tight monetary policies in the OECD countries adopted in response to the second oil shock: the slow-down of world trade following the recession of the early 1980s and the interest rate shock of the same period, followed by a whole decade of persistently high real interest rates in the world economy. These shocks affected adversely all countries in the developing world, the highly indebted economies being the most severely damaged by the sharp increase in interest rates. The only exceptions are perhaps the two largest countries, China and India, whose size, small participation in international trade, and low external debts, made them much less vulnerable than the rest to international trade and interest rate fluctuations.

A third, and most important, aspect has been the terms of trade losses affecting primary producers and exporters, most of them in Africa and Latin America, and including since 1986 the oil exporting countries. Figure 6.1 shows the evolution of terms of trade during the 1980s in different developing regions, including also for comparison the industrial market economies. Clearly, the hardest hit have been the economies of Sub-Saharan Africa where not only has the size of terms of trade losses been enormous – many times larger, for example, than the size of the terms of trade losses suffered by the OECD economies as a result of the first oil price shock in the mid-1970s (see Singh, 1990) – but its consequences have been aggravated by the high degree of specialization of these countries in primary exports and their extreme vulnerability to international commodity markets. In this case, the East Asian NICs and South Asia, which are mostly exporters of manufactures and net importers of primary goods, have in contrast benefited from the evolution of the terms of trade during the 1980s.

The fourth aspect is the capital account shock arising from declining aid flows to Sub-Saharan Africa and, among the highly indebted Latin American countries, from the sharp contraction in commercial bank lending and increased capital flight following the 1982 debt crisis. Together with the larger debt service arising from high interest rates in international markets, the reduction of capital flows to these two regions in the 1980s accounts for the negative transfer of resources abroad over most of the decade and the abrupt and massive change that has taken place in this respect from the 1970s to the 1980s. As shown in Table 6.2, Latin America alone transferred annually nearly US$40 billion in 1984–5. As highlighted by Diaz Alejandro (1984) and Fishlow (1987), the sharply reduced access to international financial markets among semi-industrial countries has been to a large extent a characteristic feature of the Latin American crisis, since some of the East Asian countries which were also highly indebted did not suffer from this capital account shock.[5]

Two main aspects have been stressed with respect to the role of domestic policy factors and development strategies in the development crisis of Africa and Latin America. The mainstream analysis of these issues is well known and we do not need to go here into a lengthy

Figure 6.1 Terms of trade, by regions, 1980–8 (1980 = 100)

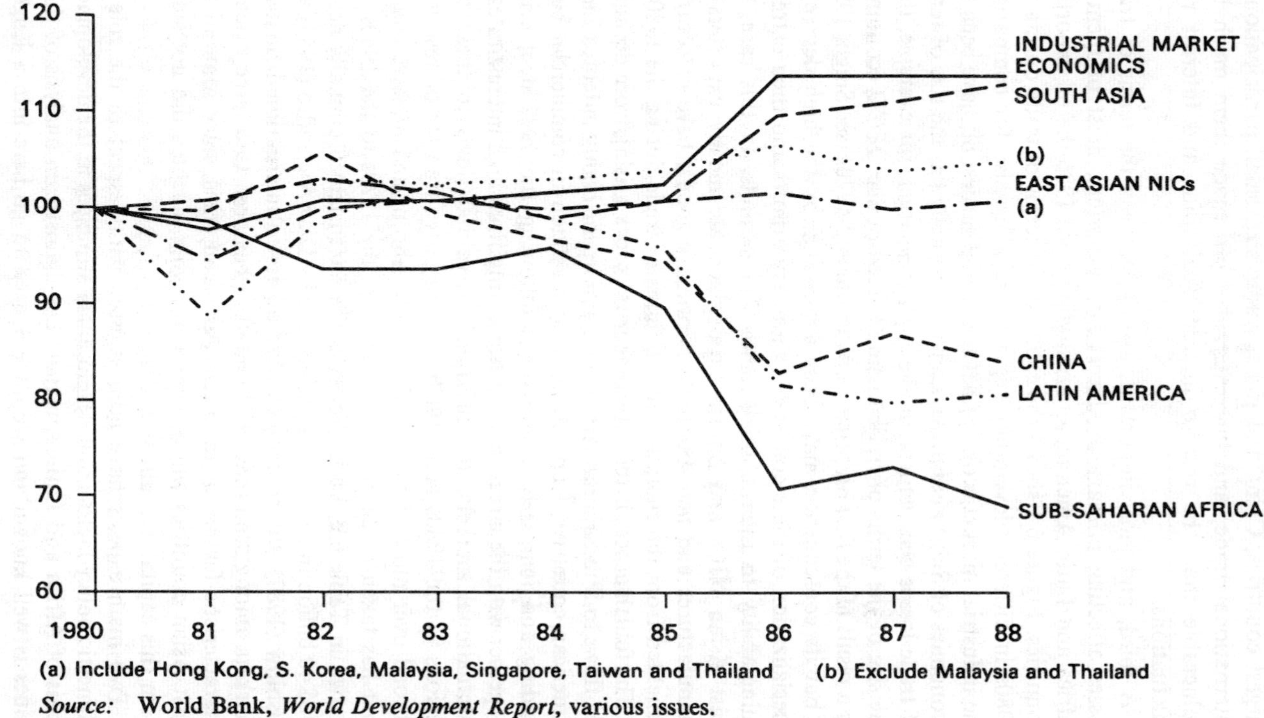

(a) Include Hong Kong, S. Korea, Malaysia, Singapore, Taiwan and Thailand (b) Exclude Malaysia and Thailand

Source: World Bank, *World Development Report*, various issues.

Table 6.2 Net resource flows to Africa and Latin America (billion US dollars per year)

	1977–8	*1984–5*
Africa	+8.6	−5.4
Latin America	+4.9	−39.0

Source: Cornia, Jolly and Stewart (1987).

presentation. It emphasizes, first, the role of macroeconomic mismanagement and policy mistakes, such as the public spending booms and excessive external deficits in the highly-indebted countries of Latin America during the years preceding the debt crisis, or the persistency of over-valued exchange rates in Sub-Saharan Africa well into the first half of the 1980s – which, in this view, contributed to postponing economic adjustment in many of these countries (for a recent analysis along these lines, see Corden, 1990). The second aspect refers to the role of long-term development strategies. The well known argument here is that the greater degree of openness of the East Asian NICs has been a major factor explaining their greater flexibility and capacity to adjust to external shocks as compared to the Latin American semi-industrialized economies or to many African countries which have followed inward oriented industrialization strategies and which, for the same reason, would have shown a smaller degree of openness, greater supply side deficiencies and resource misallocation and, hence, less resilience and capacity to adjust (see Balassa, 1984; Balassa *et al.*, 1986; Sachs, 1985; World Bank, 1987).

5 THE DEBATE AND ITS POLICY IMPLICATIONS

Several reasons point, in my view, to the role of world economic forces coupled with differences in economic structures among the various regions as by far the major factors explaining the development crisis of the 1980s as well as the divergent development performance among countries. First, it is clear that the magnitude of the external shocks and, most important, the vulnerability of different developing countries to those shocks are far from being similar across the developing world. Their role in explaining the diverging economic performances of different regions and countries emerges very clearly when comparing the number and size of the external shocks with the ranking of countries in terms of growth rates, investment coefficients or inflation during the same period. The less vulnerable countries, China and India, with low external debts and limited participation in international trade, either did not suffer (India) or suffered less (China) from external trade losses and interest rate shocks and, in any case, given their large size were much less affected than the rest of the developing world. These countries were almost the only ones which managed to improve the pace of their development in the 1980s. At the other extreme of the spectrum, the primary exporters and/or heavily indebted countries of Sub-Saharan Africa and Latin America suffered from the four major shocks of the period while, at the same time, being particularly vulnerable to these adverse developments, given the high levels of external debt, the excessive specialization of their export structure on primary products, or both of these. These were the regions where the crisis has been most severe. In between are the East Asian NICs which suffered from the slow-down in world trade growth and interest rate shocks, but were much less affected than Africa and Latin America by the international debt crisis, while benefiting from improved terms of trade during the decade. They managed only moderately to slow down the pace of economic growth. There is no doubt that this strong correlation between economic performance and the magnitude of external shocks is striking. Leaving aside India and China, it is hard to find any country which has done better in spite of an adverse external environment or, indeed, which has done worse in spite of favourable shocks, as would be the case in outstanding examples of policy mismanagement.

Policy mismanagement undoubtedly played a role, but policy mistakes were generally rapidly corrected and can hardly explain one decade or more of retrogression. Public spending booms were present in the late 1970s, in both good and bad performers thereafter (South Korea, Turkey and Sri Lanka as compared to Mexico or Brazil), and they were absent or rather moderate in both types of countries (India and Cameroon as compared to Colombia and Nigeria). The impression that mismanagement does not go a long way in explaining the crisis is strengthened by a more detailed consideration of some major cases. While there is no doubt that Mexico made policy mistakes, the major ones turned out to be so only *ex post facto*. Most of Mexico's problems in the 1980s have their origin in the fact that a substantial share of the debt acquired during the 1970s at low real interest rates was used to build and expand its oil industry and exports at a time when the oil prices were very high and expected to remain high, while interest rates were expected to remain low. It was the very sudden change in these prospects that sharply reduced the profitability of previous investments and Mexico's creditworthiness. The comparison between Brazil and South Korea is also interesting. Brazil borrowed heavily from abroad and invested during the second half of the 1970s in much the same way as South Korea did over the same period, that is in rather successful long-term industrial development programmes for the expansion of heavy industries, chemicals and capital goods sectors, while largely avoiding capital flight by residents in contrast to many other Latin American countries.

The role of long-term development strategies is also doubtful, at least as far as the evidence of the past decade is concerned. It is striking to note that those countries which performed well during the 1980s, just as those which did not, constitute two extremely heterogeneous groups with respect to the long-term development policies followed in the past and to the changes in strategies over the last decade. Many of the policies which in Africa or Latin America are blamed for their bad recent performance – such as trade protectionism, regulation of foreign investment, or an over-extended public sector – are easy to find in the countries which improved their development performance, such as China and most South Asian countries, as well as in some of the East Asian NICs, which have performed well not only in the 1980s but over a longer period of time (see, among others, Amsden, 1989; Chakravarty and Singh, 1988; Fishlow, 1987; Sachs, 1987).

This chapter started by stating that underlying the debates on development policies in the South – outward v. inward orientation, the role of the public sector and foreign investment, financial liberalization and so on – were different views on the causes of development performance in the 1980s. Yet disagreement about the causes of the development crisis need not imply disagreement about its remedies. It is possible to agree, for example, without having to go into long and sophisticated discussions about the development model of South Korea, that over-regulation of exports in countries that badly need foreign exchange is absurd and counter-productive. Or that high inflation can be a major obstacle to sustained growth, while disagreeing about what caused high inflation in the first place. The need for improving development policies is therefore not in doubt.

The policy lessons of the 1980s are, however, far from being self-evident. It is becoming increasingly clear, after a decade of experience with stabilization plans and Structural Adjustment Programmes, that the standard and universal recipes of these plans and programmes (cutting the budget deficit, getting relative prices right, and opening up the economy) may have been in too many cases inappropriate. Emphasis on cutting the fiscal deficit has often missed the critical distinction between increasing public savings – an essential element for improving the growth prospects of fiscally constrained economies – and cutting back on public investment, which simply validates the fiscal constraints. Since the burden of fiscal retrenchment often falls upon government investment programmes, the achievement of fiscal deficit reductions has accommodated the level of economic activity to higher levels of resource under-utilization, while leaving the severity of fiscal constraints unaffected. Aggressive devaluations have shown clear limitations or even counter-productive results in improving the trade balances of primary producers, let alone in promoting adjustment with growth.[6] By keeping the price of exportable goods high relative to other domestically produced goods, in spite of adverse movements in the external terms of trade, excessive devaluations, in opposition to their intended results, may well have hindered the process of transformation of productive structures among non-diversified economies with an already very limited capacity for structural adjustment. And, by stimulating the simultaneous expansion of commodity production in a large number of primary producers, they have tended to aggravate over-supply in world commodity markets, thus contributing to the prolonged depression of commodity prices and worsening even further the export earnings of these countries.

Similarly, in countries where the public sector shows a negative foreign exchange balance as a result of a large external debt service, that is all highly indebted countries with the exception of some oil exporters, real depreciation tends to worsen fiscal imbalances and thus to aggravate the fiscal constraints operating directly on public investment and indirectly on the economy's overall growth prospects.[7] The intractable macroeconomic problems facing some of these highly indebted countries – permanently on the brink of hyperinflation or a debt moratorium – are being finally recognized in some debt relief proposals, such as the Brady Plan, which explicitly or implicitly admit that, in the case of over-indebted economies, the restoration of macroeconomic stability, let alone the resumption of economic growth, may simply be impossible without a significant reduction in the value of their external debts.

The point of these concluding remarks is that the debate on the future of development policies is entirely different from the debate on the causes of the development crisis or the diverging performance of developing countries in the 1980s. In fact, the view that the adversity of the international environment has been the major single factor of the South's development crisis leads one to conclude with the imperative for developing countries to improve on their development policies. For precisely that reason and because the external environment is likely to continue to be hostile, their economic and social prospects will, with perhaps a few exceptions, largely depend on it and only on it. Moreover, as our brief discussion of the policy experience of the 1980s suggests, the issues involved can only be meaningfully discussed in a country-specific context or, at most, in the context of regions with relatively homogeneous economic structures and similar structural constraints.

NOTES

1. This has been since the early years of the decade the single major subject of every annual report by international agencies and organizations in the United Nations System: The World Bank's *World Development Report*, UNCTAD's *Trade and Development Report* or UNICEF's *The State of the World Children*. See also, for a recent and comprehensive assessment of the development crisis, the *Report of the South Commission* (1990).
2. These are Botswana, Cameroon and Mauritius, with rates of GDP growth of 5 per cent and over during 1980–8.
3. Those that come closest to being an exception are Colombia – with a small external debt at the beginning of the decade – which has avoided high inflation and managed to achieve positive growth in per capita income, and Chile in the second half of the 1980s, after a massive contraction of economic activity in the early 1980s. Yet by the end of the decade, in the Chilean economy, with probably the best record of growth and control of inflation in Latin America since the mid 1980s, unemployment was higher and real minimum wages lower by more than half than 1970 levels, while the provision for social services had been severely cut (Inter-American Development Bank, 1989).
4. The average annual inflation rates over 1980–8 for these countries are: Bolivia 482.8, Argentina 290.5, Brazil 188.7, Peru 119.1, Nicaragua 86.6, and Mexico 73.8.
5. This is the case of South Korea as compared to Mexico and Brazil and, among countries with lower debt levels, of Thailand as compared to Colombia.
6. See Faini and de Melo (1990). As reported by the authors, primary producers (including most Sub-Saharan African countries) have experienced real depreciations of nearly 40 per cent since 1980, yet, their study

found no evidence that devaluations, by themselves, have improved the trade balances of this group of countries.

7. See on these issues Bacha (1990) and the growing literature on three gap models emphasizing fiscal constraints on medium-term growth.

REFERENCES

AMSDEN, A.H. (1989) *Asia's Next Giant*, New York: Oxford University Press.

BACHA, E. (1990) 'A Three Gap Model of Foreign Transfers', *Journal of Development Economics*, April.

BALASSA, B. (1984) 'Adjustment Policies in Developing Countries: A Reassessment', *World Development*.

BALASSA, B. *et al.* (1986) *Toward Renewed Economic Growth in Latin America*, Washington, DC: Institute for International Economics/ Mexico City: Colegio de Mexico.

CHAKRAVARTY, S. and A. SINGH (1988) 'The Desirable Forms of Economic Openness in the South', mimeo, Helsinki.

CORDEN, M. (1990) 'Macroeconomic Policy and Growth : Some Lessons of Experience', *World Bank Annual Conference on Development Economics 1990*.

CORNIA, G.A., R. JOLLY and F. STEWART, (eds) (1987) *Adjustment with a Human Face*, Oxford: Clarendon Press.

DIAZ ALEJANDRO, C.F. (1984) 'Latin American debt: I Don't Think We Are in Kansas Any More', *Brookings Papers on Economic Activity*, 2.

FAINI, R. and J. DE MELO (1990) 'Adjustment, Investment and the Real Exchange Rate in Developing Countries', *Economic Policy*, October.

FISHLOW, A. (1987) 'Some Reflections on Comparative Latin American Economic Performance and Policy', Berkeley: University of California, Working Paper 8754.

HUGHES, A. and A. SINGH (1988) 'The World Economic Slowdown and the Asian and Latin American Economies: A Comparative Analysis of Economic Structure, Policy and Performance', World Institute for Development Economics Research, Helsinki.

INTER-AMERICAN DEVELOPMENT BANK (1989) *Economic and Social Progress in Latin America, 1989 Report*, Washington: IDB.

SACHS, J.D. (1985) 'External Debt and Macroeconomic Performance in Latin America and East Asia', *Brookings Papers on Economic Activity*, 2.

SACHS, J.D. (1987) 'Trade and Exchange Rate Policies in Growth Oriented Adjustment Programmes', in World Bank, *Growth Oriented Adjustment Programmes*, Washington, DC.

SINGH, A. (1990) 'The State of Industry in the Third World in the 1980s: Analytical and Policy Issues', The Helen Kellogg Institute for International Studies, Working Paper, no. 137.

SOUTH COMMISSION (1990) *The Challenge to the South. The Report of the South Commission*, Oxford: Oxford University Press.

UNCTAD, *Trade and Development Report*, several issues, Geneva.
UNICEF, *The State of the World Children*, several issues.
WORLD BANK (1987) *World Development Report 1987*, Washington, DC.
WORLD BANK (1990a) *World Development Report 1990*, Washington, DC.
WORLD BANK (1990b) *World Debt Tables 1989–90 Edition*, Washington, DC.

7 Sustainable Debts and the 'Human Factor'

Gianni Vaggi

1 INTRODUCTION

Ever since the beginning of the debt crisis many scholars have tried to assess the sustainability of foreign debts. The issue has received different interpretations, but by and large these studies have tried to spell out the conditions under which the indebted country could be expected to stay solvent and hence maintain its creditworthiness on international markets. These conditions have often been associated with the possibility of achieving a reduction of the debt to GNP ratio through time. Creditworthiness is crucial not only in international financial markets, but also in foreign trade, and for many debtor countries commercial credit is very important. Trade arrears, that is to say unpaid imports, have been one of the major causes of the rise in debt stock.

This chapter examines some attempts to establish the sustainability of the debt burden and in particular the ability to service debt satisfactorily; that is to say to pay interest and principal, without falling into arrears and resorting to rescheduling. Section 2 shows that the issue of sustainability is linked to the problem of growth rates in the debtor country. Section 3 highlights the negative impact of debt servicing on the future performance of indebted economies. Section 4 presents some arithmetic of debt servicing. Section 5 investigates a new approach to debt sustainability, by taking into account population and GNP per capita. This allows the analysis of what we could call the 'human' dimension of debt servicing, that is to say a transfer of resources to foreign creditors compatible with an acceptable growth of GNP per capita. Section 6 illustrates the new perspectives highlighted by the 'human factor' and the lessons to be derived for the future.

2 THE GROWTH RATE AND THE REAL INTEREST RATE

2.1 How to prevent a debt crisis?

The problem of the sustainability of sovereign debt has often been analysed by analogy to the problem of public debt evolution and by taking as a starting point the 'overlapping generations' model put forward by Samuelson in 1958 (see Cohen 1985, p.142). Recent literature on public debt has focused on the need to stabilize the ratio of debt to income and to prevent its growth; the debt–GDP (or GNP) ratio should approach a stationary value (see Spaventa 1987, p. 377; Congdon 1988, pp. 217–19). An even better scenario is when the debt grows at a rate lower than that of the economy, so that the debt–GDP ratio decreases through time.

Let us examine some of the arithmetic behind this theory.

D = overall foreign debt.
$X = GDP$ = Gross Domestic Product.
$g_n = (dX/dt)/X$ is the nominal growth rate.

The change of D/X over time is given by the following expression:

$$[d(D/X)/dt] = (dD/dt)/X - g_n D/X \tag{7.1}$$

Take the following definitions:

$E(M)$ = exports (imports) of goods and non-factor services,
NFI = Net factor incomes.
NCF = Net capital flows (net of changes in reserves).
i_n = nominal interest rate on foreign borrowing.

No such items as foreign direct investments, fully concessional loans, capital flights and so on exist, so that capital flows consist only of new loans and the repayment of previous ones. Net factor incomes do not include items other than interest payments abroad – in particular workers' remittances and the repatriation of profits on direct investments are ignored. Consider the balance of payment identy which states that the current account balance is equal to capital movements, net of changes in reserves (see UNCTAD 1990, p. 37):

$$E - M + NFI = -NCF \tag{7.2}$$

$E - M$ is the balance of the 'non-interest current account'; dD/dt is the net change in the debt stock over time: the new loans obtained minus the repayment of previous loans in a given year; hence $dD/dt = NCF$ and $NFI = -i_n D$, that is interest payments on existing debt. Equation (7.2) becomes:

$$E - M - i_n D = -dD/dt$$

and substituting this expression in (7.1):

$$d(D/X)/dt = i_n D/X - gD/X - (E - M)/X$$

By rearranging the terms and deflating both sides of the equation we obtain

$$d(D/X)/dt = (i - g)D/X - (E - M)/X \qquad (7.3)$$

where i and g are the real interest rate and real growth rate of GDP respectively. For debt to be sustainable D/X must not increase through time, because it is argued that there is a 'ceiling' to the debt–output ratio which, when exceeded, undermines a country's creditworthiness. When the debt stock of a country becomes too high with respect to its GDP, creditors no longer believe that the debt will be entirely repaid; there follows a confidence crisis and the debtor country is unable to obtain new loans. The debt to GDP ratio is either constant or declines if $d(D/X)/dt$ is either zero or negative. If we take as an example a zero *non-interest current account* $E = M$, this brings to the fore the relationship between the interest rate and the growth rate. When $g > i$ no problem of sustainability arises because D/X decreases through time.

It has been shown that the condition $g > i$ by itself does not guarantee that an economy will be able to avoid the debt trap (Bhaduri, 1987, pp. 270–3). In fact the trade deficit could be so large as to require new foreign borrowing which would lead to an increase in the debt–output ratio. Bhaduri shows that in order to achieve self-reliant growth with foreign borrowing, not only must the growth rate exceed the real rate of interest, but the marginal propensity to export must be higher than the marginal propensity to import.[1]

On the other hand if $g < i$ there can still be a decrease in the debt-output ratio provided that the surplus on the non-interest current account, $E - M$, is larger than $(i - g)D$ (see equation (7.3)). Thus the feasibility of obtaining new loans, fresh commercial credit on international markets and eventual repayment of debt, thereby avoiding the debt trap, depends on the ability to generate a generous surplus of exports over imports of goods and non-factor services.

A very high export growth rate is one of the most important conditions for gaining advantage from foreign borrowing and avoiding debt reschedulings and a crisis in confidence. The 1980s have shown that this condition has been very hard to achieve for most indebted countries. There is however one country, South Korea, which was able to reduce substantially her debt–output ratio in the second half of the 1980s, a result due to the very high economic growth and, in particular, high export growth rates. The decrease of the debt to GDP ratio began in 1986 and continued at least until 1989 (see World Bank, 1990b, p. 186); during these same years Korea had a notable surplus on its current account balance on goods and non-factor services (see World Bank 1990c, p. 343).

2.2 Solvency and the time element

Unfortunately South Korea is the only country, so far, in which the process of ever-increasing indebtedness has been decisively reversed without resorting to some form of cancellation of the existing debt. In fact it is clear from (7.3) that with unfavourable current accounts and low growth rates the only way of achieving *at least a once for all reduction* of the debt–output ratio is by forgiving part of the existing debt. By itself this measure does not modify the tendency of the indebted country to build up debt again in the future but it does provide temporary relief for debt servicing and reduces the debt–output ratio to more realistic levels.[2] One of the main causes of the debt crisis was the increase of real interest rates from negative levels in the late 1970s to very high positive levels in the first half of the 1980s.[3] The debt crisis emerged because most debtor countries could not regularly service their debts, a fact which made it clear that they would be unable to repay their debts within the negotiated terms.

However, the condition $g < i$ does not necessarily imply that a country will default on international financial markets. To prevent a debtor country insolvency it is sufficient that the present discounted value of all future payments should be equal to the initial face value of the debt (see Cohen 1985, pp. 142, 162). As Cohen shows this happens if the debt grows at a rate which is strictly less than the real rate of interest:

$$(D_t - D_{t-1})/D_{t-1} = i_D < i$$

In this case the discounted value of the debt at a certain time t, far in the future, will be 0 because:

$$\lim_{t\to\infty} \frac{D_t}{(1+i)^t} = 0$$

In order to achieve a situation in which the debt grows less than the rate of interest it is enough to repay part of the interest payments due each year, rolling over the principals and remaining interest payments. If at time $t-1$ neither the principals nor the interest payments are repaid the debt at time t would be $D_t = D_{t-1}(1+i)$, but the servicing of only a part of the interest payments due would satisfy the condition $i_D < i$. If this condition holds true we know that at any particular moment in the future the debt will have a market value equal to the discounted value of future payments. Therefore creditors will be able to sell the assets which represent the sovereign debt of the indebted country on the secondary market, and if all creditors share this opinion there is no reason to doubt the solvency of the debtor country (see ibid., pp. 142–3).

The condition for avoiding insolvency is that there must be a future stream of payments whose present value matches the face value of the debt. The future payments which should reduce the debt–output ratio derive from the trade surplus, as can be seen from (7.3), and in particular one can assume that they are a proportion of the export earnings of the debtor country. Cohen describes an index of solvency, b, which is the percentage of future export earnings necessary to guarantee the solvency of a country. If D_0 is the value of the debt at time '0', 'n' is the number of years during which the repayments must take place and E_j is the value of export's earnings at time j. Following Cohen's methodology (see ibid. p. 146) we have:

$$D_0 = bE_1/(1+i) + bE_2/(1+i)^2 + \ldots + bE_n/(1+i)^n \qquad (7.4)$$

Assuming that the rate of interest and the export growth rate are constant through time, and that the latter is equal to the economic growth rate,[4] the right-hand side of equation (7.4) is a geometric sequence whose ratio is $(1+g)/(1+i)$. Then (7.4) becomes:

$$D_0 = \{[1-(1+g)^n/(1+i)^n]bE_0(1+g)\}/(i-g) \qquad (7.5)$$

from which one can find the value of *b*. With reasonable assumptions about future trends of exports and interest rates Cohen finds that most debtor countries should be able to generate a trade surplus high enough to prevent them from defaulting (see ibid., pp. 149–53). For some countries the 1983 and 1984 the ratios of trade surplus to exports were well above the values of the solvency index, such that these countries exceeded the interest payments required to remain solvent.

Cohen's methodology clarifies the theoretical background and hypotheses which, both explicitly and implicitly characterized the approach to the debt crisis adopted by Bretton Wood institutions and by the Paris Club of creditors, at least until 1989.

Firstly, it should be noted that the view that debt is sustainable even if only a fraction of it is actually serviced seems to be designed to convince creditors to accept the rolling over of principal and of a part of the interest, a typical feature of many types of rescheduling. This approach shows why it is better to keep the system working instead of declaring the bankruptcy of the debtors. Given certain conditions the creditors should always be able to sell their debt denominated assets and eventually the debt will be entirely repaid. Debtors should not sacrifice the entire earnings from a trade surplus to service the debt, but should stabilize the stream of payments as a proportion of the value of exports. The scenario seems to be workable if not completely reassuring; appropriate reschedulings can be an answer to the debt crisis of the 1980s.

Secondly, the main hypothesis which allows the mechanism to work concerns the time horizon, which in Cohen's model is infinite;[5] provided that the repayment period of the debt, or maturity, is long enough, no default problem arises. Of course the longer the maturity the lower the fraction *b* of export earnings needed to pay the minimum amount of interest to be regarded as a solvent debtor.

In fact the main element in most reschedulings seems to be the increase in the maturity of the debt. Creditors accept the payments actually made and which are less than those due. The principal and the unpaid interest are rolled over, but of course the value of debt increases because only part of the interest has actually been paid. Therefore unless the interest rate decreases more payments are needed if the present value of future payments is to match a higher value of the debt. The idea of converting the debt, which was originally mainly short-term, into long-term bonds is another important aspect of the Brady Plan, which among other possibilities suggests increases in the length of the grace period, that is to say the number of years during which only the interest has to be paid.[6]

Thus the time horizon becomes a decisive element for the repayment of the entire debt and when the repayment period is not infinite the fraction b of future earnings which is needed to avoid insolvency increases. When n tends to infinity and with $i > g$, equation (7.5) becomes:

$$D_0 = bE_0(1 + g)/(i - g) \tag{7.6}$$

which is in fact the formula used by Cohen to determine the solvency index b. But when the repayment period is finite the term inside square brackets in equation (7.5) cannot be ignored any longer and the value of b rises considerably even for very long maturities.[7]

Cohen takes a lender's point of view because he provides convincing arguments to prevent the creditors from declaring the bankruptcy of the debtor; moreover, the debtor country can delay the full repayment of its debts provided that it generates an acceptable stream of interest payments in the future. However, reschedulings and the extension of maturities are no solution to the debt crisis. They cannot be a substitute for higher growth rates both for exports and for the economy, through which the economy can generate enough foreign currency to make the repayment of the entire debt stock, at some reasonable future time, credible. The strategy of delaying payments and reducing debt servicing to a minimum is a way of 'buying time', thus preventing the outbreak of a crisis and hoping for the reduction of real interest rates and, above all, for an increase in growth rates.

3 DEBT SERVICE, INVESTMENTS AND GROWTH

The main problem emerging from the debt crisis is that of having to have growth rates higher than the real rates of interest on the existing foreign debt. However, the debt itself creates negative conditions for the restoration of the growth process. First, there is the famous problem of the 'debt overhang'. This indicates the general climate of uncertainty which surrounds a heavily indebted economy. Moreover, the government may not be very keen to make sacrifices and to implement unpopular economic policies, and businessmen may not be ready to start new enterprises, when they know that the benefits will be reaped by foreign creditors (see Krugman, 1988, pp. 254ff.; Sachs,

1989). 'The debt is so large that its service acts as 100 per cent marginal tax on foreign earning' (Edwards, 1989, p.268; we are on the declining side of the debt Laffer curve) and there are no incentives for the country to improve its economic performances.

Second, the debt service itself is detrimental to growth because it affects national savings and investments in a negative way. Suppose:

Y = GNP = gross national product.
C = consumption (private and public).
I = investment (private and public).
S = domestic savings.
NS = national savings.

The following relations are valid:

$$Y = X + NFI,$$
$$X = C + I + (E - M) \text{ and}$$
$$Y = C + NS$$

Then we have:

$$C + NS = C + I + (E - M) + NFI \tag{7.7}$$

But $NS = S + NFI$, and equation (7.7) becomes:

$$S = I + (E - M)$$

From (7.2) $(E - M) = -(NFI + NCF)$, therefore we obtain:

$$I = S + (NFI + NCF) \tag{7.8}$$

Let us suppose that a country should service its debt entirely, both for interest and repayment of principal. If there are no capital flows other than the repayment of the debt due, in particular no new lending, NCF is negative and it is equal to the decrease in the debt stock: $NCF = -dD/dt$. Similarly when no factor income exists other than interest payments it is $NFI = -iD$ and the debt service, DS, is the sum of the two payments, one on the current account and one on the capital account. Equation (7.8) becomes:

$$I = S - (iD + dD/dt) = S - DS \tag{7.9}$$

From (7.9) it is easy to see why the debt service has a negative impact on the rate of growth (see Bacha 1990, pp. 73–4). Define $a = (dX/dt)/I$ as the incremental output-capital ratio, assumed to be constant, then in a Harrod-Domar model the growth rate of the economy is: $g = aI/X$ and from (7.9):

$$g = a(S - DS)/X$$

The debt service is a foreign claim on domestic savings, and if we assume that it has seniority with respect to investments, then investments must be lower than domestic savings, in other words the debt service crowds out domestic investments (see Cohen, 1989, p. 8). In all likelihood a positive debt service reduces both domestic investments and the growth rate below the level they could reach according to the value of domestic savings.

$-DS$ represents the net financial transfer from the debtor country to its creditors, and this phenomenon of negative net transfers is known to have played a major role in North–South financial relationships from 1983 (see World Bank, 1988, p. 30). Bacha shows that when there is a negative financial transfer there is also a negative real resource transfer. In fact from (7.2) and the assumptions about the signs of NCF and NFI we have

$$(E - M) = DS \tag{7.10}$$

therefore the negative financial transfer is financed with a trade surplus on the non-interest current account (see Bacha, 1990, p. 71). This is precisely what happened during the 1980s: 'developing countries have been exporting more goods and nonfactor services to the developed countries than they receive – a reversal of the pattern before the 1980s' (World Bank, 1990b, p. 9).[8] Currency depreciation is the most widely adopted policy to achieve a surplus on 'non-interest current account'. Of course devaluation implies a higher debt stock in local currency, and it may not lead to an improvement of the debt situation, because it can foster both inflation and capital flights; tariffs and export subsidies are a better way of achieving a trade surplus (see Rodrik, 1990, pp. 238–9, 245–7).

Investments and growth are influenced negatively by the need to fulfil financial obligations with foreign creditors, but consumption too may suffer because of the high debt service. Bacha describes the *vicious and self-sustaining* circle which began at the end of the 1970s for most indebted countries (see Bacha, 1990, pp. 77–8). The rise in real interest rates on international financial markets led to a decrease of new loans because creditors believed that further increases in debt stocks would have been unsustainable (see section 2.1 above). With the collapse of capital inflows and the need to pay interest abroad indebted countries had to generate a trade surplus to service the debt. This negative net transfer reduced investments, and hence GDP growth rates were below their potential level according to domestic savings. This probably reinforced the confidence crisis of private investors and commercial banks thus leading to further reductions of fresh currency for debtor countries. The adverse effect of debt and debt service on growth is clearly recognized in the 1989 *World Development Report*, which analyses the impact of a 20 per cent debt reduction on investment and growth. If 'the reduction in net resource transfer in the form of interest payments associated with the reduction in debt stocks ... is used to import needed investment goods, investment rates would rise several percentage points' (World Bank 1989, p. 21). This should lead to an additional 1 per cent increase in GDP after three years on top of the spontaneous growth rate and the improvement should even be as large as 2 per cent for Argentina, Brazil, Mexico and Nigeria (see ibid.). UNCTAD is less optimistic about the effects on growth rates of debt forgiveness, but this is because of the assumption that part of the reduction in debt service ends up in higher imports, which are not entirely made up of investment goods but can lead to higher consumption rates (see UNCTAD, 1990, pp. 64–6). The persistence of very high debt stocks and debt service ratios, particularly with respect to output, prevents the triggering of the *virtuous* circle of less debt, more investment, more growth, more creditworthiness and so on.

Finally it should be noted that consumption too may be adversely affected by the negative transfer associated with debt servicing. $X = C + I + (E - M)$ and from (7.10)

$$X = C + I + DS = DA + DS \tag{7.11}$$

where DA is domestic absorption.

Equation (7.11) shows that with a given gross domestic product, an increase in the debt service will squeeze domestic absorption. Of course a reduction of real consumption may absorb part of the impact of debt servicing on domestic investments, thus acting as a kind of buffer to prevent too sharp a fall of their share in GDP.[9] During the 1980s the average growth rates of both government and private consumption in all developing countries were remarkably lower than during the period 1965–80 (with the usual exception of Asia). However, this did not prevent negative growth rates of gross domestic investments in Latin America and in Sub-Saharan Africa (see World Bank, 1990a, pp. 192–3).

4 THE ARITHMETIC OF DEBT SERVICING

Debt service is likely to have an adverse impact on consumption and investments, as equation (7.11) clearly shows, but what is the relationship between debt servicing and the GNP? Remember that $Y = X + NFI$, and suppose that there is no repayment of principals $dD/dt = 0$; then:

$$NFI = -iD = -DS, \text{ and}$$
$$Y = X - DS \quad (7.12)$$

from (7.11) $DA = Y$. This is the situation during the grace period, when only interest accrues to foreign creditors.

However, when the grace period expires principal must be repaid in some finite period of time and not simply continuously rescheduled, at least in principle.[10] The theoretical debt service due in a certain year is $DS = dD/dt + iD$; suppose this is the amount of international currency transferred to foreign creditors. Then equation (7.12) describes the size of the impact on GNP in year 1, when for the first time a debt payment arises, after a year 0, in which $DS = 0$ and $Y_0 = X_0$. Notice that in 1990 for the group of 'all severely indebted countries' the total debt service on long-term debt actually paid, amounted to 4.5 per cent of GNP, while the debt service due was more than 8 per cent of GNP (see World Bank, 1990b, pp. 170–3; during the period 1983–8 the overall actual debt service was more than 6 per cent of GNP). Therefore there is a remarkable subtraction of resources from GDP, hence a squeeze of domestic consumption and investments.

However, the picture looks less desperate if we examine the relationship between the rates of change of GNP and of the debt service. Let us take Y as a proxy for domestic absorption, therefore equation (7.12) becomes a proxy for equation (7.11) which is $DA = X - DS$. From (7.12) we have:

$$Y_j - Y_{j-1} = X_j - X_{j-1} - DS_j - DS_{j-1}$$

and dividing by Y_{j-1} it is:

$$y_j = (X_j - X_{j-1})/Y_{j-1} - (DS_j - DS_{j-1})/Y_{j-1}$$

where y_j is the growth rate of GNP between time $j-1$ and time j. Multiply the first addendum of the right-hand member of the above equation by X_{j-1}/X_{j-1} and second addendum by DS_{j-1}/DS_{j-1}, then:

$$y_j = g_j(X_{j-1}/Y_{j-1}) - ds_j(DS_{j-1}/Y_{j-1})$$

where d_{sj} is the rate of change of debt service. If we assume $c_{j-1} = (DS_{j-1}/Y_{j-1})$, then $(X_{j-1}/Y_{j-1}) = 1 + c_{j-1}$ and from (7.12) is:

$$y_j = g_j(1 + c_{j-1}) - c_{j-1}d_{sj} = g_j + c_{j-1}(g_j - d_{sj}) \tag{7.13}$$

Equation (7.13) allows us to examine the effect on the growth rate of GNP of the rate of change of the debt service. Equation (7.13) shows the following relationships between g, y and ds for any year j, with $0 \leq j \leq n$, (where n is the repayment period of the debt stock).

(1) If $ds \geq g$ then $g \geq y$. When the equality sign is valid all magnitudes move at the same rate and c is constant.
(2) If $ds < g$ then $g < y$.
(3) $ds = 0$ corresponds to the situation during the grace period, when the debt stock is constant and only the interest, iD, is paid; of course the debt service does not change. But this would also be the situation when the yearly instalments to be repaid, including both interest and principal, are kept constant, using the formula of financial mathematics, as is often the case for the repayment of domestic mortgages.
(4) $ds < 0$ is the usual situation, when only the repayment of principal takes place at constant instalments, while each year the interest is calculated on the residual debt stock. In this case c decreases over time and so does y, but it is still $y > g$ for each year during the entire repayment period.

A simple example may illustrate the dynamics of GNP and debt service. Supposing:

$i = 5$ per cent,
$n = 18$ years,
$g = 3$ per cent,
$D_0/Y_0 = 50$ per cent[11]

At time j the debt service is:

$$DS_j = [(n+1-j)i+1]D_0/n \tag{7.14}$$

where D_0/n is the constant yearly repayment of principal. In each year equation (7.12) holds, then:

$$Y_j = X_j - DS_j = X_0(1+g)^j - DS_j \tag{7.15}$$

Suppose $Y_0 = X_0 = 1$ one can easily calculate the sequence of GNP for the eighteen years and the corresponding growth rates y_j, with $j = 1, \ldots 18$.[12] During the first year the growth rate of GNP is negative, $y_1 = -2.3$ per cent, which, of course, represents the impact of the debt service, when DS arises for the first time. But from year 2 onwards the annual growth rates of Y are higher than 3 per cent, decreasing and they tend to g.

We can also calculate the average annual growth rate of GNP over the entire period, $y_{(0-18)}$. The value of GNP after j years is given by equation (7.15), which says that Y_j is equal to the autonomous GDP at year j minus the debt service for that year. With $Y_0 = X_0 = 1$, the average annual growth rate of GNP during the first j years, $Y_{(0-j)}$, can be calculated from the following equation:

$$Y_{(0-j)} = (1 + y_{0-j)})^j \tag{7.16}$$

where Y_j is given by equation 7.15.

The average growth rate of GNP during the 18 years is 2.9 per cent; thus only 0.1 per cent lower than the autonomous rate of growth of GDP. However, during the first part of the maturity the average growth rates of GNP are much lower than those of GDP. For instance, for the first four years $y_{(0-4)} = 1.87$ per cent, therefore on average more than 1 per cent every year is lost to spontaneous growth because of the need to fulfil obligations to foreign creditors. Again the time element comes to the fore; the longer the repayment period the lower the impact on the growth rates of GNP, because the debt service is diluted.[13]

If yearly growth rates and the average rate for the entire maturity are taken into account the loss in terms of GDP due to the need to repay the debts is not too high, apart from the first year, when a debt service of 5.28 per cent absorbs growth entirely and determines a decrease in GNP, $Y_1 < Y_0$. This confirms that there are large negative effects on the standard of living of people in the debtor country whenever DS increases, but a strategy which stabilizes the debt service and possibly leads to its reduction over time is possible, at least in purely mathematical terms. Of course this strategy implies that apart from the large shock of the first year all other causes which could lead to an increase of the debt service during the remaining years should be *neutralized* in order to avoid further GNP reductions. Possible increases in real interest rates should then be compensated for either by lengthening the maturity, or by partial forgiveness of the debt; as equation (7.14) shows these are the only two possibilities to absorb an increase in i and to prevent the rise of DS.

Even more reassuring results emerge if we introduce the grace period into the example.

$m = 5$ years is the grace period.

For the debt service we have the following equations:

$$DS_j = iD_0, \qquad \text{for } j = 1, \ldots 5;$$
$$DS_j = [(n + 1 - j)i + 1]D_0/(n - m) \quad \text{for } j = 6, \ldots, 18 \qquad (7.17)$$

The average annual growth rate of GNP is roughly the same as in the case without a grace period and $y_{(0-6)} = 2$ per cent, which means that the debt service costs on average 1 per cent of growth for each of the first six years. In year 6 $ds > g$, which according to equation (7.13) implies $g > y$, and in the example $y_6 < 0$. Therefore when the country begins to repay the principal its GNP suffers a temporary halt and may even decrease, but then the debt service will begin to decrease and y_j will again be higher than g_j. The grace period allows the avoidance of large negative impacts on GNP during the first years of repayment. The negative effects on Y_1 and Y_6 are limited, in the sense that practically income does not rise during the first and sixth year of the repayment period, but no large negative growth rate arises. Hence the introduction of a grace period somehow improves the time profile of debt repayment.

The rationale for the existence of a period of time during which only interest is paid is that an *easier* debt service should facilitate the triggering of a process of economic growth. The reduction of the amount of resources which must be diverted from the domestic economy and in particular from investments (see Section 3 above) should lead to higher rates of domestic growth and should hence make the repayment of the debt at the end of the grace period less painful.

That 'buying time' and 'waiting for growth' are the major reasons for a delayed repayment schedule is also obvious if we consider the new repayment schedule, the so-called '30 years-bullet', which was one of the instruments used during 1990 for Mexico and Venezuela under the Brady initiative. The grace period is equal to the maturity, 30 years, hence the debt is repaid in one shot at the end of the period. If g does not increase over the autonomous 3 per cent during the 30 years we have the following results:

(1) The growth rate of GNP for the thirtieth year will be $y_{30} = -18.4$ per cent.
(2) The average growth rate for the three decades will be $y_{(0-30)} = 2.16$ per cent, that is to say 0.84 per cent lower than the growth rate of GDP.

After 30 years this outcome would be an obvious economic disaster. It is clear that the reduction of the debt burden to interest alone for the whole repayment period should favour the emergence of a growth path with much higher rates than those experienced during the 1980s.[14]

5 THE 'HUMAN FACTOR'

Three points emerge from the above discussion on sustainable debt:

(1) Debt sustainability leads to the issue of the relationship between the rate of growth and the real rate of interest. When an indebted country achieves a growth rate of GDP higher than the average real rate of interest on its foreign debt no serious problem of servicing the debt should arise, hence it should keep its creditworthiness on international financial markets.
(2) The time element is a crucial aspect of debt sustainability. The strategy of increasing maturities reflects the now common opinion that if the debt crisis is to have a solution, it will only be in the long run.

(3) A debt service higher than 8 per cent of GNP and service ratios exceeding 30 per cent of exports have economic, social and political costs which are unbearable for debtor countries, hence the idea of a grace period on principal repayments which should reduce the debt burden roughly by half during the first years.

Let us now consider the following question: can debt be serviced with a 'human face' approach?[15] Long before Shakespeare's *The Merchant of Venice* debt repayment did not seem to provoke emotions particularly favourable to creditors; all the more so when – contrary to Shylock and the Venetian merchant Antonio – the creditors are much richer than the borrowers. However, here we are not dealing with the question of a purely humanitarian viewpoint, rather we want to see if there are social and economic reasons which allow us to calculate a debt whose servicing will not produce unbearable conditions for the debtor. Taking into account the three points sketched above the 'human factor' introduces two more aspects: population and GNP per capita and in particular their long-term growth rates. By taking into account these two elements some of the traditional conclusions will be reinforced, while others will appear less significant.

Apart from the obvious humanitarian ones, there are good analytical reasons to examine population and GNP growth in relation to debt servicing. First, it is now clear that the debt crisis is not a short-term problem of liquidity but may have a solution only in the long term (looking at the maturities agreed for Sub-Saharan Africa we should talk of the very long term). Population growth rates are one of the few socioeconomic magnitudes which change very slowly and which allow reliable predictions about future population size. All exercises on the capability of sustaining a stream of debt service for a long repayment period are based on assumptions about the expected values of growth rates of GDP and exports, future real rates of interest, future terms of trade and exchange rates. It is difficult to predict the value of these magnitudes for more than two or three years. Hence population growth has a remarkable advantage over other socioeconomic magnitudes.

Second, debt servicing cannot result in excessive foreign subtraction from domestic production for more than a very few years without endangering the political stability of the debtor country. Of course, there is no reason to endure a severe adjustment process when the benefits of it are systematically transferred abroad. Therefore, there are good reasons for including the increase of GNP per capita in the analysis of debt sustainability as a good proxy of the trend in people's standard of living.

5.1 The debt stock

We shall now introduce population and GNP per capita into a simple model of debt sustainability, which could be described as a 'human face' approach. Take the following definitions:

Y_k = GNP per capita.
POP = population.
k = rate of growth of Y_k,
p = rate of growth of population.

We have the following identities:

$$Y \equiv Y_k POP,$$
$$y \equiv k + p.$$[16]

k and p are assumed to be constant for the entire maturity of the debt; p is a positive datum, k may be negative, but we can regard a positive k as a policy target. Therefore we define $h = k + p$ as the growth rate of Y which satisfies the condition leading to annual increases of GNP per capita equal to k, given the autonomous growth of population at rate p; we regard h as the 'human factor'. Supposing that $X_0 = Y_0$ and $DS = 0$, then

$$Y_{hj} = Y_0(1 + h)^j$$

is the value of GNP at time j which is necessary to fulfil the target of securing an average growth rate of k in GNP per capita during the period $0 - j$. We can regard Y_{hj} as that part of GNP which must be reserved for domestic absorption in order to guarantee a decent standard of living for the people (see equations (7.11) and (7.12) above).

Assume that the 'autonomous' rate of growth of GNP, y, is equal to that of GDP, that is to say g. We can calculate which part of the GNP of year j, Y_j, can be used to service the debt, without worsening the living conditions of the people inside the debtor country; this is $Y_{fj} = Y_j - Y_{hj}$.

$$Y_{fj} = Y_0(1+g)^j - Y_0(1+h)^j = Y_0[(1+g)^j - (1+h)^j] \qquad (7.18)$$

is the part of GNP which can be 'freely' transferred abroad to service the debt, compatible with the 'human face' conditions, that is an average modest increase in GNP per capita during the first j years. The sum of all Y_{fi} for the entire maturity gives the value of the debt stock at time 0 which has a repayment schedule satisfying the 'human factor' h. From (7.18) we have:

$$D_{f0} = \textstyle\sum_j Y_{fj}/(1+i)^j, \qquad \text{with } j = 1, 2, \ldots, n.$$

Notice that the sequence on the right-hand side of the above equation implies that servicing the debt allows an increase in GNP per capita *in each year* during the entire maturity.[17] In fact each Y_{fj} has been calculated in order to guarantee an average percentage rise k of GNP per capita over the period 0–j; but this is true for all periods, from 0–1 to 0–n, hence *in each year* the 'human factor' condition is satisfied. This relationship is similar to equation (7.4) above, but D_{f0} is not the actual value of the debt at time 0 but the present value of the stream of payments which may be sustained according to the 'human factor'. Hence:

$$D_{f0} = Y_0[\textstyle\sum_j (1+g)^j/(1+i)^j - \sum_j (1+h)^j/(1+i)^j] \qquad (7.19)$$

with $j = 1, 2, \ldots, n$.

Inside square brackets we find two geometric sequences whose ratios are $[(1+g)/(1+i)] = v$ and $[(1+h)/(1+i)] = u$ respectively. Therefore we can calculate their sums over n years and from (7.19) this is:

$$D_{f0}/Y_0 = [v(1-v^n)/(i-v)] - [u(1-u^n)/(i-u)]$$

from which with appropriate manipulations we derive:

$$\begin{aligned} D_{f0}/Y_0 = &\{[1-(1+g)^n/(1+i)^n](1+g)/(i-g)\} \\ &- \{[1-(1+h)^n/(1+i)^n](1+h)/(i-h)\} \end{aligned} \qquad (7.20)$$

Equation (7.20) brings to the fore the relationship between the autonomous rate of growth g and the 'human factor' h, which includes the desired rate of increase in GNP per capita k and the rate of population increase p. Assuming positive values for g and h we can examine the possible relationships between the two rates.

Case $g < h$

The value of D_{f0} is always negative, meaning that there is no positive value for the debt stock which is sustainable according to a 'human face' repayment schedule. Notice that a decrease in the real interest rate does not modify the sign of equation (7.20), not even if $0 > i > -1$, that is to say with negative real rates of interest.[18] Then even very long maturities do not make the debt stock sustainable.

Case $g > h$

This is the condition for having a positive sustainable debt, whose annual service is compatible with an increase in GNP per capita. Of course a rise of the real rate of interest increases the annual debt service and lowers the value of the sustainable debt–GNP ratio, D_{f0}/Y_0, but this ratio remains positive even for very high values of i. The higher is the positive difference $(g - h)$, the higher is the level of debt which can be sustained according to this 'human face' criteria.

Case $g = h$

Here $D_{f0}/Y_0 = 0$, confirming that this case defines the threshold above which a positive value of debt can be repaid without endangering the standard of living of a country.

Notice that with $n = \infty$ and for $i > (g, h)$ equation (7.20) becomes:

$$D_{f0}/Y_0 = (g - h)(1 + i)/(i - g)(i - h).$$

Equation (7.20) indicates the debt–GNP ratio whose value guarantees that for each year during the entire maturity the debt service to be repaid satisfies the 'human factor' conditions. A less stringent 'human face' formula can be derived from equation (7.16) by substituting $h = k + p$ for y and by solving it with respect to DS_j, which now satisfies the 'human factor' h; hence this debt service becomes DS_{fj}:

$$DS_{fj} = (1 + g)^j - (1 + h)^j \tag{7.21}$$

Equation (7.21) gives the 'human face' debt service which can be paid in year j when the growth rates of GDP g and of population p are constant during the whole period 0–j. If we assume that the repayment of the principal takes place at annual constant instalments (see equation (7.14), Section 4 above) then for $j = n$ the contractual debt service due for payment is:

$$DS_n = (1 + i)D_0/n,$$

hence: if we assume that DS_n satisfies condition (7.21) then $DS_{fn} = DS_n$, and we can calculate the 'human face' value, $D_{f'0}$, of the debt stock.

$$D_{f'0} = [(1 + g)^n - (1 + h)^n]n/(1 + i) \tag{7.22}$$

This equation does not require that the GNP per capita increases at a rate k *in every year*, but that its *average growth rate over the entire repayment period* does not violate the 'human face' conditions set by h. It can be seen that with $g > h$ the value of $D_{f'0}$ is systematically higher than that of D_{f0} derived from (7.20).

However, the 'human factor' h has not been introduced to calculate the sustainable value of D_{f0}, but to define a threshold below which there is a trade-off between debt repayment according to an agreed schedule and the increase in GNP per capita. The conditions for $D_{f0} > 0$ are not different in equation (7.20) from those of equation (7.22), that is to say, it must be $g > h$ (of course with $i > -1$).

5.2 The Debt Service

We can explore further the debt service profile when the 'human factor' is satisfied on average over a period of time and not in every single year. In fact it is possible to calculate the average value of the debt service sustainable according to the 'human factor' over a number of years $q \leq n$:

$$\textstyle\sum_j DS_{fj}/q, \qquad \text{with } j = 1, \ldots q.$$

And from (7.21)

$$\textstyle\sum_j DS_{fj}/q = \{(1 + g) + \ldots + (1 + g)^q - [(1 + h) + \ldots + (1 + h)^q]\}/q.$$

In the second term the two geometric sequences have ratios $(1 + g)$ and $(1 + h)$, therefore:

$$\sum_j DS_{fj}/q = \{[1-(1+g)^q](1+g)/g - [1-(1+h)^q](1+h)/h\}/q \qquad (7.23)$$

If $g > h$ equation (7.23) allows us to calculate the average debt service for different values of q, let us say $q=3$, 5, 10. Hence we can evaluate the amount of GNP which can be transferred to foreign creditors, without endangering at least a modest increase in domestic GNP per capita on average during the first years of maturity (remember that g is the autonomous growth rate of both GDP and GNP).

As expected this average 'human face' DS depends basically on the value of the average growth rate of GDP over the period; fractional changes in g produce very different results as to the amount of GDP which can be lost without excessive damage to the standard of living of a country. For instance take the following example where $DS_{(0-j)}$ indicates the average DS over period $0-j$ as a percentage of GDP, and where we assume growth rates of 3.5 per cent and 4 per cent respectively, and $h=3$ per cent:

g	*3.5%*	*4%*
$DS_{(0-3)}$	1	2.1
$DS_{(0-5)}$	1.6	3.3
$DS_{(0-10)}$	3.3	6.8
$DS_{(0-18)}$	6.9	14

The example highlights two facts. Firstly, it is necessary to have a growth rate g higher than the 'human factor' h during the entire repayment period, or at least for most years. Secondly, for the entire maturity the values of the sustainable average debt service are fairly high, and not too far away from the scheduled debt service, even for the case with slower growth. But during the first years it is much more difficult to fulfil the debt service due without a decrease in GNP per capita. This can be seen by comparing two groups of debt service series; the first group includes two series, DS_{fj} for 18 years, which derive from equations (7.21), with $g=3.5$ per cent and 4 per cent respectively, $h=3$ per cent. The second group includes two series derived from equations (7.14) and (7.17) respectively (for the data used in the example see footnote 11). The values of all four series are divided by the corresponding X_j (See Figure 7.1.)

The debt services in the two former series satisfies the 'human factor'; in the latter two series DS_j is the actual debt service due in

Figure 7.1 Debt service profiles (percentages of GDP)

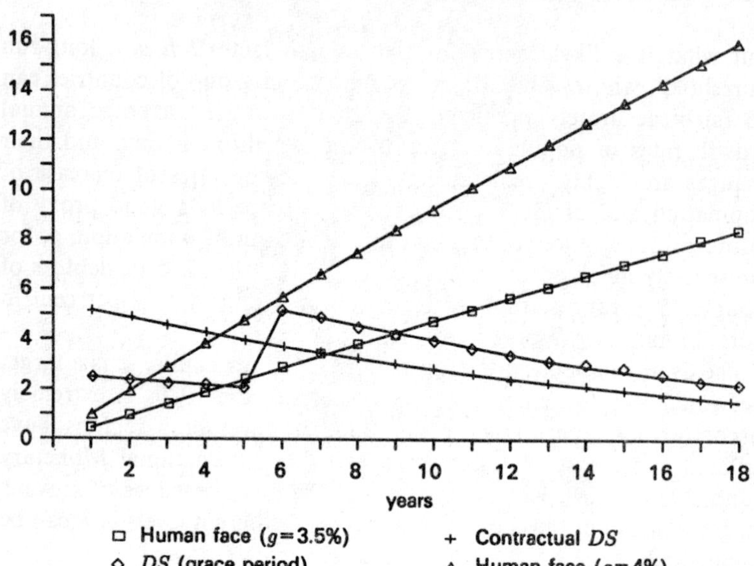

year j, 'without' and 'with' a grace period respectively. The two groups of series describe opposite 'debt service profiles'; the sustainable debt services increase with time according to the 'human factor', while the contractual debt services decrease; the debtor country's ability to pay is lower when it is needed more and it rises when the burden of the required financial transfers eases.

The situation is even more worrying if we remember that the debt service is likely to have a negative effect on investments and growth (see Section 3 above). Therefore during the first part of the repayment period the debt service may either hinder or delay the process of increase of the growth rate of the economy, the only thing which can guarantee the long-run sustainability of the debt. There is a sort of logical 'mismatch' in the timing of growth on one side and of debt service on the other; only a high long-run g guarantees the solvency of a country, but the existence of a relevant debt service in the short run makes it more difficult to achieve the required long-run growth rate. Debtors are not given enough time to trigger a process of long-run economic growth. The only way for a debtor to repay its debts without a decrease in GNP per capita is that of being already on a very high growth path.

5.3 What is the 'human factor'?

But what is a likely value for the 'human factor'? h is a long-run 'threshold', whose value for each country and group of countries can be fairly accurately predicted. As already noticed average annual growth rates of population are fairly stable through time and their changes are highly predictable. Let us take the rates of increase of population and of GDP during the last decade as a good proxy of future values.The average annual rate of growth of population, p, for the severely indebted countries was 2.1%. For the 27 large debtors of Chapter 5, p ranges from –0.1 per cent in Hungary to 4 per cent in Côte d'Ivoire (see World Bank, 1990a, p. 228–9).

The average annual rate of growth of GNP per capita, k, is a target we would like to achieve. The experience of the 1980s is extremely discomforting; apart from Asia all other developing regions have suffered a decrease in GDP per capita (see International Monetary Fund, 1990, p. 19). However, let us assume positive values of k; some suggestions about the economic meaning of different levels of k can be highlighted.

(1) $k=1$ *per cent* is the *minimal* value of the 'human factor' h; that is to say there is at least a minimum increase in the standard of living, something which should be guaranteed to all people.[19]

(2) $k=2.5$ *per cent* is a *decent* value of h; this has been the average annual growth rate of GDP per capita in the industrial countries during the period 1980–9; the expected rate for the rest of the century is in the same range (see World Bank, 1990a, p. 16). Apart from the effects of the Gulf War, during the next few years the expected rates of growth of industrial economies are around 3 per cent (see ibid., p. 186; Fardoust and Dhareshwar, 1990, pp. 47–8). Therefore a 2.5 per cent rise in real GDP per capita in the developing world should ensure that the gap between rich and poor countries does not widen. Given population increases, to fulfil this target the 'severely indebted countries' need to grow at a rate of 4.6 per cent.

(3) $k>2.5$ *per cent* shows the range of values which reduce the gap in the GDP per capita between low- and high-income economies.

(4) $k=6$ *per cent* is a *catching-up* value; that is to say the value required during the last decade of the century in order to bring the GDP per capita of Latin America and Africa in the year 2000 to the levels that they would have achieved with an annual average rate of increase $k=2.5$ per cent over the entire period 1980–2000. The figure of 6 per cent is the rate necessary to overcome the economic crisis of

the 1980s in these two regions (a period during which they lost 7–10 per cent of their GDP per capita) so that by the year 2000 the situation will be as if standards of living in rich countries and in these regions had grown at the same speed during the last two decades of the twentieth century. The wealth–poverty gap, as shown by the ratio between GDP per capita in rich and poor economies, will be the same in 2000 as it was in 1980. This target implies that, given the expected increases in population, the rates of economic growth in Latin America and Africa should be in the range of 8–10 per cent![20]

6 CONCLUDING REMARKS

The reason for including population and GNP per capita in the analysis of debt sustainability is not that of providing a new formula for the repayment schedule: however the 'human factor', as represented by $h = p + k$, brings to the fore some aspects of the problem.

Firstly, in order to secure an ordered debt servicing it is not sufficient to explore the financial and economic conditions, as described by the rate of interest and by the growth rate respectively. Social and demographic considerations must come into the picture. Equation (7.20) shows that the importance of the relationship between the rate of interest and the growth rate fades away with respect to that between g and h. A widespread opinion in the literature on debt maintains that no problem of default arises when $g > i$ (see Section 2 above). The 'human face' approach leads to partially different conclusions. In fact the desired relationship $g > i$ can be achieved thanks to a decrease in real interest rates (this has taken place in the second half of the 1980s, after the peaks of the first years of the decade); but the relationship $h > g > i$ does not reconcile an increase in GNP per capita with ordered repayments. The 'human factor' stresses the need for high rates of growth independent of the level of real interest rates on international markets. Therefore the emphasis is immediately on growth rather than on financial devices, including grace periods, long maturities, all sorts of rescheduling and so on. Of course these 'devices' ease the debt burden, and thus leave more resources for investments and growth inside the country, but by themselves they do not solve the long-term problem of a 'human face' debt sustainability.

It must be underlined that the conclusion that no solvency problem exists on foreign debt when $i < g$ derives from debates on public debt and it well suits a situation where a country, possibly a rich one, faces the problem of consumption levels of present and future generations. In this case one must decide whether to leave debts or a dowry to one's children. With rates of population growth lower than 1 per cent, high GNP per capita and no foreign sector i and g provide most of the information needed to solve the problem. But in countries where population increases at 2–4 per cent a year and development, meaning an increase in GNP per capita, is a compulsory, and not simply a desirable, objective growth rates must take into account the 'human factor' h.

Secondly, the 'human factor' sets a threshold on the rate of growth, below which a country will never be able to repay its foreign debts according to the 'human face' criteria, notwithstanding the financial conditions. This implies that some countries with very high population growth and bad records on economic growth will hardly be able to be good debtors. This is the case of most Sub-Saharan countries, with the possible exception of some oil exporters in the Gulf of Guinea. Very long maturities, long grace periods and negative real rates of interest are now the typical conditions for the debt of heavily-indebted countries south of the Sahara; these measures are also part of the so called 'Toronto Terms' of rescheduling for the poorest countries. These conditions ease the debt burden, but do not make low-income debtors able to fulfil their past financial commitments, nor do they help them to borrow on financial markets with a reasonable rating. These economies are too weak to comply with the rules of the international credit markets where commercial banks are the main lenders.[21] These countries are like children who cannot enter a casino and play the game; if they decide to enter and play, two things can happen: (1) no private creditors will lend them money, because of the very high possibility that they will default on their commitments; and (2) if they obtain private loans they are quite likely to face a debt crisis within a few years, with considerable transfer of resources abroad.

Therefore other instruments must be used to provide the necessary resources for the development of the poorest countries and to increase their growth rates; for the time being the financial game does not suit them. Similar considerations have been made in the course of the debate on debt rescheduling; different terms and financial instruments have been used for various debtor countries, in particular a distinction has been made between middle- and low-income debtors. The latter have been offered much more favourable terms. However, the 'human factor' shows that a simple increase in the degree of concessionality of loans does not reduce the risk for the debtor country of facing a trade-off between servicing the debt and securing humane living conditions at home. The 'human factor' approach may help to differentiate the countries which can be reasonable borrowers from those who need different kinds of aid and it could help to avoid a new debt crisis in the future.

The 'human factor' shows that we must realistically accept a twofold channel to provide developing countries with the foreign currency needed for investments: (1) private lending by commercial banks, and (2) grants from rich countries and from multilateral organizations. Some LDC countries are already eligible to be borrowers on private credit markets, while many others must *first* be helped to achieve high growth rates of both GDP and exports. This is confirmed by the reluctance of commercial banks to lend money to poor countries since 1982; however shortsighted commercial banks may be, this situation is likely to continue for many years to come. In a sense the 'human factor' highlights another aspect of the 'debt overhang'. Thus the present pattern of a high share of official over private financement towards low-income countries is not likely to be reversed soon. Therefore the 50 billion dollars of Official Development Assistance (ODA) yearly disbursed from the Development Assistance Committee (DAC) of the OECD should be increased, and the grant element in it should rise.

Of course there is also the positive side of the story; commercial banks could well take care of loans to those countries where $g > h$, that is with high past growth rates of GDP and of exports and where the expected future ones look promising. In some circumstances the 'human factor' approach may thus be used to overcome banks' preoccupations. Of course in this case the terms of foreign borrowing, and in particular the level of interest rates, come to the fore; lending terms should be linked to some indicators of domestic growth.

Thirdly, equation (7.20) sets a theoretical limit to all kinds of payments which must be made to foreign creditors, and it also applies to such things as profit repatriation. Hence foreign direct investments by private investors of rich countries may lead to the same problem as loans from commercial banks as far as the sustainability of a future stream of payments is concerned. From a purely financial point of view foreign direct investments are no solution to the financial needs of the poorest countries.[22] This implies that new financial instruments and much higher development aid are needed to help the poorest countries, as indicated in the United Nations Report on debt voted by the General Assembly in December 1990 (see United Nations, 1990, paras 132–7).

Fourthly, the purpose of the 'human factor' is not so much that of asking for the cancellation of debts of the poorest countries; that most 'low-income severely indebted countries' will never repay their debts was already obvious at the outbreak of the crisis in 1982. It is now equally clear that for most middle-income debtors the percentage of debt forgiven must be substantially higher than that indicated in the Brady Plan. A substantial debt cancellation is now widely regarded as a condition to remove the 'debt overhang' and to restore growth. However, only at the end of 1991 the World Bank has clearly indicated 'debt retrenchment' as the main problem to solve in order to ease the debt crisis (World Bank, 1991, pp. 1ff.). Unfortunately these recommendations have not yet been put into practice; apart from a few countries such as Mexico, Egypt and Poland, where geopolitical reasons have led to major debt cancellations, we shall have to wait well into the 1990s to see substantial reductions of the debt stocks and of the debt service.

However, forgiveness and cancellation are not the points we want to stress. The 'human face' approach to debt sustainability highlights a 'flaw' in the discussions on debt of the 1980s, which can be traced back to the failure to give due consideration to long-term economic features. The elements which characterize the 'human factor' and the considerations leading to equation (7.20) were available both in 1982, at the outbreak of the debt crisis, and in the 1970s, when borrowing by the developing world and lending by northern banks were in high fashion.

In 1982 the priority was to avoid a major crisis of the financial and banking system of the United States. But even so the theory might have provided better guidance for international agencies and for governments. The following points are now well known: the inadequacy of continuous rescheduling; the costs of debt servicing for the debtors; the negative impact on domestic investments; the need to restore growth first in order to make the debt sustainable; the impossibility of solving the problem simply by means of financial gimmicks; the fact that it was not simply either a liquidity crisis or a problem of short-term macroeconomic imbalances. All these elements were predictable, but perhaps too much attention was paid to the short-term aspects of the crisis. The 'human factor' approach has the advantage of bringing the analysis back to the issue of long-term conditions of economic growth.

During the first years of the debt crisis the prevailing attitude was that of 'buying time': let us keep the financial markets working until the situation improves. However, some time has also been lost and in many severely indebted countries there are now much worse conditions for economic growth than in 1980. Infrastructures, the capital stock and 'human' capital are now in a very poor condition. Debtors have probably learned a lot from the crisis, but in Africa, Latin America, the Middle East and even in some parts of Asia the economic and humane costs of the lesson have been extremely high.

APPENDIX

International agencies have produced forecasts of the growth rates in developing countries for the rest of the twentieth century. Table 7A.1 summarizes some of them. Columns *a* and *b* give the data from the *World Development Report 1989* (see World Bank, 1989, p. 21) and are respectively the baseline and the low scenario for 1988–95. Column *c* is the 1989–2000 forecast from the *World Development Report 1990* (see World Bank, 1990a, p. 16). Columns *d* and *e* are the baseline and alternative scenario from the *World Economic Outlook* (see International Monetary Fund, 1990) for 1992–5. Columns *f* and *g* are respectively the 'high' and the baseline 1990–2000 projections given by UNCTAD (see UNCTAD, 1990, pp. 63, 65). Thus *a, d* and *f* are the 'optimistic' forecasts, while *b, e* and *g* are 'low' scenarios; *c* looks on the optimistic side.

Table 7A.1 Alternative projections of real GDP growth, 1988–2000 (average annual increase, per cent)

	a	*b*	*c*	*d*	*e*	*f*	*g*
Africa				3.8	3.0	4.2	2.4
Sub-Saharan Africa	3.2	3.1	3.7				
Asia	6.0	4.9		5.4	5.3	5.8	4.5
East Asia			6.6				
South Asia			5.1				
Europe, Middle East and North Africa	3.5	2.8	4.3				
Middle East				3.4	3.4		
Eastern Europe			1.9				
Latin America	3.1	2.3	4.2	5.0	3.7	3.4	2.6
Highly indebted countries	3.2	2.3		4.5	3.2		

Sources: World Bank (1989), (1990a); International Monetary Fund (1990); UNCTAD (1990).

Figure 7A.1 gives the relationship between the expected growth rate of the GDP(GNP), *g*, and the 'human factor', *h*, for some geographical regions in the developing world and for the group of highly indebted countries.

For each region there is an optimistic and a pessimistic scenario. In the 'high' scenario, represented by triangles, the expected average annual growth

Figure 7A.1 Growth and the 'human factor' – projections in the 1990s by regions (average annual increases, per cent)

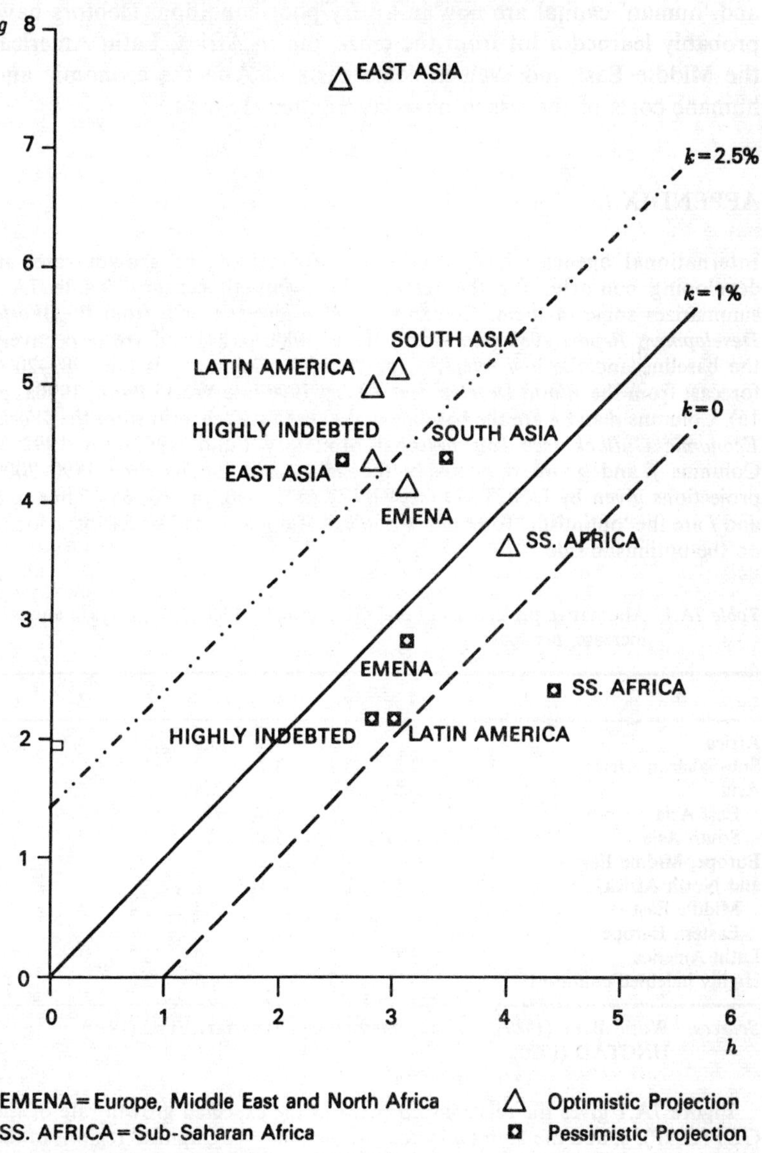

Source: As Table 7A.1.

rate of GDP is the highest among the values of Table 7A.1, and population grows at the rate projected for the period 1988–2000. The 'low' scenario is represented by small boxes and takes the average annual growth rate of population for the period 1980–8 and the lowest value of g in Table 7A.1. Therefore the 'high' scenario is based on high economic growth and low population increase; the opposite is expected to take place in the 'low' scenario. The 'human factor' h, is obtained by imposing an annual average increase in GNP per capita of 1 per cent, that is to say $k=1$ per cent is added to the average annual rate of population growth.

The 45 degree line from the origin separates the regions where GNP per capita is expected to increase more than 1 per cent from those where it will not satisfy the 'human factor'. The $k=0$ line corresponds to the case of invariant GNP per capita and $k=2.5\%$ is the situation in which GNP per capita grows at the same rate as in the OECD countries, so that the 'gap' between rich and poor nations does not widen. Even in the optimistic forecast Sub-Saharan Africa will not meet the 'human factor' requirement of $k=1\%$, while Asian countries will satisfy it also in the 'low' scenario. In general we see that unless we take the most optimistic projections the group of highly indebted countries and three regions – Latin America, Sub-Saharan Africa, Europe/Middle East and North Africa – will continue to have problems in guaranteeing a decent increase in the standard of living of their people. Therefore, apart from some Asian countries, the rest of the developing world may well have to face the trade-off between debt repayment and more resources for their people.

Figure 7A.2 describes the conditions of the 27 'large debtors' during the period 1980–8 (see Chapter 5 Appendix). The growth rates of GDP and of population are taken from the experience of the 1980s (see World Bank, 1990a, pp. 180–1, 228–9; for the average annual growth rate of Poland from 1980 to 1989 see Moct-Most, 1991, p. 124). Notice that in all but three countries – South Korea, India and Bangladesh – growth has been remarkably lower during the last decade than in the 1960s and 1970s.

The countries where GNP per capita has decreased from 1980 to 1988 are shown below the $k=0$ line. In Figure 7A.2 the situation does not look terriable, but some comments are needed.

First, GDP and GNP are calculated in local currency, which seems to be a good indicator of the standard of living. In terms of dollars the trend of GNP per capita would be much worse. In eight countries above the $k=0$ line – Brazil, Chile, Colombia, Indonesia, Algeria, Morocco, Turkey and Yugoslavia – GNP per capita in dollars has either decreased or stagnated during the 1980s (see World Bank, 1990c, pp. 3–5). Of course the dollars GNP per capita represents a better indicator of the possibility of entering international markets, of the capacity to import and of the relative position with respect to rich countries (it should be remembered that some countries, for instance Algeria, import food, hence changes in the GNP per capita in dollars also have an immediate bearing on living conditions).

Second, for some countries, the performances since 1988 are much less brilliant than during the period 1980–8. From 1985 to 1988 the average annual growth rate of GDP of Egypt has been only 2.6 per cent; this condition would bring the country below the 'human factor', $k=1$, line. Of course Egypt might now benefit from large debt cancellations (50 per cent) plus increased foreign

Figure 7A.2 Growth and the 'human factor' in the 1980s for 27 'large debtors' (average annual increases, per cent)

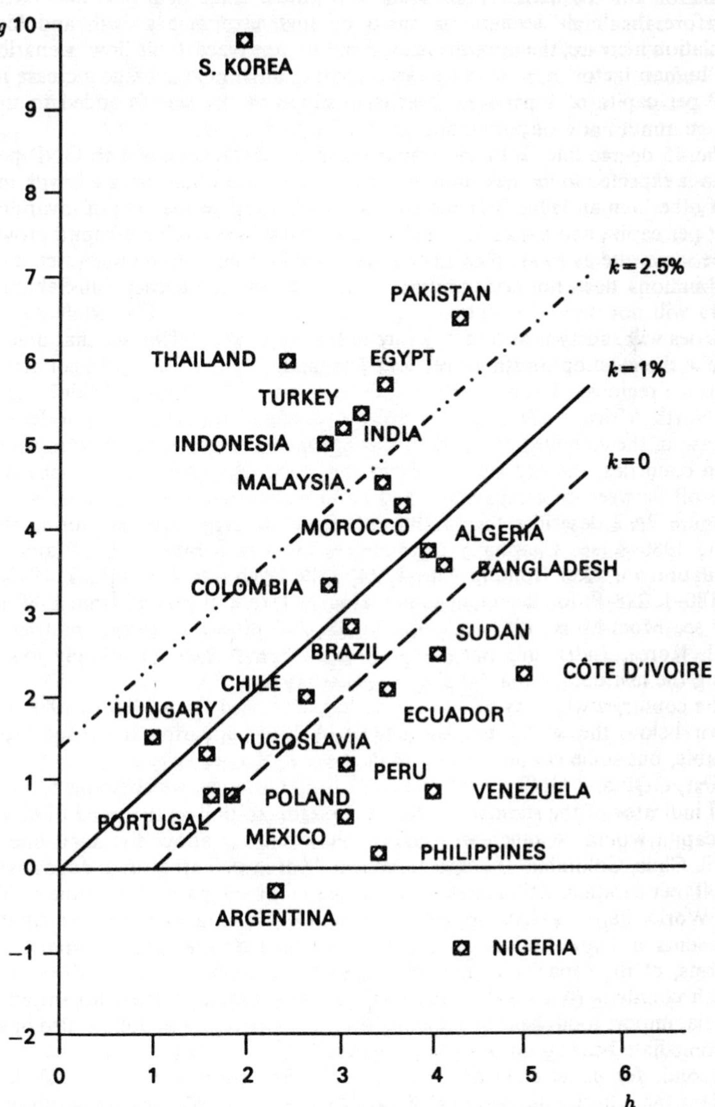

Sources: Elaborations on World Bank, *World Development Report* (1990a) and for the growth rate of Poland, Moct-Most (1991).

aid. After remarkable performances in the mid-1980s, since 1988 Turkey has entered a period of slowdown and of macroeconomic imbalances whose outcome is not yet clear; here too, foreign aid could help the post-Gulf War situation. Both India and Pakistan are now experiencing some macroeconomic imbalances, such as accelerating inflation, worsening current accounts and a drop in foreign-exchange reserves. It must be remarked that, because of the Afghanistan war and of its consequences, during the 1980s Pakistan's adjustment programmes were generously supported by western governments and international agencies with several billion dollars of development aid.

Third, the situation is likely to improve in some countries of Latin America such as Mexico, which has obtained very favourable reschedulings along the lines of the Brady Plan and where, above all, investments from the United States seem to have produced an economic boom. The performances of some oil exporting economies, such as Indonesia, will depend on the future price of oil. Malaysia has experienced large current account deficits both in 1990 and 1991.

To sum up, we can see that there are only two countries with unambiguously good performances: South Korea and Thailand.

NOTES

1. For the analysis of the conditions in which foreign borrowing allows the achievement of self-reliant growth, see Bhaduri, 1987, p. 271; Bianchi, 1991, 32ff; Cantalupi and Ricottilli, 1987. The problems of North–South financial integration are also examined in Darity 1987, pp. 216–18. It has been shown that four Latin American countries – Argentina, Brazil, Mexico and Chile – did not particularly benefit from commercial bank lending in terms of long-run output growth (see Kamin, Kahn and Levine, 1989, p. 23).
2. On the relationship between debt, debt servicing the rate of growth and the positive feedback of debt forgiveness on economic growth, see below, Section 3.
3. See World Bank, 1988, p. 29. The real interest rate is deflated by the change in the export price index of developing countries, thus the increase of the real interest rate reflects also the fall in the terms of trade suffered by most indebted countries during this period.
4. Cohen also discusses the case in which both the rate of interest and the growth rate vary through time (see Cohen, 1985, pp. 146, 163–5).
5. See Cohen, 1985, pp. 142–3, 147, 156.
6. The agreements reached in 1990 for Mexico and Venezuela under the Brady Plan include the conversion of debt into bonds with a single, so called 'bullet', repayment of the principal after 30 years: no repayment is due until the year 2020.
7. Suppose $i=8.5$ per cent, $g=4$ per cent, $D_0/E_0=300$ per cent; according to equation (7.6) $b=13$ per cent, but the solvency index is 22.7 per cent and 18 per cent if calculated with equation (7.5) for maturities of 20 and 30 years respectively. Moreover the size of the *error* included in equation

(7.6) rises when the real rate of interest decreases. Now suppose $i=6$ per cent, from (7.6) we have $b=5.8$ per cent, but from (7.5) b is 18 per cent for a maturity of 20 years and 10 per cent for a repayment period of 40 years. With $n=60$ the solvency index b is 8.46 per cent, that is to say almost 50 per cent higher than the value calculated with $n=\infty$.

8. Apart from Asian countries a trade surplus has been achieved mainly through drastic cuts in imports (see World Bank, 1990a, pp. 204–5; Dakolias and Lawrence, 1990, pp. 4–5). On the distinction between real and financial net transfers see Bacha, 1990, pp. 78ff. For a detailed analysis of the direct and indirect costs of the transfer for Mexico see Brailowsky, 1989, pp. 37ff.
9. The mechanisms which lead to sharing the debt burden between consumption and investments are analysed in Dakolias and Lawrence, 1990, pp. 7ff, where particular attention is dedicated to the role of the terms of trade in the case of Latin America.
10. We assume that there are no new 'disbursements' to match 'principal repayments' hence only the latter make up the (negative) 'net flows on debt' which appear in the *World Debt Tables* (see World Bank, 1990b, p. 115).
11. The figures adopted for this exercise refer to the conditions of the group of 'Severely Indebted Countries' and describe a sort of baseline scenario with some optimism about growth possibilities: 5 per cent is roughly the 1+LIBOR forecast included in the *World Economic Outlook* of October 1990 (see IMF 1990, p. 186; see also World Bank, 1990b, pp. 56, 59); 50 per cent is the debt–output ratio, taking into account the grant element, and 18 years is the average maturity (see World Bank, 1990b, pp. 170–2); 3 per cent is a rather optimistic growth rate of GDP for this group of countries; during the 1980s the severely indebted countries experienced much lower rates of growth (see World Bank, 1990a, p. 181; IMF, 1990, p. 117).
12. We assume that the growth rate of GDP, g, is constant over the entire repayment period and it is not negatively influenced by debt servicing. The same is true for the real rate of interest. The debt service is supposed to be paid back all in one go, at the end of the period.
13. The results of the example are obviously quite sensitive to the value of g. Suppose a 50 per cent reduction in the growth rate of GDP to the value $g=2$ per cent, it will take almost three years for the GNP to go back to its initial value $Y_0=1$. The average annual growth rate during the first three years will be only $y_{(0-3)}=0.37$ per cent. Suppose now a 50 per cent increase in the real rate of interest to $i=7.5$ per cent; it takes only slightly more than two years for the GNP to go back to its initial value and $y_{(0-3)}=1.04$ per cent. Therefore the situation is much worse when the growth rate decreases than when the real rate of interest increases by the same percentage.
14. During 1980–8 the average annual rate of growth of GDP was 0.5 per cent and 0.9 per cent in Mexico and Venezuela respectively; both countries are oil exporters and their economic performances are largely infuenced by international oil prices. Between 1965 and 1980 the average growth rate was 6.5 per cent in Mexico, almost an East Asian rate, while

Venezuela did not fare particularly well with an average rate of 3.7 per cent (see World Bank, 1990a, p.181).

15. This terminology is taken from Cornia, Jolly and Stewart (1987).
16. The correct formula is $y = k + p + kp$, but for values of k and p which are of the order of magnitude of 1–3 per cent the difference is negligible.
17. The stream of payments is calculated with respect to the revenues of the debtor country as approximated by the value of the GNP and not of exports as in (7.4). For a discussion of the better proxy of a country revenue in both the short and long run see Cohen, 1985, pp. 145–6.
18. If $i < -1$ equation (7.20) shows that D_{f0}/Y_0 is either positive or negative depending on whether n is odd or even respectively.
19. Policy measures of poverty relief are possible also with very low economic growth (see World Bank, 1990a, chs 4–6; Cornia, Jolly and Stewart, 1987, vol. 1, chs 7, pp. 10–13). However it seems very unlikely that the living conditions of the poor could improve if the GNP per capita stagnates for a long time.
20. For the Middle East the growth rate should be higher than 10 per cent, given the marked decrease in GDP per capita during the last decade.
21. Of course banks might have other reasons to invest in a poor country.
22. Foreign investments may be a more efficient way of triggering economic growth, but the size of profit repatriation should be linked to growth rate for a fairly long period.

REFERENCES

BACHA, E. L. (1990) 'Debt crisis, net transfers, and the GDP growth rate of the developing countries', mimeo, Geneva: UNCTAD Secretariat.

BHADURI, A. (1987) 'Dependent and self-reliant growth with foreign borrowing', *Cambridge Journal of Economics*, vol. 11, no. 3, September.

BIANCHI, C. (1991) 'The Balance of Payments Constraint and the Growth of the Italian Economy', in C. Bianchi and C. Casarosa (eds), *The Recent Performance of the Italian Economy*, Milan: F. Angeli.

BRAILOWSKY, W. (1989) 'The Macroeconomic Implications of Paying: Policy Responses to the Debt 'Crisis' in Mexico, 1982–88', *Political Economy – Studies in the Surplus Approach*, vol. 5, no. 1.

CANTALUPI, M. and M. RICOTTILLI (1987) 'A development strategy with foreign borrowing; a neo-Austrian approach', *Department of economic science – Research Series*, no. 35, University of Bologna.

COHEN, D. (1985) 'How to evaluate the solvency of an indebted nation', *Economic Policy*, November.

COHEN, D. (1989) 'Slow Growth and Large LDC Debt in the Eighties: an Empirical Analysis', mimeo, Paris: CEPREMAP, November.

CONGDON, T. (1988) *The Debt Threat*, Oxford: Blackwell.

CORNIA, G. A., R. JOLLY and F. STEWART (1987) *Adjustment with a human face*, Oxford: Clarendon Press.

DAKOLIAS, M. and R. LAWRENCE (1990) *The Terms of Trade, Debt and Growth in Latin America*, Geneva: UNCTAD Secretariat.

DARITY, W. Jr (1987) 'Debt, finance, production and trade in a North–South model: the surplus approach', *Cambridge Journal of Economics*, vol. 11, no. 3.

EDWARDS, S. (1989) 'A market solution for the debt crisis?', in Luciani, G. (ed.), *La finanza americana fra euforia e crisi*, Fondazione Adriano Olivetti.

FARDOUST, S. and A. DHARESHWAR (1990) 'A long-term outlook for the world economy – Issues and projections for the 1990s', *The World Bank Policy and Research Series*, no. 12, September.

INTERNATIONAL MONETARY FUND (1990) *World Economic Outlook*, October, Washington, DC.

KAMIN, S.B., R.B. KAHN and R. LEVINE (1989) 'External debt and Developing Country Growth', *Board of Governors of the Federal Reserve System – International Finance Discussion Papers*, no. 352, May.

KRUGMAN, P. (1988) 'Financing vs. Forgiving a Debt Overhang', *Journal of Development Economics*, vol. 29, no. 3, November.

MOCT-MOST (1991) *Economic Journal on Eastern Europe and the Soviet Union*, no. 1.

RODRIK, D. 'The Transfer Problem in Small Open Economies: Exchange Rate and Fiscal Policies for Development', *Ricerche Economiche*, no. 2–3, April–September.

SACHS, J.D. (1989) 'The debt overhang of developing countries', in Findlay, R. (ed.), *Debt, Stabilization and Development: Essays in Memory of Carlos Diaz-Alejandro*, Oxford: Basil Blackwell.

SPAVENTA, L. (1987) 'The growth of public debt', *IMF Staff Papers*, vol. 34, no. 2.

UNCTAD (1990) *Trade and Development Report*, New York, October.

UNITED NATIONS (1990) *External debt crisis and development*, New York.

WORLD BANK (1988) *World Development Report 1988*, Oxford: Oxford University Press.

WORLD BANK (1989) *World Development Report 1989*, Oxford: Oxford University Press.

WORLD BANK (1990a) *World Development Report 1990*, Oxford: Oxford University Press.

WORLD BANK (1990b) *World Debt Tables 1990–91*, 2 vols, Washington, DC.

WORLD BANK (1990c) *World Tables*, Baltimore: The Johns Hopkins University Press.

WORLD BANK (1991) *World Development Report 1991*, Oxford: Oxford University Press.

Part III

International Agencies and Structural Adjustment Policies in Developing Countries

8 The International Monetary Fund and the Creation of an Enabling Environment[1]

Peter M. Keller

1 INTRODUCTION

While the tasks of the International Monetary Fund (IMF) are quite distinct from those of development organizations, such as the World Bank or some of the other institutions, they are highly relevant to global interrelationships and for development as: (1) the IMF has the responsibility of fostering economic conditions that are conducive to sustainable growth, with low inflation and avoidance of balance of payments problems in all of its member countries, most of which are developing countries, (2) while the Fund has lent to a number of industrialized countries, all of its lending operations in recent years have been with developing countries, including those in Central and Eastern Europe – currently almost 50 developing countries have programmes supported by the Fund, with outstanding loans at about $30 billion in addition to large amounts in the pipeline, (3) even developing countries that are not currently borrowers benefit from the Fund's work in the areas of statistics, economic analysis, policy advice, technical assistance, and through the provision of resident experts, and (4) the Fund's surveillance function/policy co-ordination role with groups of industrial countries helps create an enabling external environment for the developing countries, as do its efforts to support the functioning of an efficient multilateral payments system as a crucial ingredient of the General Agreement on Tariffs and Trade (GATT)'s role in the promotion of trade.

2 CREATING AN ENABLING EXTERNAL ENVIRONMENT

As with much of the United Nations system and its specialized agencies, the Fund has its origins in the experience of the 1930s, in particular the 'beggar-my-neighbour' policies that countries adopted during the Great Depression, as each took defensive action to maintain its own living standards in the face of shrinking domestic and external markets and thereby contributed to a downward spiral of world trade, output and employment. To avoid a repetition of this collectively self-destructive behaviour, including mounting restrictions on trade and payments and competitive devaluations, a major effort was made to develop a system that would preclude it. As part of this system, the Fund was created – and remains today – as an international financial co-operative, with, like any co-operative, its rules of conduct and its mutual support system.

A major responsibility of the Fund is one based on the conviction (born out of the experience of the 1930's) that an open multilateral payments system was essential to foster economic growth. Therefore, the Fund's Articles of Agreement enjoin members to move progressively towards establishing payments systems for current transactions (in other words imports, exports, travel expenditures and so on) that are free of discriminatory and restrictive practices. The GATT's open multilateral trading system, which has served the world of the last half century so well, became a crucial counterpart.

With the abolition of the fixed exchange rates or par value system – which had been the 'linchpin' of the Fund's policy until the early 1970s – we now have a system under which member countries are free to choose their exchange arrangements, although the Fund has developed principles to guide members in the conduct of their exchange rate policies. Furthermore, it has developed an extensive system of surveillance over the full range of domestic and external policies that bear on the exchange rate. To enable the Fund to carry out this surveillance function, member countries are required to provide it with the necessary information and to consult with it on their exchange rate policies when the Fund requests them to do so. In addition to these special consultations, the Fund is routinely engaged in virtually round-the-year surveillance, through the regular and generally annual consultations that it has with each member, the twice yearly world economic outlook exercise, the role that management and staff play in the G-7 co-ordination exercises, and the routine informal contacts between staff and country authorities that take place on a continuing basis in between these formal surveillance exercises.

In exercising its surveillance functions, the Fund provides the industrial countries with a frank evaluation of their economic policies and draws the attention of each of these countries to the impact of its actions on other countries – all with a view to generating strong, non-inflationary, and sustainable world economic growth; a strong expansion of world trade based on an open, multilateral trading system; and, generally, an international economic environment that is supportive of development efforts.

3 CREATING AN ENABLING DOMESTIC ENVIRONMENT

3.1 The macroeconomic environment

Appropriate macroeconomic and structural conditions are an essential prerequisite for successful development – stable prices, interest rates which encourage domestic savings and appropriately channel investment, a budgetary policy which does not pre-empt the credit requirements and initiatives of the private sector (a sector which is crucial to successful development), pricing, exchange rate and trade policy supportive of export growth and an efficient pattern of investment and resource allocation in general.

Changes are occurring in the developing world that are leading to a growing acceptance of market-based reforms. The experience of outward-oriented Asian economies is emerging as a model. In most developing countries, especially those in Africa, there is evidence of greater receptivity to many of the tenets of Fund policy advice which in turn continues to be informed by countries' experience. Furthermore, countries in Central and Eastern Europe are undertaking major economic reforms and the international community must be responsive to these countries' needs at this critical juncture. It was, therefore, essential that the IMF be endowed with the necessary increase in its resource base to handle this challenge. It is also essential that the international community, including the IMF, encourage and support this movement towards greater market orientation with consistent policy advice.

The Fund, through its surveillance function, can assist developing countries in evaluating policy choices by drawing on 45 years of often intense experience with its member countries. And the Fund provides advisors and technical experts, with such assistance ranging from the collection of important statistics to advising on tax reforms – the VAT for example – to helping develop institutions, such as central banks, tax administration. And institution building is an important development task.

As regards borrowing countries, the Fund can assist in designing strong growth-oriented adjustment programmes and monitoring their implementation – programmes that aim to increase domestic savings; to eliminate the causes of capital flight and encourage a return of flight capital; to ensure that these resources are put to the best possible use and that impediments to productive investment are eliminated; and thereby to prepare the ground for the effective mobilization of foreign resources, whether these be in the form of grants, new loans, non-debt creating flows (such as foreign direct investment), or operations that reduce debt and debt service.

3.2 Provision of finance

The Fund also has, of course, an important financing function, in addition to generating the conditions for the successful catalysis of financing from official and private sources. The Fund assists its members in trouble by enabling them to make purchases of exchange through a variety of instruments and facilities which enable it to tailor its assistance to the requirements of the situation at hand. Thus the Fund may help by allowing outright purchases of foreign exchange or measure out its loans in instalments over periods ranging from one year to three years; the lending may be linked to particular circumstances (cataclysmic natural disasters, temporary export shortfalls, contributions to buffer stock facilities) or to programmes of domestic policy reform – and lending in support of policy changes is very much at the core of its work and perhaps even a unique feature of the institution – special contingency mechanisms can be used to provide additional financing in the face of unexpected shocks and thereby help to keep the programmes on track; finally, there are structural adjustment facilities – the Structural Adjustment Facility (SAF) and the Enhanced Structural Adjustment Facility (ESAF) – on terms especially suited to the needs of the poorest member countries. A total of 33 of the poorest of the developing countries, mainly in Sub-Saharan Africa, are now eligible for some $8 billion of highly concessional assistance available with interest rates of 0.5 per cent and with 10 years' maturity.

3.3 Conditionality

Balance of payments problems require adjustment; it is inevitable and will take place whether or not the IMF is involved. The only question then is whether that adjustment will be orderly and coherent or not. Orderly adjustment is in the best interest of the deficit country, in terms of the contribution it makes to future growth and development, the confidence it gives to investors, savers, farmers, exporters, the protection it can provide to the poorest and most vulnerable members of society and, not least, the inducement it provides to the international community for providing assistance to help smooth over a difficult period.

The purpose of the Fund's conditionality is to ensure that its resources are used in accordance with the Fund's purposes, and specifically to foster and monitor such orderly adjustment so as to lay the foundation for sustained growth and to safeguard the revolving nature of the Fund's resources, that is, that they are repaid so that they can be recycled to other countries when they encounter problems at some future date. The resources of the Fund constitute a communal kitty. A failure to replenish the kitty on the part of one country threatens the ability of other members to draw on it in a time of need. This is why the Fund has a natural interest in seeing to it that borrowing members adjust successfully and emerge from their need.

Much is said in the popular press about the Fund 'imposing austerity' by insisting on raising taxes and cutting expenditures, including on those subsidies that hold down the prices of essentials. While this is of course a confusion of the sickness and the cure, it does not mean that the process of healing is not painful. But the blame must rest with the circumstances that have led to problems arising in the first place: external shocks, such as worsening terms of trade, protectionism and high real interest rates, but also external and domestic instability and poor macro-economic policies, poor investment choices ('white elephants'), wasteful government consumption, policies which discouraged farmers from tilling the land, exporters from exporting, savers from saving and private industries from investing.

4 THE ROLE OF THE FUND IN THE DEBT STRATEGY

Much has been written about the enormous difficulties many of the developing countries are facing in dealing with the effects of the burden of their external indebtedness. At the same time, however, it should be stressed that there is little justification for despair. After all, many developing countries have successfully avoided debt difficulties and much ground has been gained over the years that the present, continuously evolving debt strategy has been pursued: thus (1) the threat to the international financial system from this source has receded and, indeed, the industrial countries have registered eight years of uninterrupted economic growth which has helped improve the environment in which the developing countries are operating; (2) the danger that the debt crisis might spread to a wider range of more creditworthy debtor countries has been considerably reduced – for example, with the major exception of the Philippines, most developing countries in Asia, including countries like China and India, which account for most of the World's poor, have successfully avoided debt problems and at the same time registered considerable growth in per capita income; and, indeed, the economies of South Korea, Taiwan, Thailand, and others have experienced spectacular growth and rapid transformation and are shedding the typical attributes of developing countries.

Figure 8.1 illustrates the success of Asian countries and the marked regional differences in the growth of real GDP per capita. Interestingly enough, several of the Asian countries have, at times, relied heavily on foreign borrowing and the accumulation of debt to finance their development efforts but without 'falling into a debt trap'; (3) the Fund and other international co-operative institutions have adapted and made more effective their instruments of assistance; (4) the industrial countries have provided steady financing, including large-scale debt rescheduling, in support of the efforts of developing countries; and (5) many of the indebted developing countries have begun to put in place, despite enormous difficulties faced, far-reaching policy reforms that can pave the way to strong sustainable growth and eventually to the resolution of their debt problems.

In analysing these debt problems, it is important not to gloss over the varied experience of developing countries and, even in Sub-Saharan Africa, one of the poorest and most affected regions in the world, experience was not uniform and there are valuable lessons to be learned from this. By and large, our experience shows that it was the economic policies pursued in a particular developing country which determined whether it encountered debt problems or not. Despite, at times, very large borrowing, many countries have managed to avoid debt difficulties through good policies; they escaped high inflation by

Figure 8.1 Developing countries: real GDP per capita, by region (1970=100)

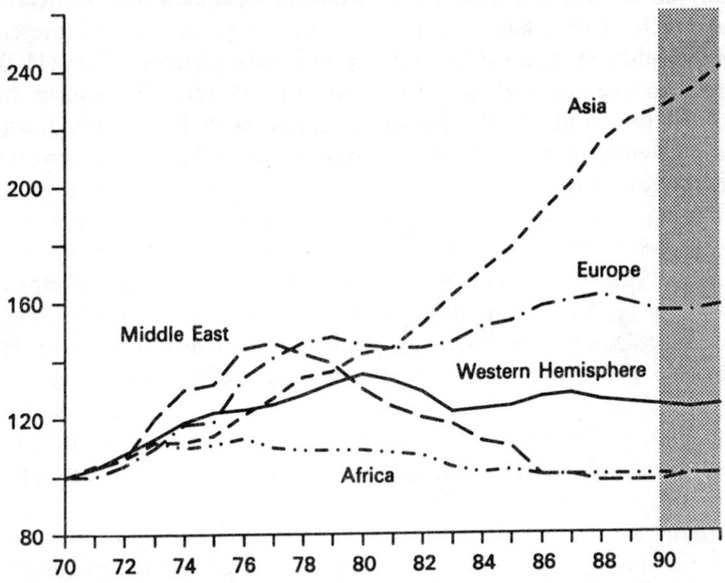

1. Composites are averages of percentage changes for individual countries weighted by the average US dollar value of their respective GDPs in 1988.
2. The shaded area indicates staff projections

Source: International Monetary Fund (1990) *World Economic Outlook*, October.

keeping their budgets and monetary policies under tight control, they have pursued realistic exchange rate policies and more broadly avoided wide-ranging distortions of their economies. They have relied on market forces and private initiatives. On the other hand, many of the countries now burdened with debt difficulties have a history of poor governance and instability not conducive to economic growth, of relatively poor economic management, a high percentage of budgetary expenditures going to unproductive projects, including military expenditures, and corruption.[2] This, of course, is not to say that unfavourable external events, including high interest rates and low prices for exports, did not contribute to the debt difficulties. However, there is also clear evidence which suggests that countries in similar external circumstances, which pursued appropriate economic policies, including an openness and export orientation of their economies, were more successful in dealing with these external difficulties and in avoiding debt problems.

All this being said, there is no reason for complacency. Despite the fact that, in recent years, on average, exports and national income have grown faster in the indebted developing countries than debt and debt service, daunting problems persist for many developing countries (see Figure 8.2).

The experience of the 1980s has, however, shown that very substantial efforts have been made under the debt strategy to assist countries that undertake strong adjustment efforts. In particular, assistance by multilateral agencies like the Fund was less constrained by the availability of financing than by the time it took indebted countries to develop solid programmes worthy of support and to sort

Figure 8.2 Net debtor developing countries: ratio of debt to exports (per cent)

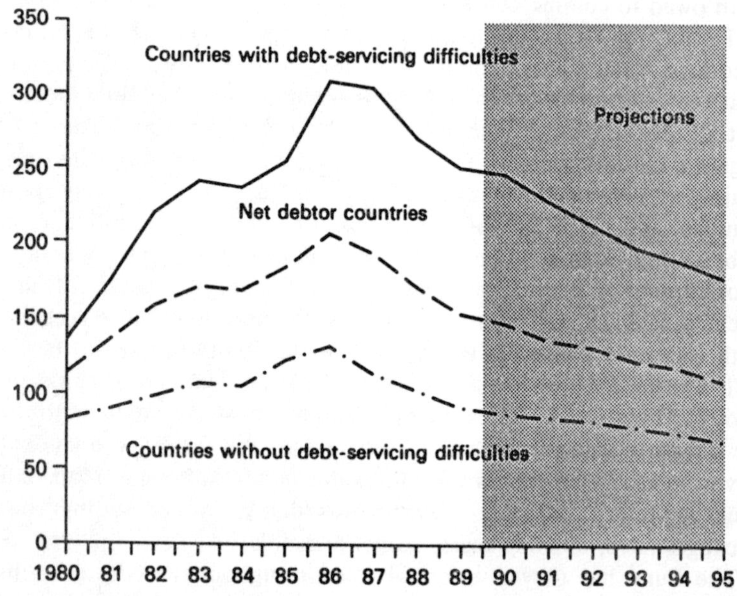

Source: International Monetary Fund (1990) *World Economic Outlook*, October.

out problems with commercial banks. The major components of support from official sources were balance of payments lending from the Fund, adjustment and investment lending by the World Bank, more recently, provisions of resources from both institutions for debt and debt service reduction, expanded programmes of multilateral development assistance, reschedulings by governments through the 'Paris Club' closely linked to Fund programmes, and the provisions of new finance, including bridge loans, and export credits. Official creditors have been applying concessional or 'Toronto Terms' in Paris Club reschedulings already to over a dozen low-income countries in Africa, but also to Bolivia and Guyana. ('Toronto Terms' refers to a 'menu' of options for the poorest countries that include partial cancellation of debt, extension of rescheduling maturities and interest rate concessions.) Also, a number of industrial countries have already forgiven very significant amounts of ODA loans and have in recent years generally based their development assistance to the poorest countries on grants rather than new loans. As a result, there has been a continuing and a significant net flow of resources to the low-income African countries whose debt is mainly with official creditors rather than owed to commercial banks.

Turning to those developing countries with large debt to official creditors which fall into the lower middle-income categories, one finds that the traditional Paris Club reschedulings, by rescheduling most, if not all, of the debt service, have alleviated the cash flow squeeze. As regards the problem of those middle-income countries with debt mainly to commercial banks, the situation has been relatively more complex and more difficult. The approach taken by the Fund in the debt strategy was to encourage a rescheduling where necessary and the provision of 'concerted new money'. Such financing packages have been typically linked to programmes with the Fund. More recently, with the move from the Baker Plan to the Brady initiative, the so-called 'menu approach' has evolved, which gives commercial banks the choice of continuing new lending to the indebted countries or to opt for debt and debt service reductions instead, and the Fund and Bank have already used their own resources in a handful of cases to facilitate such reduction schemes. Nevertheless delays in concluding such packages have, in some cases, been worrisome.

The Fund has played a central role throughout the debt crisis by providing both policy advice and financial assistance. Such assistance, in turn, catalyses funds from other sources because it assures the international community that appropriate policies are being pursued.

Immediately following the outbreak of debt difficulties in the early 1980s, the Fund's Executive Board approved 87 new lending arrangements for SDR 35 billion over a three-year period. This was totally unprecedented, and reflected the systemic nature of the problem which required a systemic response. It was therefore natural for the pace of new lending to slow in the following years. More recently, however, during the fiscal year 1989/90, the Fund's Executive Board approved 26 new lending arrangements amounting to more than SDR 11 billion, including three SAF and four ESAF arrangements which provide highly concessionary terms for the poorest countries.

5 THE TASK AHEAD

Unfortunately, the legacy of the past presents formidable hurdles. All parties must continue to deal with the debt burden inherited from the past decade and the challenges of environmental deterioration; most developing countries will also continue to face the realities of recent and ongoing pressures of rapid population growth.

Policy efforts that produce more efficient governmental activities and an environment conducive to private initative, and that are appropriately financed, should lead to a sustained improvement of growth performance. However, given the depth and complexity of the problems facing many countries, this development process is likely to be lengthy. In the developing countries, resources need to be directed away from less productive expenditures, including excessive military establishments, and towards more economically productive uses. To fulfil these potentials, the international community must work effectively to create an environment that fosters these tendencies. The Fund has a central role to play in this.

NOTES

1. The views expressed are those of the author and do not necessarily represent the official views of the IMF.
2. The *World Development Report 1990* by the World Bank shows that developing countries, as a whole, have spent a higher percentage of their budget and of their national income on military expenses than the NATO countries.

9 Is Adjustment Conducive to Long-Term Development? The Case of Africa in the 1980s

Giovanni Andrea Cornia

1 INTRODUCTION

The economic difficulties of the 1980s led to a phenomenal increase in the number of countries in Africa south of the Sahara (henceforth referred to as Africa *tout court*) undertaking stabilization and structural adjustment programmes with the assistance of the IMF and of the World Bank. Given the persistence of the problems most countries are facing, it is likely that stabilization and structural adjustment will continue dominating policy making for the rest of the century.

The adjustment policies introduced in the 1980s were primarily designed to restore macroeconomic balance over the short and medium term. Long-term development was not emphasized, although it is obvious that such an objective could not be achieved in the presence of persistent macroeconomic disequilibria and that, therefore, some 'stabilization' was required. Even the World Bank's more recent emphasis on 'structural adjustment' does not deal explicitly with the removal of those structural weaknesses and distortions (in human capabilities, production and trade structures, and in transport and rural infrastructure) which are to a large extent responsible for the macroeconomic disequilibria and the consequent need to adjust. It is not self-evident, therefore, that the emphasis of most adjustment programmes on external and fiscal balance, privatization and export orientation is consistent not only with the preservation of economic growth and of the welfare of the population over the short term, but also with the achievement of long-term development goals.

This chapter is aimed at assessing whether orthodox adjustment policies are consistent with the long-term development objectives of the

African countries or whether such adjustment policies are pushing the African economies away from a development path which is desirable and necessary from a long-term perspective. In Sections 2 and 3, the structural weaknesses of the African economy at independence and the extent to which the development policies followed during the first two decades have succeeded in lessening them are reviewed. In Section 4, the economic shocks of the early 1980s are briefly illustrated, together with the adjustment policies introduced to deal with them. Finally, Section 5 assesses the impact of the orthodox adjustment policies and their consistency with the long-run objectives of African countries, while Section 6 presents some conclusions.

Much of the discussion which follows refers to 'Africa' as if it were a homogeneous whole. This represents an obvious oversimplification as economic, social and ecological conditions vary remarkably between countries and, often, within each country. Important distinction ought to be made according to their size (Nigeria has at present over 100 million inhabitants, while nine countries have less than one million), income per capita (which varies by a factor of 20), location (15 countries are landlocked, while six are islands), population density (which varies from less than a person per square kilometre in Mauritania to 250 around Lake Victoria), availability of fertile land and mineral wealth as well as according to their colonial inheritance, past policies and political systems. Despite this diversity, which would require a more detailed approach, there are two important reasons for most of the subsequent discussions in relatively aggregate terms. First of all, there are striking commonalities with the problems facing the African countries. And, second, the adjustment policies adopted by the African countries in collaboration with the IMF and the World Bank in the 1980s are little differentiated by country. An assessment of their impact and consistency with long-term development does not require, therefore, a country-by-country evaluation.

2 THE AFRICAN ECONOMY AT INDEPENDENCE

With the exception of Liberia, which acceded to independence in 1847, and of Ghana, Guinea, Sudan and Ethiopia, which saw the end of colonial rule shortly before 1960, most African countries became independent between 1960 and 1963. For a few of them, such as Angola and Mozambique, colonization ended in 1975 and in the case of Zimbabwe and Namibia not until 1980 and 1990. In 1991, Western Sahara remains the only country which is not independent. Although the situation varied from country to country, five main structural weaknesses characterized the economies of the Sub-Saharan African countries in the early 1960s.

First, *distorted trade structures*. During the colonial period, Africa represented a main supplier of raw materials and tropical products to the metropolitan economies of Europe from which it imported manufactured goods, machinery and food. Africa's dependence on primary exports was such that immediately after independence, in 1965 (the first year for which comprehensive continent-wide data are available), mineral and agricultural primary commodities represented 92 per cent of total exports, with peaks of 99 or 100 per cent in countries such as Zambia, Ethiopia and the Gambia (World Bank 1989). In several cases, the export basket included only one or two commodities (such as coffee in Ethiopia, copper in Zambia, or tea and tobacco in Malawi), making such countries entirely dependent upon some form of monoculture as the unique source of export earnings. In the same year, imports of manufactured goods and food accounted on average for 75 and 14 per cent respectively of total imports. Inter-African trade was practically non-existent, while about 80 per cent of total trade originated from or was directed to the OECD countries and, in particular, to Western Europe. Transport and communication infrastructure and monetary arrangements were all reinforcing such distorted trade patterns. The problems of over-dependence on a narrow export basket and limited market outlets were compounded by substantial differences in price and income elasticity of demand for the goods exported versus the goods imported. Indeed, the demand for traditional agricultural exports (such as coffee, cocoa, tea, sugar and bananas) is characterized by low price elasticity and low income elasticity (Godfrey, 1985), while the reverse is true for the demand of imported manufactured goods, foods and fuel which tend to be price inelastic, while having a high income elasticity.

Second, a *desperately extensive agriculture* with abundant low-fertility land but with limited availability of good agricultural land, a difficult climate and a skewed network of transport, credit and extension services – favouring the large farmers and the plantation sector – constituted a major hindrance to the evolution of rapid and sustainable growth in agriculture. In spite of the alienation of land that occurred during colonization and the incipient spread of commercial farming, communal land tenure was still prevalent at independence.

Cultivation, carried out on a slash-and-burn basis and with long fallow periods (from a minimum of 6–7 years up to 10 years), was mainly geared to subsistence needs. Production depended essentially on land and labour, using extremely simple manual techniques. Outside the plantation sector there was little or no capital accumulation or use of intermediate inputs or irrigation, and output could only be increased by extending cultivation into new areas through a greater application of labour inputs and not from an intensification of farming techniques. Except under climatic changes, output per head and yields per hectare remained constant. Under this stationary state, there were few changes in social differentiation (as land was in unlimited supply), nutritional standards (as land and labour productivity were constant) or soil fertility (as long fallow periods allowed for an appropriate reconstitution of soil nutrients).

Third, a *limited industrial base*, the result of implicit or explicit colonial policies aimed at preventing Africa from engaging in import substitution. Not surprisingly, most African countries found themselves at independence with levels of industrialization that were far below the 'historical norms' for countries with their level of per capita income (Gulahati and Sekkar 1981). Even in relatively better off countries, such as Zambia, Kenya and Tanzania, the GDP share of value added in manufacturing was 45 to 80 per cent less than the expected 'Chenery Norm' (calculated by regression on the basis of GNP per capita and population size). In 1965, therefore, manufacturing accounted for 9 per cent of GDP compared to 14 per cent in South Asia, 23 per cent in Latin America and 27 per cent in East Asia.

Fourth, the *extremely low level of development of human resources* represented a formidable obstacle to the development of new productive activities, enhancement of farming techniques, creation of the necessary administrative structures, improvement of the health and educational status of the population and control of high levels of fertility.

During the colonial period, modern health services and educational facilities were largely neglected and available only in urban areas and plantation enclaves. In Burkina Faso (then Upper Volta), for instance, despite an infant mortality rate of 252 per 1000 live births, there was at independence only one doctor (including the expatriates) per 100 000 people, while more than half of the country completely lacked any modern medical services (Savadogo and Wetta, 1991). Figures on educational enrollment indicate that in 1960 the proportion of school-age children participating in primary education was 31 per cent in the former French colonies, 40 per cent in the anglophone territories, 50 per cent in the former Belgian colonies and around 10 per cent in Somalia, a former Italian colony (World Bank, 1988a). In contrast, primary enrollment rates were close to 70 per cent in South Asia which had an average GDP per capita of roughly half that of Sub-Saharan Africa. The situation was substantially worse in the field of secondary and tertiary education. In 1960, there were only 1200 indigenous graduates in the whole of Sub-Saharan Africa (UNESCO, quoted in World Bank, 1988a). In Malawi and Ghana, for instance, there were only 29 and 90 graduates respectively, while when Botswana became independent in 1966, 96 per cent of the higher level posts in the country were filled by expatriates (World Bank, 1988a). In addition, the school system of the time reflected in its structure, curriculum and language of instruction the need of the colonial apparatus.

This acute shortage of indigenous technical, managerial and administrative cadres imposed a continued reliance on expatriate manpower recruited at internationally competitive pay scales and, thus, inhibited the compression of an extremely dualistic and distorted public-sector pay structure inherited at independence.

Fifth, with the exception of the limited infrastructure supporting the export needs of the plantation or mining enclaves, there was an *almost complete absence of public infrastructure* in transport, communication, power generation, trading and storage. This situation was largely responsible for the high degree of disarticulation among agriculture, industry and services, and for the high import elasticity of GDP growth of the African economies. Because of this, growth stimuli originating in one sector often leaked out of the country or fizzled away and therefore had a limited multiplier effect on the rest of the economy. Empirical analysis, for instance, has shown that agriculture–non-agriculture linkages in Africa south of the Sahara were consistently weaker than in South Asia (Haggblade *et al.*, 1989).

3 DEVELOPMENT POLICIES AND FAILURES IN THE 1960s AND 1970s

3.1 The development experience of the 1960s and 1970s

It is impossible to do justice in a few pages to the diversity of development approaches of the African countries in the first two decades after independence. Experiences varied from that of a large number of countries (including, for instance, Kenya, Côte d'Ivoire and Malawi) opting for a capitalist development path characterized by large direct foreign investment, an important export-crop sector and a relatively important domestic private sector, to that of countries such as Tanzania which, after the Arusha Declaration of 1967, adopted 'African Socialism' as the guiding principle for their development. Such an approach placed a strong emphasis on self-reliance and attempted to address the structural weaknesses outlined above by aiming simultaneously at growth maximization and at the redistribution of income through public sector enlargement and through an ambitious programme of free health care, education and other social services. Only a few countries such as Guinea and, more recently, Ethiopia, Angola and Mozambique opted for a centrally-planned, state-controlled development.

In spite of this diversity of development philosophies, there are startling elements of commonality in the policies followed in the 1960s and 1970s by the majority of African countries in a number of crucial sectors. Such common elements did indeed reflect the development thinking – often originating from Western academic circles and development agencies – which prevailed in those years. Such thinking, which with hindsight appears somewhat simplistic or even misplaced, was almost universally accepted at that time (Singer, 1989). To begin with, there was a heavy and almost exclusive emphasis on physical capital accumulation as a source of growth (and not so much on human factors, such as education, skills and training-market size and other factors not explicit in the Harrod–Domar model) and on the related need to increase saving ratios (even if this had led to the persistence or even growth of income inequality). In addition, in view of the limited entrepreneurial tradition of indigenous elites in most countries, the state was fairly universally expected to play a major role in the process of accumulation and modernization.

Similarly, the restrictions on industry which had existed in many countries under colonial rule, and the uncertain outlook dominating commodity exports by developing countries in the late 1950s, gave legitimacy to the views of those emphasizing import-substituting industrialization as the most obvious way to diversify out of primary commodities. While, again with the benefit of hindsight, it appears that export-substitution was not given sufficient attention, most development economists of the time did find it difficult to visualize the rapid growth of the exports of manufacturers achieved by the Asian NICs in the late 1960s and 1970s because of the gross inadequacy of the transport infrastructure needed for export industries. In addition, in Africa development approaches were influenced by the Lewis model, another of the theoretical pillars upon which rested the development thinking of the post-Second World War period. The Lewis model, with its emphasis on the ancillary role of the rural sector and the preponderance of urban-based industrialization, perhaps contributed to the comparative neglect of agriculture (see later).

Although it is currently fashionable to suggest that Africa's economic troubles started with independence – and in spite of what may now appear to some as obsolete development thinking and a perverse political economy – it is undeniable that during the 1960s and 1970s (and particularly up to 1973 and between 1976 and 1978) the African economy performed, in aggregate terms, relatively well. GDP and exports grew at rates similar to those of the other main developing regions and, overall, faster than South Asia (see Table 9.1).

Manufacturing production in particular rose at sustained rates, although from very low levels, and in sectors with relatively simple technologies such as processed food, textiles, construction material and in other simple consumer goods. Such efforts were sustained by an important mobilization of domestic savings (and particularly since 1974 of foreign resources) which raised the overall investment ratio from 14 per cent in 1965 to 20 per cent in 1980 and by a massive expansion in primary education (World Bank, 1989). The average primary enrollment rate doubled from about 38 per cent in 1960 to 79 per cent in 1980. Because of the rapid growth of the population, this progress represented a fourfold increase in the number of school-age

Table 9.1 Average annual growth rates of selected macroeconomic indicators in Sub-Saharan Africa (SSA) and South Asia

	Population		*GDP*		*Agriculture*		*Manufacturing*		*Export*	
	65–73	*73–80*	*65–73*	*73–80*	*65–73*	*73–80*	*65–73*	*73–80*	*65–73*	*73–80*
Sub-Saharan Africa										
Low-income	2.6	2.7	6.0	2.8	2.2	0.0	10.7	10.2	16.9	−0.6
Mid-income	2.8	3.3	5.2	1.4	2.2	−1.7	–	2.5	7.2	3.8
Total	2.6	2.8	5.9	2.5	2.2	−0.3	10.1	8.2	15.1	0.2
South Asia	2.4	2.4	3.7	4.3	3.4	2.4	4.1	5.2	−0.7	5.8

Source: World Bank (1989)

children in primary school over the same period. Similar progress was achieved in the field of adult literacy and, to a lesser extent, in the health sector. Clearly disturbing was, in contrast, the performance of agricultural production and traditional food crops in particular, which already in the 1960s was growing more slowly than the population (whose growth rate increased from about 2.4 per cent in the 1960s, to 2.9 per cent in the 1970s, and to 3.1 per cent in the 1980s). The poor performance of agriculture was also responsible for the stagnation of agricultural exports in the second half of the 1970s and was one of the main factors behind the rapid rise of Africa's long-term external debt, which grew from US $5.6 billion in 1970 to US $43 billion in 1980 (World Bank, 1989).

The relatively positive aggregate performance of the African economy until 1973 and in some respects between 1976 and 1978, that is in a period broadly characterized, with the exception of 1973–5, by a rapid expansion of world trade, favourable borrowing conditions and relatively favourable terms of trade for the majority of countries until 1978 (except for 1973–75), does not allow the conclusion, however, that two decades of economic development had, in fact, reduced the structural weaknesses afflicting the African economy at independence and made it more resilient to changes in the international economic environment and in weather conditions.

If such a question is raised, the record of the first two decades of economic development appears substantially less favourable. Despite progress in a number of fields, in 1980 the African economy was broadly as 'dependent', 'vulnerable' and 'monocultural' as in 1960. In addition, the debt-led growth of 1974–80 made the African economies vulnerable on an additional score, that is, the potential changes in interest rates and borrowing conditions on the foreign debt. In this sense, the process of economic development was not associated with any significant process of structural transformation. While the share of primary activities in total output dropped significantly (from 43 to 30 per cent between 1965 and 1980), most of this shift favoured sectors (often including informal low-productivity operations) other than manufacturing, whose share stagnated at around 9 per cent.

The African economy, therefore, entered the 1980s – a decade during which exogenous factors such as the international environment, natural disasters and civil strife turned out to be less favourable than in the 1960s and most of the 1970s – under conditions of similar or greater vulnerability than in 1960.

3.2 Development failures

The most common explanation of the policy failures of the 1960s and 1970s states that African governments have relied too much on state and price controls and have, in this way, stifled market forces (World Bank, 1981). According to this view, a coalition of bureaucrats, industrialists and urban workers shaped distorted macroeconomic policies (in the trade, exchange rate, pricing and fiscal areas) favouring an inefficient industrialization and leading – because of the rapidly deteriorating internal terms of trade of agriculture – to serious balance of payments disequilibria as a result of declining exports of primary commodities on the one hand and rapidly surging food imports on the other. According to this view, as price distortion was the major culprit, 'getting the prices right' constituted the main element of the policy reforms.

Despite its popularity in donor circles, this view does not adequately capture the factors behind the development failures of the 1970s. Four specific policy failures which should have been addressed in the 1980s are instead considered in this chapter as the main causes of the lack of structural change since independence, the stagnation in the second half of the 1970s and, as it will clearly appear later on, the poor performance of the 1980s. These failures are discussed hereafter.

The Neglect, Growing Differentiation and Lack of Modernization of Agriculture

The problems of African agriculture started becoming evident in the late 1960s. Since then production has been growing more slowly than population, leading to a growing food crisis which occasionally reaches famine proportions. The reasons for such poor performance are many and complex and include factors such as adverse pricing policies, and in particular over-valued exchange rates and depressed farm-gate prices. An examination of empirical evidence on the extent and effects of 'price discrimination' indicates, however, that the importance of this factor, while real, has been over-stated, particularly for food crops (Ghai and Smith, 1987; Beynon, 1989; Bond, 1983). Other factors bear a greater responsibility for the failure of African agriculture.

First, with the commercialization of agriculture, land became vastly more valuable. In Ghana and Nigeria, as well as several East African and Sahelian countries, significant land markets developed alongside the beginning of a system of tenancy and share cropping (Ghai and Radwan, 1983). This was one of the first steps in the process of growing social differentiation observed over the last 30 years in rural areas.

Second, population growth substantially altered farming systems, ecological balance and yields. While initially the increasing demand for food was satisfied by extending the surface of good quality land under cultivation, at a later stage it encouraged migration to marginal land and the shortening of the fallow period. In the absence of improvements in irrigation, farming techniques and soil fertilization practices, and in view of the growing demand for wood for fuel and construction, shorter rotations and farming of marginal land led to declining average yields, rapid decreases in output per capita and, in extreme cases, to soil erosion and desertification. These well-documented processes, affecting Rwanda, Burundi, Ethiopia, Mali, Burkina Faso and the other Sahelian countries on a massive scale, are at work in varying degrees in most African countries. In all of them, the most tragic failure has been the inability to 'manage the transition' from a land-abundant, shifting agriculture to more input-intensive settled farming systems. In the early 1980s, the input intensity of production (proxied by the extent of irrigation and fertilizer consumption) in land-poor countries was as low as in land-rich countries. Also, the extent of irrigation and fertilizer use in land-poor African countries was about 23 and four times lower, respectively, than in the Asian countries with similar land scarcity and GDP per capita (Cornia and Strickland, 1990). As expected, land yields correlated closely with the input intensity of production (see Table 9.2).

Third, in the 1960s and 1970s, public expenditure in agriculture was inadequate in both volume and pattern. In the early 1960s, the share of agriculture in total government expenditure rarely exceeded 10 per cent (Ghai and Radwan, 1983). Data for 1979–81 (Norton, 1987) and the 1971–3 to 1985 period (Mosley and Smith, 1989) confirm this situation. In addition, public expenditure on rural road and transport infrastructure, input subsidies, price support, extension, R&D and irrigation has favoured large-scale farmers and the plantation sector at the expense of small farmers. In 1981, for instance, export crops received an average of 32 kg of fertilizer per hectare, as opposed to 5 kg for the food crops (FAO, 1986, Annex 5). Similarly, in 1976, US $39 million were spent on research for coffee, while in the same year no significant research was carried out on 'poor people's staple,' such as sorghum, millet and tubers.

Table 9.2 Agricultural inputs and yields in Sub-Saharan Africa and South East Asia, 1982–4

Country	*GDP per capita (1987 US$)*	*Arable land per agric. worker (ha)*	*Irrigated land on arable land (%)*	*Fertiliser consumption (kg/ha)*	*Yields of cereals (tonnes/ha)*
			Land-rich Sub-Saharan countries		
Cameroon	970	3.0	0	12	1.0
CAR	330	5.5	0	1	0.5
Zaire	150	1.9	0	2	0.9
Average	480	3.5	0	5	0.8
			Land-scarce Sub-Saharan countries		
Burundi	250	0.4	1	2	1.1
Ethiopia	130	1.0	0	5	1.2
Kenya	330	0.7	1	27	1.6
Lesotho	370	0.5	0	24	0.8
Malawi	160	1.1	1	18	1.2
Nigeria	370	1.4	0	9	0.7
Rwanda	300	0.3	0	1	1.2
Somalia	290	0.8	4	3	0.6
Uganda	260	0.9	0	0	1.7
Average	270	0.8	1	10	1.1
			Land-scarce South East Asian countries		
Bangladesh	160	0.5	16	41	2.0
India	300	0.9	25	38	1.5
Indonesia	450	0.7	26	65	3.3
Nepal	160	0.4	24	13	1.6
Pakistan	350	1.4	–	62	1.6
Sri Lanka	400	0.7	28	73	2.8
Vietnam	–	0.4	17	44	2.5
Average	300	0.7	23	45	2.2

Source: Cornia and Strickland (1990).

The successive unfolding and interaction of these three phenomena led to an extremely slow growth in agricultural value-added as well as to radical changes in land use, tenure and yields, and to a rapidly growing rural differentiation which compounded further the poor performance of African agriculture and, by implication, of the African economy. With the exception of a few countries (such as Zambia, Zaire and the Central African Republic), by the early 1980s farmable land had become increasingly scarce and its distribution more uneven.

Already in the late 1960s and early 1970s, land concentration appeared to be more pronounced than generally assumed, with Gini coefficients ranging between 0.4 and 0.7, that is, values not too dissimilar from those of countries such as Pakistan and the Philippines where land reform was a key policy issue. With few exceptions, land concentration and the proletarianization of rural labour continued over the subsequent 15 years. As a result, in 1985 15 per cent of rural households was estimated to be landless, while another 30 per cent, mostly women-headed, were near-landless (FAO, 1988; Alexandratos, 1988; Durring, 1989). Large commercial farmers and the plantation sector were estimated to own, already in the early 1970s, between 20 and 40 per cent of the fertile land and an even larger share of other productive resources. The limited information on changes in income inequality over the two decades 1960 to 1980 confirm the view of growing differentiation within the rural sector. In Madagascar, for instance, income concentration in rural areas (as measured by the Gini coefficient) increased between 1962 and 1980 from 0.29 to 0.43. This increase in income inequality was greater than that observed in urban areas and for the country as a whole (Pryor, 1990). Similar changes were observed for Malawi over the 1968/9 to 1984/5 period (ibid.).

The Failure to Modify the International Trading Position of Africa

Broadly speaking, the export and import structure (by types of goods traded and countries of destination or origin) did not change. The share of primary commodities in total exports even grew (from 92 per cent in 1965 to 96 per cent in 1980), the only noticeable difference being the increasing importance of fuels for the five African oil exporters. In only six countries (out of 45), that is, Mauritius, Zimbabwe (then Rhodesia), Botswana, Mali, Kenya and Lesotho, did manufacturing exports increase substantially. In addition, Western Europe alone continued to absorb about 50 per cent of Africa's exports.

Attempts at modifying the import structure were carried out mostly through the strategy of import-substituting industrialization. This strategy failed for its lack of depth and its excessive concentration on consumer goods and virtually no promotion of capital or intermediate goods. Its technological base was inflexible and depended on the importation of capital goods and raw materials that were neither available locally nor reflective of the continent factor endowments and whose rate of employment generation was very low. Its output structure reflected an unequal pattern of income distribution and not the need for simple consumer goods of the population as a whole. Because of the extreme narrowness of most domestic markets, and in the absence of export quotas, that is norms requiring the exportation of a given share of domestic production, local industries were little exposed to competition, operated at chronically low capacity utilization rates and could not therefore benefit from economies of scale. The main failure of such strategy, however, was that it did not accomplish its goals of substituting domestic production for imported manufactured goods. Indeed, while imports of consumer goods declined, those of intermediate and capital goods increased (see Table 9.3), not allowing any foreign exchange saving and a strengthening of Africa's balance of payments.

Table 9.3 Africa's import structure[a]

Import type	*1960s*[b]	*1972*	*1979–82 (average)*
Consumer goods	42	32	20
Intermediate goods	34	39	48
Capital goods	24	29	32

Notes
a Unweighted mean for seven African countries.
b Relates to several years in 1960s.
Source: Van der Hoeven (1992).

The emphasis on import substitution furthermore diverted attention from export diversification and did not reduce the vulnerability to price fluctuations and the long-term decline in the terms of trade of primary commodities.

The Substantial Worsening of the Fiscal and Foreign Debt Position

This was a factor that proved to be extremely detrimental in view of the adverse changes intervening on the international markets in the 1980s.

The fiscal crisis of the 1980s had its origins in three policy choices made in the 1970s. The first was the inability to properly manage commodity booms. Cyclical swings in commodity prices are well known for having disastrous effects on government budgets. Under such conditions it is advisable to set the level of government expenditure in relation to the 'permanent' component of government revenue and not in relation to the 'current' (that is, 'permanent' plus 'transitory') revenue. During the commodity price booms of the 1970s, most governments increased expenditures in line with the current revenue, particularly on projects with low rates of return and high future recurrent costs. Urban infrastructure, import-substituting industries and the plantation sector absorbed most of these resources without, however, being able to expand the tax base. Investment in rural infrastructure and the modernization of food crop agriculture, in contrast, was inadequate. The collapse of commodity prices at the end of the 1970s and in the early 1980s was the first factor which precipitated this creeping 'fiscal crisis'. Of course, not all countries fell into the 'commodity cycle trap'. Cameroon, for instance, managed its boom prudently and used much of the extra revenue from the 1979–81 oil boom to repay its external debt.

The second policy choice which contributed to the fiscal crisis of the 1980s was the euphoric indebtedness strategy followed since 1973 by many countries in Africa, Latin America and the OECD – with the encouragement of the international financial institutions – to offset the deflationary effect of the first oil shock. Some African countries, in addition, increased the recourse to foreign financing also on occasion of commodity booms, in view of what was then seen as a permanently increased repayment capacity. Niger's debt, for instance, which was equivalent in 1976 to only 13 per cent of GDP, more than doubled between 1978 and 1981, precisely the years of the uranium boom (Tinguiri, 1991). As a result of these two trends, the foreign debt of Africa as a whole (excluding Nigeria) rose from close to zero in 1960 to US $5 billion (or 18 per cent of GDP) in 1970 and to US $37 billion (or 38 per cent of GDP) in 1980.

A third factor in the fiscal crisis of the early 1980s has been the lack of any serious attempt to diversify the tax base. In most African countries the principal source of public revenues was trade taxes, especially levies on one or a handful of primary commodity exports. In mineral economies, such as Zambia (copper), Botswana (diamonds), Sierra Leone (iron ore) and Nigeria (oil), the extractive sector accounted for well over half the government's income in the form of taxes on employees' income and corporate profits, royalties and export duties. In countries exporting agricultural commodities, export levies –

normally collected by state marketing boards, which passed on to the producers only a fraction of the export proceeds – accounted for between one-quarter and one-third of total government revenue. In both types of countries, attempts at diversifying the sources of government revenue (by taxing informal sector income, introducing progressive indirect taxes, taxing wealth and improving tax collection) have been rather modest and generally unsuccessful throughout the 1960s and 1970s.

The Weak Human Infrastructure

Fourth, despite the growth in the number of university graduates, the rapid progress in primary education and health care, and the improvement in living conditions, several African countries did not manage to create an adequate human infrastructure. This lack of infrastructure has been felt in technical and scientific fields, in food research and in the inability to reduce high fertility rates or improve the health status of the population. This, in part, reflected the recent development of the new educational, training and health systems, the distortions inherited at independence, the persistence of gender biases and the high degree of centralization of services. For instance, despite far-reaching reforms, curricula in primary and secondary schools continued to bear little relevance to required labour market or life skills. In addition, the language of instruction was still a foreign language (generally western) in 18 out of 39 African countries (World Bank, 1988a). And finally, while enrollment in secondary and tertiary education remained understandably below the level of other developing regions, the proportion of students in science, engineering and technical training was also in this case much lower. This led to the absurd situation, typical of several African labour markets, of large numbers of (expensive) expatriates employed in key positions coexisting with substantial unemployment among African graduates.

4 THE EXPERIENCE OF THE 1980s: EXOGENOUS SHOCKS AND MACROECONOMIC ADJUSTMENT

At the beginning of the 1980s, the African economies were hit by a series of powerful external shocks due to the second increase in oil prices and the ensuing recession which affected the industrialized countries. Because of this:

(a) The volume of world trade – which had expanded at 5.7 per cent a year in the 1970s – virtually stagnated between 1981 and 1983. With the real GNP growth rate of trading partners falling from an average of 4.4 per cent a year in the 1970s to 1.8 per cent a year between 1981 and 1983, the growth rates of the demand for primary products and fuel fell between the 1970s and 1981–3 from about 2.0 and 0.5 per cent a year to 1.0 and −11.0 per cent a year (IMF, 1989). The overall volume of African exports stagnated completely, losing in this way market shares (ibid.). Even if Africa had maintained its export shares, however, the overall decline in world demand and prices for primary commodities would have had a serious negative impact on Africa's export earnings.

(b) With a sharp decline in commodity prices and an increase in the prices of manufactured products, the overall terms of trade of Africa fell by 7 per cent between 1981 and 1983 (ibid.).

(c) Nominal interest rates on the foreign debt increased to the record high levels of 18–20 per cent during 1980–3. The decline observed since then was not paralleled by a commensurate decline in real interest rates.

(d) Because of the accumulation of debt which had occurred since 1973, and in view of the debt crisis of 1982, gross capital flows declined sharply from 1983. Net capital flows dropped even more drastically, from US$10 billion in 1982 to about US$2.5 billion in 1985.

In addition to these four external shocks, economic conditions in Africa were negatively affected by the severe drought of 1984–5, continued civil strife and the explosion of the AIDS pandemic – now estimated to affect, on average, 5 per cent of the total population (and close to 10 per cent of the labour force in the 15–45 age bracket) in ten Eastern and Central African countries. AIDS has already caused considerable, and growing, economic losses, mainly in terms of greater medical costs and lower labour productivity (Becker, 1990).

These exogenous shocks produced immediate adverse effects on inflation, the government deficit and the current account balance of most African countries. Initially, when these macroeconomic problems were considered only as symptoms of a payment crisis resulting from a temporary deterioration of the terms of trade, IMF-supported stabilization programmes – that is Stand-By Agreements (SBA) and Extended Fund Facility (EFF) programmes – were introduced as a matter of urgency in a large number of countries to avoid the disruptions which could have followed uncontrolled payment crises. Structural adjustment programmes, in contrast, were much less frequent.

At a later stage, when it became obvious that the African economic crisis had deeper roots, efforts at stabilization were complemented by a greater number of World Bank-sponsored Structural and Sectoral Adjustment Programmes (SALs and SECALs) and by the Fund's Structural Adjustment Facility (SAF) and Enhanced Structural Adjustment Facility (ESAF) which started operating in 1988.

Altogether between 1980 and 1989, 241 programmes were initiated in collaboration with the IMF and the World Bank (see Table 9.4). Most countries have had a succession of programmes. On average, the 36 countries of Table 9.4 have undertaken about seven adjustment programmes over the 1980s, while 11 countries initiated ten or more adjustment programmes.

Only Burkina Faso, Rwanda, Angola and a few very small countries such as Botswana, Swaziland, Cape Verde, Djibouti and Comoros (whose combined population accounts for less than 6 per cent of the total population of Sub-Saharan Africa) had not initiated an adjustment programme in the 1980s. During the 1980s, therefore, adjustment had become the main focus of economic policy making and had virtually replaced any other policy objective.

Although they share several common elements (see later) and although the division of labour between the IMF and the World Bank has become increasingly less clear in the 1980s, it is useful to distinguish analytically between IMF-supported stabilization programmes and World Bank-supported structural adjustment programmes. At the cost of some simplification, it can be argued that stabilization programmes aim at re-establishing macroeconomic balance within the context of existing economic structures. Structural adjustment, in contrast, aims at removing the structural problems leading to macroeconomic disequilibria. From the World Bank's perspective, the most important structural adjustments required are those in prices and incentives structure and towards greater privatization and export orientation. It is claimed that, if such adjustments are introduced, all structural distortions (such as those discussed in Section 2) would be removed automatically through the free play of market forces.

Stabilization programmes generally include three sets of policies (Cornia *et al.*, 1987): (1) *expenditure-reducing policies* aimed at

Table 9.4 **Stabilization and structural adjustment programmes in Africa (initiated in the 1980s)**

	In co-operation with the IMF				*In co-operation with the World Bank*[a]				*Year of first programme in 1980s*
	SBA	*SAF*	*ESAF*	*EFF*	*SAL*	*ER*	*SECAL*	*Total*	
Benin		1			1		1	3	1989
Burundi	1	1			2		1	5	1986
Cameroon		1			1			2	1988
Central African Republic	6	1			2		1	10	1980
Chad		1					3	4	1987
Congo	2				1			3	1986
Côte d'Ivoire	5			1	3		3	12	1981
Eq. Guinea	2	1					1	4	1980
Ethiopia	1							1	1981
Gabon	2			1	1			4	1980
Gambia	1	1	1					3	1982
Ghana	3	1	1	1	2	1	4	13	1983
Guinea	3	1			2		1	7	1982
Guinea-Bissau					1	1		2	1981
Kenya	6	1	1		2		3	13	1980
Lesotho		1						1	1988
Liberia	5							5	1980
Madagascar	7	1	1				2	11	1980
Malawi	3		1	1	3		2	13	1980
Mali	4	1					3	8	1982
Mauritania	5	1	1		1		3	11	1980
Mauritius	5				8		1	14	1980
Mozambique		1	1			3		5	1987
Niger	4	1	1		1		1	8	1983
Nigeria	2						3	5	1983
Sao Tome		1			1	1		3	1985
Senegal	6	1	1	1	4		2	15	1980
Sierra Leone	3	1		1				5	1981
Somalia	5	1					2	8	1980
Sudan	3			1				4	1982
Tanzania	2	1					2	5	1980
Togo	7	1	1		3			12	1981
Uganda	4	1	1			2		8	1980
Zaire	6	1		1			2	10	1981
Zambia	3			1		1		5	1981
Zimbabwe	2			1		1		2	1981
Total	108	24	11	9	39	9	41	241	

SBA = Stand-By Arrangement; SAF = Structural Adjustment Facility; ESAF = Enhanced Structural Adjustment Facility; EEF = Extended Fund Facility; SAL = Structural Adjustment Loans/Credits; ER = Economic Recovery/Rehabilitation; SECAL = Sector Adjustment Loans.

[a] Some subjective judgements have been made for the assignment of credit granted before 1988 in the three types of World Bank programmes listed in the table.

Source: *IMF Survey* (various issues), World Bank (1990a)

curtailing domestic aggregate demand and, consequently, imports. They generally include public expenditure cuts and, somewhat less frequently, increases in fees and indirect taxes, tariffs and fees, tighter money supply and reduced credit ceilings, wage control or more general policies aimed at restricting real income; (2) *expenditure-switching policies* aimed at increasing the supply of 'tradables', that is, export and import substitutes, by switching productive resources (labour and capital) from the 'non-tradable' to the 'tradable' sector. The switch is normally induced by a change in the relative prices and terms of trade of the two sectors obtained by policy instruments such as exchange rate devaluation, product pricing, trade interventions (export subsidies, import controls, tariffs and so on) and by measures enhancing factor mobility; and (3) *institutional reforms*, such as privatization, fiscal reform, reform of the financial markets, and price and trade liberalization which are aimed at increasing overall efficiency, improving production incentives and stimulating savings and investment.

Stabilization programmes have been characterized by a short time horizon (between 12 and 18 months), the predominance of macroeconomic (as compared with mesoeconomic, sectoral and targeted) policies, the neglect of distributive and social issues, and the prevalence of expenditure-reducing policies (which emphasize demand restraint and produce results rapidly) over expenditure-switching policies (which emphasize an increase in the supply of 'tradables' and normally require more time and new investments) (IMF, 1986).

The World Bank-sponsored Structural Adjustment programmes (SALs) normally include five sets of policy measures (Mosley, 1987): (1) *mobilization of domestic resources* through fiscal and financial reforms and improved performance of public enterprises; (2) *efficiency enhancing* measures through privatization or reform of public sector companies, price and import liberalization and encouragement to direct foreign investment; (3) *trade liberalization* through the removal of import quotas, the reduction of tariffs and the promotion of exports; (4) *strengthening of the public sector* through the reform of the civil service and of public companies and improvement in management and institutions to support the public sector; and (5) *social policy reform* through rationalization, the introduction of user fees, greater privatization of services and some attempts to redirect resources to basic services. Originally, SALs had a duration of two to three years, but more recently they have been extended to three to five years.

The World Bank-sponsored Sectoral Adjustment programmes (SECALs) have a similar orientation to the SALS but are sector-specific and, consequently, include more detailed measures. The sector most frequently selected has been agriculture, where dismantling of parastatal organizations, suppression of input subsidies and price support have been the most frequent measures.

5 AN ASSESSMENT OF THE EFFECTS OF STABILIZATION AND STRUCTURAL ADJUSTMENT

The success of the 1980s adjustment efforts can be assessed from two interrelated perspectives. First of all, it is necessary to examine whether the IMF- and the World Bank-supported adjustment programmes have succeeded in stabilizing the economy by restoring non-crisis conditions in the balance of payments and fiscal sector, and in controlling inflation, so as to allow the normal functioning of the economy, the resumption of investment and growth, and the necessary efforts for the diversification of the production and export basket. Of course, it is necessary to know also at what costs stabilization has been achieved. If the losses of output, investment and human welfare have been large, adjustment will have temporarily solved one problem, but at the expense of reducing the utilization of domestic resources below full employment, sacrificing capital accumulation and the development of human capabilities. Ideally, stabilization should be accompanied by 'non-negative' changes in output growth, investment activity and human development, as underscored by the growing literature on 'growth-oriented adjustment', 'adjustment with a human face' and 'the social dimension of adjustment'.

From the second perspective, adjustment programmes are assessed in terms of their success in removing those distortions and bottlenecks (such as those illustrated in Section 2) responsible for the development failures of the 1970s and which made the African economy even more vulnerable to the exogenous shocks of the early 1980s. If such distortions were removed, future balance of payments and fiscal crises would be less likely, while balanced growth and long-term development goals would be more attainable.

Consistent with the analysis of the structural weaknesses of the African economy presented earlier on, the following questions would need to be asked:

- Have the distortions preventing an equitable modernization of agriculture and leading to ecological degradation been removed?
- Have production and export structures become more diversified? Has dependence on imported food been reduced?
- Has the supply of human skills and the general level of education, health and nutrition improved?
- And finally, has the resource base of African countries improved?

The evaluation of stabilization and structural adjustment performance is presented below in sub-sections 5.1 and 5.2. It is important to stress that the performance discussed below is the joint result of *both* IMF and World Bank policies (as well as of other factors). Indeed, despite the division of tasks highlighted above, in the 1980s both institutions have increasingly dealt with both aspects of adjustment. In addition, it is impossible to separate the impact of the policies of either institution, as in most cases their programmes are developed simultaneously.

The empirical information used for the evaluation of the adjustment performance is summarized in Table 9.5. The latter includes all countries of Table 9.4, with the exception of Equatorial Guinea, Gabon, Gambia, Guinea, and Sao Tome – for which it was not possible to compile the necessary information – and of Mozambique, Benin, Burundi, Cameroon, Chad, Lesotho and Congo, which initiated their adjustment efforts only in the late 1980s. The data of Table 9.5 allow the illustration of the various facets of the African adjustment experience in the 1980s. The first three variables measure the success of *macroeconomic stabilization*. The average yearly growth rate of real GDP per capita over 1981–88 allows the assessment of whether adjustment has been *growth-oriented*, while changes in investment/GDP ratios can offer useful insights about the way *future growth* has been affected in this process. The changes in primary school enrollment rates allow the assessment of whether adjustment has entailed *social costs*. (A more accurate measurement of such social costs would require an analysis of a broader set of indicators, including, for instance, the infant mortality rate and nutritional status of the population. Empirical information on these two variables is, however, extremely rare.) Finally, changes in the share of manufacturing in total value added and the growth rate of the volume of exports over the 1980s – together with data on changes in investment ratios and enrollment rates – allow an initial assessment of how 'structural' has been changing in the 'adjusting' countries in the 1980s.

Table 9.5 Selected macroeconomic indicators for adjusting countries in Africa, south of the Sahara, in the 1980s*

	CA/GDP		*Inflation*		*B. Deficit[g]/GDP*	
	81–2	*87–8*	*73–80*	*81–8*	*80–1*	*87–8*
CAR	−13.2	−17.1	14.9	7.0	−3.9	−0.2[j]
Côte d'Ivoire	–	–[d]	15.6	3.1	−11.1	−3.4[k]
Ethiopia	−6.1	−9.0	5.4	1.8	−4.2	−7.4
Ghana	−8.4	−4.3	43.0	47.0	−5.6	0.5
Guinea-Bissau	−48.0	−42.5	6.3	47.0	−25.0	−15.7
Kenya	−7.8	−8.1	11.6	9.6	−6.6	4.4
Liberia	−3.7	−14.3	10.2	1.5	−8.9	−7.3
Madagascar	−15.2	−12.7	11.2	18.4	−12.5	−4.4
Malawi	−14.8	−1.6	9.7	12.7	−14.2	−7.5
Mali	−17.0	−17.3	10.6	3.5	−4.2	−3.8
Mauritania	−42.3	−22.1	9.1	8.8	−8.5	0.0
Mauritius	−9.8	−0.2	17.2	7.9	−10.3	−1.8
Niger	−19.7	−10.3	8.2	4.2	−7.8	
Nigeria	−7.1	−1.9	18.0	13.1	−7.4	−1.0
Senegal	−21.6	−9.7	10.0	7.3	−1.2	−3.0
Sierra Leone	−14.7	−5.7	14.8	42.0	−11.1	−9.0
Somalia	−34.7	−39.8	22.0	38.0	−7.7	–[e]
Sudan	−14.2	−7.4	16.7	32.0	−3.5	−13.8
Tanzania	−6.1	−23.1	15.4	26.0	−7.5	−3.3
Togo	−16.1	−11.0	9.9	6.2	−3.8	−4.3
Uganda	−8.5	−6.4	39.0	105.0	−3.9	−2.6
Zaire	−5.4	−13.7	40.0	17.5	−3.3	−12.7
Zambia	−17.8	−7.0	9.0	33.0	−15.7	−12.0
Zimbabwe	−11.1	−0.7	2.2	12.1	−8.4	−9.2
Improving (or positive)	16			12		16
No change[f,h]	2			1		2
Worsening (or negative)	6			11		6

Notes

[a] Industry; [b] over 1980–7 period; [c] taken from Tinguiri (1991): [d] improved; [e] deteriorated; [f] no change is assumed whenever the share of manufacturers in GDP or the growth rate of the volume of exports does not change (±) by at least 1.5 per cent; [g] including grants; [h] no change (in constant prices) is assumed whenever ratios change less than ±0.5 per cent; [i] 1986; [k] 1985; [l] 1987; [m] GNP.

GDP/c Gr.	Inv./GDP		Primary ER		Manuf./GDP[a]		Gr. of exports
81–8	80–1	87–8	82	88 or MRY	82	88[f]	82–8[f]
−0.4	7.8	12.7	74	66	6.4	5.9	−0.2
−5.0	27.1	13.7	74	70	11.1	13.4	−3.6
−1.0	10.2	15.1	40	37	11.3	12.5	0.4
−2.0[m]	5.1	11.6	77	71	5.5	7.3	6.9
1.8	27.6	26.0	63	56	19.7[a,b]	5.8[a,b]	2.6
0.0	29.2	25.2	107	96	18.8[a,b]	16.4[a,b]	3.0
−5.3[m]	21.8	9.2	47	40	6.8	6.1	−4.3
−2.8	20.8	15.6	136	94	19.0[a,b]	15.8[a,b]	−3.7
0.0	21.1	15.0	62	66	16.0[a,b]	16.5[a,b]	5.3
0.2[m]	17.2	15.7	24	23	9.3[a,b]	11.6[a,b]	9.2
−1.2	39.0	19.1	37	52	24.4[a,b]	19.3[a,b]	5.5
4.7	23.0	25.7	114	106	15.7	22.5	12.2
−4.0	28.4	9.5	27[c]	22[c]	–	–[c,e]	−5.5
−3.9	21.0	12.4	97	77	12.5	9.7	2.7
1.4	15.8	14.9	51	60	16.4	16.6	8.7
−1.2[l]	17.6	10.6	–	–[e]	6.5	4.8	−3.3
−0.2	35.2	34.3	29	15	4.4	3.4	−15.2
−0.2	14.7	10.2	50	49	7.0	8.5	1.8
−1.3	21.8	22.0	90	66	9.4	7.6	−2.2
−2.1	30.0	22.6	111	101	9.7	8.1	2.1
−1.4	6.5	13.5	58	70	4.4	4.9	5.4
−1.0	15.0	11.8	94	76	3.1	3.1	−3.4
−4.1	21.3	12.0	90	97	20.4	24.8	−2.3
−1.5	20.9	19.8	130	128	24.4	23.7	1.5
5	4		5		6		11
3	1		3		9		4
16	19		16		9		9

CA/GDP = current account balance/GDP ratio; Inflation = average yearly change in GDP deflator; B. deficit/GDP = government budget deficit (including grants)/GDP ratio; GDP/c gr = average annual growth rate of real GDP per capita in constant prices; Inv/GDP = gross investment/GDP ratio; Primary ER = gross enrolment rate in primary education; Manuf./GDP = share of value added (manufacturing) in GDP in constant prices; Gr. of Exports = average annual growth rate of the volume of exports; MRY = most recent year.

Sources: UNDP and World Bank (1989); World Bank (1990b)

5.1 Stabilization performance

An examination of macroeconomic data for Africa as a whole (that is, including 'adjusting' and 'non-adjusting' countries) shows that, in spite of the large number of IMF- and World Bank-supported programmes undertaken in the 1980s, the objective of macroeconomic stabilization has been achieved only partially. In 1989, the deficit of the current account balance had declined to only $7.8 billion from the level of $9.6 and $8.3 billion respectively recorded in 1981 and 1982 (IMF, 1989 and 1990). Furthermore, in 1988, the regional budget deficit relative to GDP (6.9 per cent) was as large as in 1981–2. In the meantime, the average regional inflation rate had remained at around 21 per cent throughout the 1982–9 period, with no improvement over the average rate of 20.8 per cent recorded over 1972–81 (ibid.).

Stabilization performance has varied of course from country to country. A more detailed analysis based on the data of Table 9.5 shows that, of the 24 countries which undertook adjustment programmes in the 1980s, only six managed to achieve simultaneously lower inflation rates and lower deficits (relative to GDP) in the current account balance and government budget. While 12 other countries managed to achieve at least two of these three objectives, for six countries macroeconomic imbalances at the end of the 1980s were as severe as before adjustment efforts got under way.

In addition, in seven of the 18 countries which showed some movement towards stabilization, the deficit of the current account balance in 1987–8 was still in excess of 10 per cent of GDP, while in Guinea-Bissau and Zambia the budget deficits also exceeded this critical level.

These relatively modest results have been obtained despite large real exchange rate devaluations, substantial cuts in public expenditure and credit ceilings, and the introduction of support prices. While external factors have been in part responsible for these modest achievements (see later), in the African context the standard approach to stabilization suffers from a number of limitations which reduce its expected impact. Given the price and income elasticities of imports and exports prevailing in most African economies, devaluation produces limited effects on the deficits of the balance of payments. Furthermore, devaluation tends to be deleterious whenever all African countries producing the same primary commodities with low demand elasticities devalue simultaneously, triggering in this way a global increase in their export volume. In addition, devaluation, producer price increases and the withdrawal of subsidies contribute to the persistence or acceleration of inflation, in spite of tight fiscal and monetary policies. There is also evidence that supply responses to higher prices have been sluggish (Beynon, 1989; Bond, 1983). Although there is no conclusive evidence in this regard, it is plausible that large cuts in public expenditure for infrastructure and maintenance have offset part of the production inducements offered by higher producer prices. Similarly, trade liberalization and the overall contraction in imports and economic activity resulting from expenditure-reducing (demand-restraint) measures negatively affect tax receipts, making the achievement of fiscal balance even more problematic in spite of drastic expenditure cuts. In addition, devaluation increases the fiscal cost (in domestic currency) of public debt servicing, thus making the achievement of fiscal balance more difficult. Because of this and other factors, interest payments on the public debt of a group of 13 African countries with comparable government expenditure data increased from 7.7 per cent in 1980–1 to 12.5 per cent in 1985–7 (Cornia and Stewart, 1990).

With few exceptions, the achievement of stabilization has entailed severe losses in the field of growth, investment and welfare. Of the 18 countries which managed to stabilize their economy in the 1980s, only five recorded a positive growth of GDP per capita. In all the others, macroeconomic stability was achieved at the expense of growth (Table 9.5). In some of these countries, such as Kenya, Malawi and a few others, the stagnation or decline in GDP per capita was in part due to persistently high, and in a few cases accelerating, growth rates of the population. It must be noted also, however, that if the assessment of the growth performance were effected on the basis of gross national income per capita data (which include an adjustment for terms of trade changes), the growth performance would appear even less satisfactory.

This poor growth performance seems to suggest an excessive reliance on expenditure-reducing policies and the limited effects of expenditure-switching and growth-enhancing policies, particularly if external financing is inadequate (Helleiner, 1991). The decline in enrollment rates is indicative also of the *social costs* associated with the economic crisis of the 1980s and the adjustment measures introduced to deal with it.

5.2 Structural adjustment performance

In spite of some early claims that the IMF- and the World Bank-supported programmes had generated slightly better results in countries with 'strong reform programmes' (World Bank/UNDP, 1989), the available evidence shows that, with a few exceptions, by the late 1980s, structural conditions had not improved in the 24 countries which had initiated adjustment programmes since the early 1980s. This unsatisfactory performance has been obtained despite profound reforms in the field of privatization, liberalization of prices and foreign trade, mobilization of resources, foreign investment and others (Table 9.5; see also UNECA, 1989, which contradicts conclusively the above claims).

To start with, capital accumulation slowed down in five-sixths of these countries. In 1987–8, the average (unweighted) *gross* investment–GDP ratio was about 30 per cent lower than in 1981–2. If the comparison were carried out on the basis of *net* investment, such decline would be even greater. Public investment dropped sharply, leading to a deterioration of the limited public infrastructure painfully created in the past. There is now evidence that also private investment declined in parallel with public investment (World Bank, 1990a), while direct foreign investment stagnated at very low levels. Structural adjustment measures might have increased microeconomic ('X') efficiency and productivity by cutting wasteful investment programmes, eliminating distortions, providing better incentives, and through the rationalization of loss-making public enterprises. However, rapidly declining capital accumulation has represented a major obstacle to the improvement of overall efficiency (which depends also on the 'external efficiency' of public transport, communication, power and human infrastructure) and to the diversification of production (which requires new investment in non-traditional sectors producing 'tradables').

Similarly, enrolment rates in elementary education, which had increased rapidly between 1960 and 1980, declined over the 1980s in 60 per cent of the countries undergoing adjustment (Table 9.5). There is scattered evidence that secondary and higher education were also affected. These adverse trends are the result of a contraction of both demand and supply of educational services. To start with, the drop in household income has increased the opportunity cost of children's and adolescents' time, as well as the need to save on educational expenditures among low-income families, thus leading to a contraction in the demand for education (Tinguiri, 1991). In addition, the drop in government expenditure on education (which declined from US$10.7 billion in 1980 to $7.7 bn in 1985 for Africa as a whole) caused a substantial contraction in the supply of primary education, despite the shift in a greater share of government expenditure on education towards the primary level in 15 of the 22 countries with available information (Brestecher and Carr-Hill, 1990). The decline in government expenditure on education resulted from the fiscal crisis of the 1980s (see Section 3) and, in particular, from the continued over-dependence on trade taxes, cuts in overall government expenditure contemplated in all adjustment programmes, and the decline in the share of government spending on education caused by the increase in interest payments on the foreign debt (Ebel, 1991). In Tanzania, for instance, government expenditure for the servicing of interest and principal on the foreign debt increased from 2.6 per cent of total government expenditure in 1980–1 to about 19 per cent in 1987–8. This increase was accompanied by a commensurate decline in expenditure on health and education (Wagao, 1990). While the decline in enrollment rates and the overall weakening of the educational sector may not have an immediate impact on growth and economic structure, they negatively affect the quality of the labour force and labour productivity over the medium term and perpetuate in this way the problems caused by insufficient human capabilities and over-dependence on expatriate expertise.

The belt-tightening imposed on most African countries would perhaps have been acceptable if adjustment had triggered a radical change in economic structures, eventually leading to an increase in food production, an expansion of manufacturing activities, and a rapid growth of non-traditional exports. Also from this perspective, however, the changes which intervened in the 1980s are not satisfactory.

The share of manufacturing in GDP increased between 1982 and 1988 in only six of the 24 countries included in Table 9.5. Of these six countries, only in Mauritius and Zambia was the increase greater than three percentage points, while only in Mauritius was such change accompanied by a rapid growth of output and exports (see later). In the remaining 18 countries, the share of manufacturing stagnated or declined, an outcome to be expected in view of the almost universal decline in investment ratios. So, while the development policies of the 1960s and 1970s led in several cases to an inefficient import-substituting industrialization, the adjustment efforts of the 1980s seem to have led to, or not to have been able to prevent, a shrinking of an already under-developed industrial base.

Broadly similar conclusions are arrived at when examining the data on the growth of the volume of exports. The latter increased in 11 countries (of which in only six at rates above 5 per cent). In the other

13 countries, the volume of exports stagnated or decreased. Even in the 11 countries experiencing an increase in exports, the impact on the balance of payments has almost always been negligible because of the decline in the export prices of primary commodities. It is hardly surprising, therefore, that the modest improvements in the current account balance realized in the 1980s had to be achieved in most cases through a substantial contraction of imports. If the assessment of export performance was effected on the basis of the growth of 'non-traditional exports' (whose data for most countries are, however, not readily available), the picture would appear much less favourable. Yet this – and not a generalized expansion of Africa's export bundle – should be the true objective of 'structural adjustment' in the external sector.

Lastly, agricultural production improved somewhat in 1985–6 and 1989. It is not clear, however, whether the increase in food production is the result of better incentives and the liberalization of agricultural trade or of improved weather conditions. Typical adjustment measures, in fact, have not addressed – and in some cases made even more binding – the long-term non-price constraints to agricultural growth, such as an inadequate rural infrastructure, the growing differentiation between a landless and smallholder subsector mired in poverty and a rapidly growing commercial farming subsector, the low and declining use of fertilizers and irrigation, and the risk of ecological degradation caused by an accelerating population growth (Lele, 1990; Tinguiri, 1991).

With the exception of very few countries, changes in production structures and export baskets have therefore been extremely limited, while in a few areas (such as industrialization) there has been retrogression. At the end of almost a decade of adjustment efforts, Sub-Saharan Africa found itself still faced with the usual problems of over-dependence on primary commodities, stagnant or shrinking industrial output and sluggish and highly unstable growth in the food crop sector. In addition, in 75 per cent of the countries undertaking adjustment programmes, capital accumulation and primary enrollment rates were lower than in the early 1980s.

While the cause of this unsatisfactory situation has to be found mainly in the vulnerability of the African economy in the early 1980s and in the persistence of negative external conditions through the decade, it is clear that the structural adjustment efforts of the 1980s have not been able to offset these negative influences, nor to induce those structural transformations which are desirable and necessary from a long-term development perspective. As noted in the first World Bank evaluation of the first ten years of adjustment lending,

> the supply-response to adjustment lending . . . in Sub-Saharan Africa has been slow because of the legacy of deep-seated structural problems. Inadequate infrastructure, poorly developed markets, rudimentary industrial sectors, and severe institutional and managerial weaknesses in the public and private sectors have proved unexpectedly serious as constraints to better performance – especially in the poorer countries of SSA. (World Bank. 1988b, p. 3)

5.3 The combined stabilization – structural adjustment experience

The variety of adjustment experiences in the African countries undertaking economic reforms in the 1980s is summarized below in Table 9.6 which cross-classifies the 24 countries of Table 9.5 according to four variables: the achievement of stabilization objectives, preservation of positive growth in GDP per capita, protection of human welfare (proxied by primary enrollment rates) and structural transformation of the economy (proxied by an increase in the share of manufacturing in GDP).

Of the 24 countries which underwent stabilization and structural adjustment reforms in the 1980s, only Mauritius appears to have achieved simultaneously the four objectives of stabilization, growth, structural adjustment and protection of vulnerable groups. Another five countries – Guinea-Bissau, Mauritania, Senegal, Mali and Zambia – have achieved simultaneously three of the above four objectives (although for Mali and Zambia this was obtained at a high cost in terms of growth of GDP per capita). The largest number of countries accomplished only one or two of these objectives (stabilization being the most frequent, and growth and the removal of structural bottlenecks the least frequent), while Ethiopia, Somalia, Tanzania and Zaire did not manage either to stabilize their macroeconomic imbalances and sustain the growth in GDP per capita, or to remove structural bottlenecks and protect human conditions in this process.

The picture presented by Table 9.6 reflects, of course, the conventional (and somewhat arbitrary) criteria adopted. Such a picture would likely change if the periodization chosen (1980–1 or 1981–2 *vis-à-vis* 1987–8), or the thresholds and conventions adopted for its construction, or the variables used to proxy 'structural transformation' and

Table 9.6 Variety of adjustment experiences in Africa, south of the Sahara, in the 1980s

		Stabilization[a]		*No stabilization*	
		With structural transform.	*Without structural transform.*	*With structural transform.*	*Without structural transform.*
Positive GDP/c growth	With human protection	Mauritius	Mauritania Senegal	–	–
	Without human protection	Guinea-Bissau Mali	–	–	–
Zero or negative GDP/c growth	With human protection	Zambia	Malawi Togo Uganda	–	Zimbabwe
	Without human protection	Côte d'Ivoire Ghana	CAR Kenya Liberia Madagascar Niger Nigeria S. Leone	Sudan	Ethiopia Somalia Tanzania Zaire

Note

[a] Stabilization is considered achieved if there was an improvement in at least two of the following three variables: deficit in the current account balance, budget deficit and inflation.

Source: Elaboration of data in Table 9.5.

'social costs' were modified. Sensitivity analysis would show, however, that the results of Table 9.6 are fairly robust and that the above broad conclusions would not change substantially.

5.4 Possible causes of the failure to achieve structural adjustment

There is a legitimate controversy over the causes of the failure of adjustment policies in the 1980s in Africa south of Sahara. Four sets of factors can be singled out as possible causes of such failures:

- inadequate implementation of the adjustment programmes;
- a deterioration in exogenous conditions;
- inadequate external funding;
- policy conflicts in the design of the adjustment programmes.

Their relative importance is discussed hereafter.

First, not all of the 241 adjustment programmes initiated in the 1980s have been completed or implemented as consistently as demanded by the IMF and the World Bank. However, this has been a relatively rare occurrence, as only 21 of these 241 programmes were abandoned or terminated before the agreed upon deadline. In addition, while there are differences in viewpoints between the officials of the IMF and the World Bank and those of many African governments about the 'desirability' and 'ownership' of the IMF- and World Bank-supported adjustment programmes (Helleiner, 1991), two major evaluations of the concurrent adjustment operations of these two institutions in the 1980s found that in Africa 75 per cent of all programme conditions had been fully or substantially implemented (World Bank, 1988b, 1990a).

Second, exogenous factors have certainly exerted a negative influence on the performance of the adjustment programmes. Except for 1983–4, the terms of trade of Africa south of the Sahara worsened steadily throughout the 1980s. Between 1982 and 1990, the combined terms of trade loss in Africa as a whole was about 30 per cent (IMF, 1990). The decline in terms of trade was particularly acute for the five oil exporting countries, but it affected in an equally disruptive manner the exporters of agricultural products and minerals. Their terms of trade fell respectively by 26 and 10 per cent over the same period (ibid.). Other exogenous factors such as the 1983–4 drought and continued war or civil strife have also exerted a negative influence on the performance of adjustment programmes. Civil wars and insurrections have caused huge loss of lives, output and considerable destruction of infrastructure in four of the 'adjusting countries' included in Table 9.5 (Ethiopia, Sudan, Uganda and, to some extent, Zimbabwe) as well as in Mozambique, Angola and Chad (Sandbrook, 1989).

Third, inadequate external financing has also contributed to the poor performance of adjustment in the 1980s. First of all, the huge loss in Africa's terms of trade was not compensated by an increase in the amount of new financing. Furthermore, the protracted deadlock on the debt problem led to a growing drainage of resources for debt servicing. As a result, the net transfer of resources not only did not offset the terms of trade losses, but even declined until 1985 (see Table 9.7).

Despite a 23 per cent increase in the volume of exports over the 1980s, the adjustment of Africa's balance of payments had therefore to be achieved through an 18 per cent decline in the level of imports (IMF, 1990). It is now beyond dispute that this import strangulation has exerted a depressive effect on growth and investment and, presumably, even on the growth of non-traditional exports. Recent econometric investigation has shown that there is a positive and statistically significant correlation in recent years between increased imports and improved growth of output (Faini *et al.*, 1989).

Particularly relevant to this discussion is that, despite contrary statements of intent over the last several years, the IMF and the International Bank for Reconstruction and Development (IBRD), the non-concessional credit window of the World Bank, have become net recipients of resources from Africa and aggravated in this way the inadequate funding of adjustment programmes (see Table 9.7).

Fourth, the poor performance of adjustment is also the result of problems in the design of adjustment packages. As noted earlier on, in the African context some of the tools of stabilization produce results which are less pronounced than or may even conflict with those normally expected. In addition, while several of these tools are consistent with the achievement of long-run development objectives (such as the diversification of exports, capital accumulation, the development of human capabilities, greater food self-reliance and so on) and with the removal of the structural bottlenecks illustrated in Sections 2 and 3, others, though contributing to the stabilization of macroeconomic imbalances, make the achievement of these long-term objectives more problematic.

Table 9.7 Net transfer to Africa, south of the Sahara, 1980–9

	1980	*1983*	*1984*	*1985*	*1986*	*1987*	*1988*	*1989*
Total debt-related net transfer	5 657	4 092	1 727	2 067	−856	3 185	1 712	2 307
Of which:								
Total IMF/ World Bank	1 205	1 742	986	399	385	632	382	455
IMF	730	879	−41	−434	−954	−863	−462	−728
World Bank	72	270	305	31	33	−75	−725	−391
IDA	403	593	722	802	1 306	1 570	1 569	1 574
Multilateral[a]	707	664	442	487	650	709	672	607
Bilateral[a]	1 657	2 295	1 925	472	1 210	1 194	630	945
Private	2 818	270	−1 667	−2 648	−1 132	−213	−434	−428
Total non-debt-related net transfer	186	2 514	2 733	4 069	4 294	4 441	6 261	7 113
Of which:								
Grants	177	1 475	1 993	3 032	3 414	3 943	–	–
DFI[b]	9	1 039	740	1 037	880	498	–	–
Total net transfer	5 843	6 606	4 460	3 213	6 163	7 626	7 973	9 420

[a] Excluding grants.
[b] Based upon UNDP/World Bank (1989).
Source: Derived from Helleiner (1991).

From this perspective prevailing adjustment policies can be classified in three categories (Stewart, 1992): *contradictory* policies, that is policies which conflict directly with long-run objectives; *incomplete* policies, which could support the achievement of long-term objectives with some modifications; and *additional* policies which are not included in the usual adjustment programmes.

Contradictory policies

(a) Conflicts between cuts in government expenditure and the need to sustain or expand public infrastructure and human capabilities The combined effect of public expenditure cuts and growing expenditure on debt servicing has led to large contractions in public investment programmes, and indirectly in private investment, and to declines in recurrent government expenditure on health, education, training, agricultural research and extension and fertilizer subsidies. As

already noted, however, these trends conflict directly with the well-established needs of ensuring the maintenance of the existing capital stock, investing in new sectors (so as to diversify the production and export basket), and expanding human capabilities. They conflict also with the needs of enhancing rural infrastructure and R&D, increasing expenditure on fertilizer subsidies, the modernization of agriculture and the improvement of agricultural practices, two steps without which in Africa long-term development will remain elusive.

To sustain expenditure on investment, key inputs and human capabilities, more expansionary adjustment programmes are required. Reducing the African external debt will help finance the increasing need for external resources inherent to such approach. Significant improvements over the 'Toronto Terms' regulating debt relief are absolutely necessary if debt-distressed, low-income African countries are to have any prospect of increased net transfers of resources and stimulus to investment and growth over the coming decade.

On the domestic front, greater efforts should be placed on achieving fiscal balance also through increases in revenue from consumption, income and wealth taxes, so as to avoid excessive expenditure cuts (Tanzi, 1990; Cornia and Stewart, 1990). Examples from Burkina Faso, Zimbabwe, Botswana, Mauritius and Cameroon show that it is possible to increase tax ratios within a reasonable period of time with no adverse effects on growth (ibid., see also Savadogo and Wetta, 1991). In addition, public spending priorities must increase the proportion of public sector resources going to key areas.

(b) Conflicts between undifferentiated and sudden import liberalization and the need to diversify production towards manufacturing

This policy stance tends to compound the negative influences exerted on domestic investment in manufacturing by the compression in public expenditure, devaluation and interest rate increases. While a gradual move towards liberalization may increase competition and thus facilitate the establishment of an efficient industrial base, sudden and sharp changes in protection rates tend to lead to de-industrialization, thus preventing the build-up of essential industrial experience and prolonging dependence on primary commodity exports.

Instead, selective and temporary protection on a sliding scale (over a 5–10-year period) is more consistent with the goal of establishing an efficient manufacturing sector. Such measures should be accompanied by measures aimed at increasing domestic and intra-regional competition and by the imposition of 'export quotas'. In this regard, a much greater degree of liberalization could be immediately introduced among African countries.

(c) Conflicts between policies encouraging an expansion of traditional primary commodity exports and the need to diversify the export basket (and stabilize the balance of payments) The promotion of traditional primary commodities, which forms the pivot of most adjustment strategies, runs precisely against these two objectives. Some 60 per cent of Africa's agricultural exports appear to come from commodities (coffee, cocoa, sugar, tea, groundnuts and sisal) whose price elasticity of demand is so low and whose share of world exports is so high that an increase in export volume would *reduce* dollar export earnings and thus worsen the deficit of the balance of payment (Godfrey, 1985). The decline in the world prices of several primary products (such as cocoa and coffee) and the deterioration in Africa's terms of trade in the 1980s were in part the direct consequence of the generalized increase in the export of these goods by African and other third-world countries.

While insistence on the need for increasing export earnings is entirely justified, 'the emphasis should rather be on *diversification* of products, from 'high-share' to 'low-share' (and manufactured products), and of markets, from low-elasticity to high-elasticity' (ibid., p. 171).

Incomplete policies

A number of policies which are part of the orthodox adjustment packages have both positive and negative effects over the long term – positive because they correct past distortions, but negative because they do not sufficiently emphasize essential complementary changes. Aims should include the following:

(a) To complement measures on pricing and privatization of marketing boards in agriculture, with investment in rural infrastructure and key inputs While an improvement in the terms of trade of agriculture was desirable (particularly for food crops), given the previous discrimination against the sector, pricing policies alone are not able to generate meaningful supply responses. A review of econometric estimates of aggregate supply responses in agriculture shows that low values (0.005–0.35) are prevalent in the short run, while slightly higher

elasticities (0.1–0.5) are most common over the long term (Beynon, 1989). Complementary measures would include adequate investment in both the public and farm-level rural infrastructure and research and development, particularly in the area of indigenous food crops. Complementary measures should also comprise the provision of sufficient credit and, in some cases, of fertilizers and other input subsidies which are essential to raise agricultural production over the medium term and – where land is getting scarcer and rotations are becoming shorter – to preserve soil fertility.

(b) To complement policies for a market-based allocation of resources with measures ensuring that an adequate share of such resources reaches small producers Current adjustment packages tend to attribute to the market a main role in the allocation of scarce foreign exchange and credit. While a more market-oriented approach may be desirable, this new approach does not ensure that an adequate share of such resources goes to key sectors or efficient small-scale producers which normally lack the collateral or adequate money balances to bid effectively in such market. During the adjustment of Zambia in the 1980s, for instance, most of the auctioning of the foreign exchange went to large foreign companies, while small local enterprises, agriculture and the social sector were starved of foreign exchange (Seshamani, 1990). It is necessary therefore to ensure that the market-based allocation of resources is complemented, for instance, by the *a priori* assignment of a given share of resources to the small producers sector (Stewart, 1992).

Additional Policies

Not all the policy changes necessary for the restoration of growth and the achievement of long-term development are included in the adjustment packages of the World Bank and IMF. These additional policies include measures aimed at strengthening or modifying the institutional environment (national or regional) within which economic activity takes place in Africa, among them:

(a) Where landlessness is already acute, *land reform* is needed to redistribute surplus land in the plantation and large farmer sector, or land still under customary tenancy, to the landless and the land-deficient farmers, and particularly to land-poor female-headed households. This measure will help to reduce rural differentiation while contributing to the growth of output, because of the greater efficiency in the use of resources of smallholders (Cornia and Strickland, 1990). Where landlessness has not emerged on a large scale, land-ceilings may be instituted to prevent future land concentration from arising. Taxation of land in excess of agreed ceilings, particularly if the land is left idle, would also contribute to prevent the rise of excessive rural inequality, while improving fiscal revenue. Tenure systems should also be re-examined in those land-abundant countries which are gradually experiencing a shortening of the fallow period and a decline in soil fertility. Under such conditions, the recognition of individual property rights would increase the incentives to invest in the land in order to preserve or improve its fertility.

(b) The reform or *creation of institutions to serve smallholders* and small producers in the field of R&D in food crops, the dissemination of appropriate and affordable technologies of credit (see above) and recurrent inputs.

(c) A major effort to *sustain and reform public services for the development of human capabilities.* Over the 1980s, only 24 per cent of the World Bank-supported adjustment measures have included specific measures in this field (World Bank, 1990a). The IMF-sponsored stabilization programmes, while agnostic in principle, tend to exert undifferentiated downward pressures on all types of public expenditures, including that for the social sector. An expansion of human capabilities in key sectors requires that the 'fiscal squeeze' experienced by most African countries in health care, education, potable water supply, training and similar sectors in the 1980s be reversed.

While a restoration of adequate levels of public (and private) expenditure would be an enormous step forward, profound reforms are also necessary to improve the relevance of existing approaches to social service delivery for the production, health and educational needs of the population; to adjust the standards of service and salary structures (which often still reflect 'dualistic' structures inherited at independence) to the needs and resource base of the African countries; and to enhance the participation of the population, and of the poor in particular, to the design, management and delivery of social programmes.

(d) Policies to *create or improve regional institutions* in the field of R&D in agriculture, public health, trade, transport and other forms of economic co-operation. However difficult, a move in this direction is highly desirable from the long-term perspective.

6 CONCLUSIONS

Compared with the other developing regions, relatively little structural change occurred in the first two decades after independence in Africa. Overall, the problems caused by the over-dependence on primary commodity exports, the neglect and backwardness of agriculture, and inadequate manufacturing production, industrial skills and know-how were as acute in the late 1970s as at independence. While sustained growth and remarkable improvements from the unfavourable conditions inherited at independence have been realized in a few areas (such as growth, urban infrastructure and education), additional problems – such as debt and environmental degradation – emerged between 1960 and 1980.

With the negative changes in the international economic environment that intervened in the early 1980s, the pressures to overcome such structural bottlenecks became even more pressing. However, while the shortcomings of African stabilization and structural adjustment are obviously controversial, it appears that the adjustment policies applied on a massive scale in the 1980s have not been able to provide a solution to Africa's old and new problems.

A few difficulties and inconsistencies have plagued such policies. First, adjustment has achieved some positive but extremely limited results in producing economic stability. Progress has been hindered by the inadequate appreciation of the consequences of devaluation in the African context, and by the fiscal implications of reform packages which incorporate sharp devaluations and interest rate increases.

Second, excessive reliance on demand restraint measures – partly caused by the inadequate funding of adjustment programmes and by the deterioration in terms of trade in the 1980s – has resulted in significant losses of output, investment and human welfare. In particular, adjustment policies can be faulted for sacrificing the provision of crucial public goods such as agricultural infrastructure, for relatively neglecting human capital development and for failing to minimize the impact on the poor.

Finally, in response to the question raised in the title of this chapter, adjustment has not removed most structural obstacles to sustainable long-term development. While it is likely that microeconomic efficiency has been improved, IMF and World Bank's insistence on increased exports of traditional primary commodities, rapid import liberalization and drastic cuts in public investment are retarding Africa's recovery, and pushing many African economies away from achieving the long-term objectives of greater food self-sufficiency, an efficient manufacturing sector, diversified export composition and markets, and increased export volume. In the African context the almost exclusive emphasis of structural adjustment on relative price changes, privatization, financial and trade liberalization, and interest rate increases has generated extremely modest supply responses which are much smaller than those anticipated at the beginning of the decade.

REFERENCES

ALEXANDRATOS, N. (ed.) (1988) *World Agriculture Toward 2000: An FAO Study*, London: Belhaven Press.

BECKER, C. M. (1990) 'The Demo-Economic Impact of the AIDS Pandemic in Sub-Saharan Africa', *World Development*, vol. 18, no. 12, pp. 1599–1619.

BEYNON, J. G. (1989) 'Pricism v. Structuralism in Sub-Saharan African Agriculture', *Journal of Agricultural Economics*, vol. 40, no. 3, September, pp. 323–35.

BOND, M. (1983) 'Agricultural Response to Price in Sub-Saharan African Countries', *IMF Staff Papers*, vol. 30, no. 4.

BRESTECHER, D. and R. CARR-HILL (1990) *Primary Education and Economic Recession in the Developing World since 1980*, Paris: UNESCO.

CORNIA, G. A. and F. STEWART (1990) 'The Fiscal System, Adjustment and the Poor', *Ricerche Economiche*, XLIV, no. 2–3, pp. 349–79, Venezia: Dipartimento di Scienze Economiche, Università degli Studi Ca' Foscari.

CORNIA, G. A. and R. STRICKLAND (1990) 'Rural Differentiation, Poverty and Agricultural Crisis in Sub-Saharan Africa: Toward an Appropriate Policy Response', *Innocenti Occasional Papers*, no. 4, Florence: UNICEF–ICDC.

CORNIA, G. A., R. JOLLY, and F. STEWART (eds) (1987) *Adjustment with a Human Face*, vol. 1, New York: Oxford University Press.

DURRING, A. B. (1989) 'Poverty and the Environment: Reversing the Downward Spiral', *Worldwatch Paper* 92, November 1989, Washington, DC: Worldwatch Institute.

EBEL, B. (1991) 'The Pattern of Government Expenditure during the 1980s: Implications for the Social Sectors', (forthcoming) in *Innocenti Occasional Papers*, Florence: UNICEF–ICDC.

FAINI, R., J. DE MELO, A. SENHADJ-SEMLALI and J. STANTON (1989) 'Growth-oriented Adjustment Programs: A Statistical Analysis', *Development Studies Working Paper*, no. 14, Torino and Oxford: Centro Studi Luca d'Agliano–Queen Elisabeth House.

FAO (1986) *African Agriculture: The Next 25 Years: Main Report*, Rome: FAO.

FAO (1988) *The Impact of Development Strategies on the Rural Poor*, Second Analysis of Country Experiences in the Implementation of the WCARRD Programme of Action, Rome: FAO.

GHAI, D. and S. RADWAN (eds) (1983) *Agrarian Policies and Rural Poverty in Africa*, Geneva: ILO.

GHAI, D., and L. SMITH (1987) *Agricultural Prices, Policy and Equity in Sub-Saharan Africa*, Boulder, Colorado: Lynne Rienner.

GODFREY, M. (1985) 'Trade and Exchange Rate Policy: A Further Contribution to the Debate', in T. Rose (ed.), *Crisis and Recovery in Sub-Saharan Africa*, Paris: OECD, pp. 168–79.

GULAHATI, R., and C. SEKKAR (1981) 'Industrial Strategy for Late Starters: The Experience of Kenya, Tanzania and Zambia', *World Bank Staff Working Papers*, no. 457, Washington, DC.

HAGGBLADE, S., P. HAZELL and J. BROWN (1989) 'Farm–Non Farm Linkages in Rural Sub-Saharan Africa', *World Development*, vol. 17, no. 8, London.

HELLEINER, G.K. (1991) 'The IMF, the World Bank and Africa's Adjustment and External Debt Problems: An Unofficial View', paper presented to the symposium on 'Structural Adjustment, External Debt and Growth in Africa', jointly sponsored by the Association of African Central Banks and the IMF, 25–27 February 1991, Gaborone, Botswana.

IMF (1986) 'Fund-supported Programs, Fiscal Policy and Income Distribution', *Occasional Paper* 46, Washington, DC: IMF.

IMF (1989) *World Economic Outlook, October 1989*, Washington, DC: IMF.

IMF (1990) *World Economic Outlook, October 1990*, Washington, DC: IMF.

IMF Survey, various issues.

LELE, U. (1990) 'Structural Adjustment, Agricultural Development and the Poor: Some Lessons from the Malawian Experience', *World Development*, vol. 18, no. 9, Oxford and New York, pp. 1207–19.

MOSLEY, P. (1987) *Conditionality as Bargaining Process: Structural Adjustment Lending, 1980–86*, Princeton, New Jersey: Princeton Paper in International Finance.

MOSLEY, P., and L. SMITH (1989) 'Structural Adjustment and Agricultural Performance in Sub-Saharan Africa 1980–87', *Journal of International Development*, 1 (3), pp. 321–55.

NORTON, R.D. (1987) 'Agricultural Issues in Structural Adjustment Programs', *FAO Economic and Social Development Paper*, Rome: FAO.

PRYOR, F.L. (1990) 'Changes in Income Distribution in Poor Agricultural Nations: Malawi and Madagascar', *Economic Development and Cultural Change*, vol. 39, no. 1, October, pp. 23–45.

SANDBROOK, R. (1989) 'Economic Crisis, Structural Adjustment and the State in Sub-Saharan Africa', paper presented at the conference on Economic Crisis and Third World Countries: Impact and Response, 3–6 April, Kingston, Jamaica.

SAVADOGO, K., and C. WETTA (1991) 'The Impact of Self-imposed Adjustment: The Case of Burkina Faso, 1983–1989', *Innocenti Occasional Papers*, no. 15, Florence: UNICEF–ICDC.

SESHAMANI, V. (1990) 'Toward Structural Transformation with a Human Focus: The Economic Programmes and Policies of Zambia in the 1980s', *Innocenti Occasional Papers*, no. 7, Florence: UNICEF–ICDC.

SINGER, H. (1989) 'Lessons of Post-War Development Experience: 1945–1988', *Discussion Paper* no. 260, London: Institute of Development Studies, April.

STEWART, F. (1992) 'Shorter Term Policies for Longer Term Development', (forthcoming) in G.A. Cornia *et al.* (eds), *Africa's Recovery in the 1990s: From Stagnation and Adjustment to Human Development*, London: Macmillan.

TANZI, V. (1990) 'Fiscal Issues in Adjustment Programs', *Ricerche Economiche*, XLIV, no. 2–3, pp. 173–94, Venezia: Dipartimento di Scienze Economiche, Università degli Studi Ca' Foscari.

TINGUIRI, K.L. (1991) 'Structural Adjustment, Growth and Human Welfare: The Case of Niger, 1982–1989', *Innocenti Occasional Papers*, no. 14, Florence: UNICEF–ICDC.

UNDP/WORLD BANK (1989) *African Economic and Financial Data*, New York and Washington DC: UNDP and World Bank.

UN ECONOMIC COMMISSION FOR AFRICA (1989) *African Alternative Framework to Structural Adjustment Programmes for Socio-Economic Recovery and Transformation*, Addis Ababa.

VAN DER HOEVEN, R. (1992) 'External Dependence and Structural Adjustment in Sub-Saharan Africa: The Need for a New Approach', (forthcoming) in G.A. Cornia *et al.* (eds), *Africa's Recovery in the 1990s: From Stagnation and Adjustment to Human Development*, London: Macmillan.

WAGAO, J.H. (1990) 'Adjustment Policies in Tanzania, 1981–1989: The Impact on Growth, Structure and Human Welfare', *Innocenti Occasional Papers*, no. 9, Florence: UNICEF–ICDC.

WORLD BANK (1981) *Accelerated Development in Sub-Saharan Africa* (Berg Report), Washington, DC: World Bank.

WORLD BANK (1988a) *Education in Sub-Saharan Africa: Policies for Adjustment, Revitalization and Expansion*, Washington, DC: World Bank.

WORLD BANK (1988b) 'Adjustment Lending – An Evaluation of Ten Years of Experience', *Policy and Research Series*, Washington, DC: World Bank.

WORLD BANK (1989) *Sub-Saharan Africa: From Crisis to Sustainable Growth: A Long-Term Perspective Study*, Washington, DC: World Bank.

WORLD BANK (1990a) *Report on Adjustment Lending II: Policies for the Recovery of Growth*, Washington, DC: World Bank.

WORLD BANK (1990b) *World Tables: 1989–90 Edition*, Baltimore: Johns Hopkins University Press.

WORLD BANK/UNDP (1989) *Africa's Adjustment and Growth in the 1980s*, Washington, DC: World Bank.

10 The Sequence of Stabilization and Liberalization

Francesco Daveri

1 SEQUENCING POLICY REFORMS

Policy reforms imply institutional changes in the environment where people operate and take decisions. They are usually undertaken for either of the following reasons:

- as a response to perceived permanent shocks, starting from an unsustainable position in order to restore equilibrium;
- in order to get out of an inefficient equilibrium position to reach a new equilibrium position;
- starting from an unjust initial position, to reach a more equitable outcome.

However desirable, reforms rarely take place all at once. Determining whether an optimal sequencing exists and is feasible is thus an important element in the design of policy reforms, given that not all sequences end up producing ultimately identical results. Domestic market disruption and temporary unemployment of people fired in the previously protected sectors, and external and domestic macroeconomic imbalances are examples of transitional costs due to all sorts of pre-existing market imperfections and externalities, which may injure the success of overall well conceived and socially advisable reforms. They are the price paid for a change of regime to take place and are often considered unavoidable, at least in the short run.

In countries subject to rather severe imperfections, it comes as no surprise that reforms encounter some flaws: costs are usually immediate and highly visible, while the most relevant gains from reforms are delayed, dynamic and hard to measure. For all such reasons, recommending a specific sequencing has proved a difficult task, mainly because the optimal path of sequencing depends on the kind of distortions initially affecting the economy and on the way governments evaluate each of them. The theory of the second-best is not helpful in this respect because, in the presence of non-zero cross-sectoral elasticities, partial reforms may generate any result in terms of welfare, so that very little guidance is provided to ascertain whether reforms are inappropriately sequenced and either too rapidly or too slowly implemented.

In practice, reforming governments and international organizations proved more eager to address budgetary and trade distortions, taking the rigidities in labour markets and the apparent biases in the composition of government expenditure as given. Yet this most likely occurred because labour markets and government expenditure have been considered politically contentious areas rather than as a consequence of the application of welfare maximization criteria.

In the absence of general guidelines, the economists' perspective on how to sequence reforms has taken quite a narrow view and the discussion, especially stimulated by the policy experiments carried out in the Latin American Southern Cone, dealt with few issues, such as the precedence of stabilization over liberalization and the order of liberalization (current versus capital account, domestic versus external financial liberalization).

Some statements concerning the principal steps to undertake in economic reforms have been formulated and are sometimes taken for granted. First, stabilization is a precondition to any form of liberalization, because trade and financial liberalization are likely to have adverse macroeconomic implications. Second, domestic capital market liberalization is a precondition to external capital market liberalization, because otherwise foreign capital would flow out, thus destabilizing an economy with poorly working financial markets. Third, external goods market liberalization should precede external capital market liberalization, because otherwise major foreign capital inflows would cause the real exchange rate to appreciate, at variance with the requirements for a successful trade liberalization.

In what follows some points are discussed with reference to the sequence of stabilization and liberalization.

2 STABILIZATION FIRST

High and unstable inflation and persistent balance of payments deficits as well as microeconomic distortions are undoubtly costly. However, they often coexist in many developing and socialist countries. High inflation by itself is often said not to be too damaging (at least, as long as it is fully anticipated and institutions are inflation-proof), while the welfare costs of price and exchange rate instability are to a greater extent emphasized. In an inflationary environment, the use of money as a unit of account is undercut, for contracts become riskier (the phenomenon called 'dollarization' can be taken as an extreme case of the progressive loss of confidence in local currency as the relevant unit of account). Moreover, the increased uncertainty due to instability reduces the informational content of relative prices, potentially worsening centralized as well as decentralized resource allocation. Productive factors are devoted to exploiting opportunities for arbitrage, while the planning horizon of firms shrinks; a defensive and waiting attitude develops in the private sector as a whole and capital flight may take place either officially (when capital movements are allowed) or unofficially (through over-invoicing and under-invoicing of trade transactions or outright smuggling). In turn, persistently negative external balances cause, in the absence of exchange rate corrections, unsustainable foreign indebtness and/or drawing down of hard currency reserves.

Microeconomic distortions due to both 'market failures' and 'government failures' involve static and dynamic resource misallocation, which decreases the overall efficiency of the economy. Take trade restrictions as an example: protection results in distorting the use of inputs into production and the overall pattern of production and consumption, because price signals do not reflect the actual trading opportunities open to the country. Moreover, these costs are probably outweighed by the additional costs of protection due to administration and compliance tasks and individuals' rent-seeking behaviour. Administration and compliance costs are often very high in the presence of a licensing system, which also generates rent-seeking costs as a result of wasteful competition in order to obtain the licences.

In conclusion, both stabilization and liberalization reforms would very often be necessary to restore the potential for growth as well as to enhance welfare and equity. Yet many economists, such as McKinnon (1982), Edwards (1985), Corbo and de Melo (1987), and Dornbusch (1983), addressing this question in the last ten years, seem to agree that liberalization and stabilization packages should not be undertaken together. Let us consider why.

3 MACROECONOMIC IMPLICATIONS OF TRADE LIBERALIZATION

As to foreign trade liberalization, wrong sequencing (such as an abrupt move from quotas to free trade) as well as excessive speed may contribute to the adverse effects of welfare-improving liberalizations on the external balance, thereby triggering stabilization problems, especially in economies with no access to international capital markets. This adverse effect (external liberalization not compatible with the maintenance of external equilibrium) is likely to be exacerbated the more heavily protected is the domestic market before the liberalization takes place.

Moreover, historical episodes, such as the much discussed ones in the Southern Cone, have shown that even liberalization programmes which appeared to be compatible with balance of payments equilibrium from an *ex ante* point of view turned out to be harmful if implemented simultaneously with exchange rate based stabilization policies. The use of the exchange rate as a nominal anchor narrows the feasible path for obtaining the real devaluation necessary when liberalizing trade so as to materially support the desired expenditure switching, while maintaining the balance of payments in equilibrium. To put it another way, a liberalization that is compatible with the maintenance of external equilibrium may not be compatible with an exchange rate-based stabilization, for too many tasks are simultaneously assigned to the exchange rate.

Alternative ways of phasing out trade restrictions are also likely to have implications for the government budget constraint. While a move from quotas to tariffs is presumably relatively soft on the fiscal side, leaving a tariff-based regime towards free trade would probably involve the need to find alternative sources of revenues so as to respect the government budget constraint. This raises the additional complication that, being a tax reform a 'distortionary' measure by definition, it may well end up jamming the desired welfare effects of trade liberalization.

4 MACROECONOMIC IMPLICATIONS OF FINANCIAL LIBERALIZATION

As a first approximation, financial liberalization appears to be harmful to stabilization purposes if undertaken early, no matter whether it is domestic or external. On the one hand, liberalizing domestic financial markets, before stabilization takes place, reduces government revenues from seigniorage for any level of the budget deficit (through the reduced real demand for money consequent to the increased availability of interest-bearing instruments for saving allocation), thereafter potentially fuelling the rate of inflation. Moreover, the underlying macroeconomic instability is likely to originate high domestic real interest rates, which would increase the burden of government debt repayment and the likelihood of default. On the other hand, opening up the capital account when stabilization reforms are still under way would permit capital flight and further worsen the external accounts.

5 EVALUATION

The seemingly adverse macroeconomic implications of trade and financial liberalization establish a case for stabilizing first, in order to respect domestic and external budget constraint. Yet, though liberalizing first appears not to be advisable, it ought to be borne in mind that stabilizing a distorted economy is costlier than stabilizing a no-distortion, perfectly competitive economy. Members of organized coalitions, such as farmers, landlords, or unionized workers, may collude with the goal of appropriating a higher share of national income during the disinflation, thereby increasing price stickiness and slowing down the speed of disinflation.

The way in which stabilizations are carried out is not at all neutral on the possibility of successfully liberalizing afterwards. For instance, tariffs are often employed to raise government revenues rapidly and effectively in the short run for stabilization purposes: if this is the case, today's stabilization undermines the successful undertaking of future trade liberalization for it does not provide the country with permanent and reliable rules for fiscal discipline.

Stabilization policies based on temporary price, wage and exchange rate freezes appear to reverse significantly the timing between costs and benefits of reforms. Benefits accrue quickly and at low costs, while costs in terms of real exchange rate over-valuation and balance of payments emerge more slowly. However, after an initial honeymoon period, when net benefits are positive (rapid disinflation and no output contraction), the wedge between the sharply rising costs of real exchange rate appreciation and freeze-induced rigidities in resource allocation and the thin benefits of temporary disinflation widens, so that, at some point in time, the reform becomes unsustainable and is abandoned: this was the case in Argentina, Peru and Brazil in 1985–6. Two elements counter-balanced the drawbacks usually brought about by heterodox policies in the Israeli success story: the substantial inflows of US foreign assistance, which helped avoid balance of payments difficulties, and the switch to a non-accommodating behaviour of the Central Bank, which has no longer validated inflationary expectations.

When stabilizations are systematically delayed, as is the case in many Latin American countries, structural reforms may run the risk of waiting forever. In such a case, the claim 'stabilization first' appears to conflict with common sense, which would suggest that some liberalization steps could be cautiously initiated. However, the 'common sense' solution is not a panacea: the most effective steps on the way to liberalization may not actually ease the way to stabilization. Dismantling the oligopolistic structure of labour and goods markets, aimed at reducing price and wage stickiness, would also presumably contribute to a deterioration in the social climate, thereby laying the foundations for either a rekindling of inflation or a loss of consensus for the manoeuvre.

It must finally be pointed out that grouping public and private capital flows together, often done when arguing against an early opening of capital markets, can be somewhat misleading. Unlike export credits, private investment and lending, which are usually heavily correlated to business expectations about the evolution of the local economy, foreign aid is meant to obey different goals, one of which is to soften the effects of sharp changes and external shocks in countries undertaking adjustment efforts. A distinction between official and private capital inflows, while not weakening the argument for postponing the opening of the (private) capital account to the latest possible stage, highlights the potentially stabilizing role of foreign aid.

REFERENCES

CORBO, V. and J. DE MELO (1987) 'Lessons from the Southern Cone policy experiments', *World Bank Research Observer*, July, pp. 111–43.

DORNBUSCH, R. (1983) 'Real interest rates, home goods and optimal external borrowing', *Journal of Political Economy*, 91, February, pp. 141–53.

EDWARDS, S. (1985) 'Stabilization with liberalization: an evaluation of ten years of Chile's experience with free market policies', *Economic Development and Cultural Change*, 33, January, pp. 223–54.

McKINNON, R. I. (1982) 'The order of economic liberalization: lessons from Chile and Argentina', in K. Brunner and A. H. Meltzer (eds) *Economic Policy in a World of Change*, Amsterdam: North Holland.

11 Aid Agencies and the Promotion of Foreign Investments in Developing Countries: Between Market and Co-operation – A Short Note

Giorgio Barba Navaretti[1]

1 INTRODUCTION

Bilateral and multilateral aid agencies are extremely active in promoting foreign investments to developing countries (LDCs). Their action in this domain reflects the wider goal of strengthening the private sector in LDCs, one of the major objectives of aid in the 1980s.[2] There are three main areas of intervention related to the promotion of foreign investments:

(1) financial incentives;
(2) diffusion of information and technical assistance;
(3) enhancement of the transfer of skills.

This chapter is focused on the use of financial incentives which, in the last few years, has generated much controversy amongst donors. The origin of the controversy is a contradiction. Strengthening the private sector means strengthening markets. However, aid agencies, in promoting foreign investments, aim at channelling financial resources that would not be attracted on a mere market basis towards the third world. Their intervention would otherwise not be justified. But how can they go beyond the market without interfering with the market mechanism?

Of course, financial incentives can be justified because of the existence of market imperfections. Market imperfections certainly interfere with foreign investment flows to LDCs. First, in industrialized countries there is a limited availability of information on investment opportunities in LDCs. Second, the perception of the risk of investing in LDCs is often distorted, particularly for categories of investors like small and medium enterprises (SMEs) which are not used to investing abroad and even less in the third world. Third, there are imperfections arising from the need to train locals.

A second justification for financial incentives is that markets do not always fulfil development objectives. As an example, we can consider low income countries that need foreign technology and capital but that cannot provide many appealing investment opportunities.

Donors are divided between those that argue that they are acting on a pure market basis, without distorting markets, and those that make large use of financial subsidies, arguing that markets are distorted and need to be corrected. In this chapter the two approaches will be compared, examining, as an illustration, the issue of the compensation for risks. The next section will consider how the perception of risk may affect the decision to invest in LDCs and how different types of financial incentives act in order to compensate for risks. In the following section the intervention of different agencies will be examined.

2 THE REDUCTION OF RISK AND THE IMPACT OF DIFFERENT FINANCIAL INCENTIVES

The first step is to define what is meant by risk in this context. We need to distinguish the objective risk of the investment from the subjective perception that the investor has of the risk of the investment:

(1) Objective risk, determined by specific features of the investment (such as investments with a high commercial risk) or by the environment where the investment is made (such as low-income countries with an unstable political and economic framework).
(2) Subjective perception of the risk of the investment, commonly shared between potential investors (for example, investments in countries or sectors where there are no previous foreign investments). This gives rise to a problem of externality: the performance of the first investor represents a signal to subsequent investors on the

riskiness of the investment. The non appropriability of the benefits deriving from the signalling to subsequent investors acts as a deterrent to the first mover.

(3) Subjective perception of the risk of the investment, differently shared between potential investors. This is the consequence of (a) asymmetry of information (such as between firms that are used to investing abroad or that are already present in the host country and firms that are not); (b) different amounts of resources available in reserve, should the investment not give the expected results (for example, between small and large firms or private and public firms); (c) other things equal, a different propensity towards risk (for example, between conservative and innovative firms).

If incentives are effective, aid agencies can affect the decision to invest abroad at three different levels: destination (country and sector), category of the investor (small or large firms) and the form of the investment (equity participation in the new firm in the host country or non-equity foreign investment). The objective of aid agencies should be to channel resources towards LDCs that are not attracted on a mere market basis. Thus financial incentives should channel foreign investments in low-income countries or in risky sectors with a high developmental impact (reduction of the objective risk), promote investments from SMFs or other categories of firms not used to investing in LDCs and in forms that imply a long-term commitment of the foreign investor (reduction of the subjective risk).

The distorting impact of financial incentives depends on both the type of risk and the type of intervention of aid agencies. When the goal is to compensate for objectively high risks that make the investment unattractive on a market basis, the use of financial incentives aimed at reducing the risk and the cost of the investment is necessarily distorting. Aid agencies can justify their intervention on development grounds, but they would, in any case, be in conflict with the market. On the other hand, a wrong perception of risks is a market imperfection that could be compensated by financial incentives without causing distortions. Financial incentives can be grouped into four broad categories:

(1) subscription of a minority equity share by the aid agency in the capital of the new firm (IFC, CDC, Proparco, DEG, OECF);
(2) loans at a market interest rate (IFC, DEG);
(3) subsidized loans (CDC, CCCE, KFW, OECF);
(4) investment insurances (MIGA, SACE, OPIC).

Subsidized loans can be granted (a) to the investor of the advanced country to finance its equity share in the new firm (Italian Co-operation) or (b) to the new firm, either directly or through a local public intermediary (two-step loans), usually to finance the import of machinery or other long-term expenses.

Of course, loans at a market interest rate do not reduce the cost and the risk of the foreign investor unless there are alternative market sources of financing. This is not the case for subsidized loans and subscriptions of an equity share in the new firm. It is interesting to compare these two forms of incentives. Curiously enough, in the controversy amongst donors, the subscription of an equity share is not considered to be distorting. The reason will be examined in what follows.

It is possible to demonstrate that, whereas subsidized loans always provide a subsidy to the foreign investor, which amounts to the difference between market and subsidized interest rates, in equity subscriptions the subsidy increases when the revenues from the investment decrease. For the purpose of this illustration, only subsidized loans to finance the equity share of the foreign investor are considered. It is assumed, for simplicity, that the foreign investor borrows at a market rate to finance the share of capital not covered by the subsidized loan or directly subscribed by the aid agency and that both subsidized and market loans are reimbursed at the same time and in one instalment. It is also assumed that the foreign investor will buy back the equity subscribed by the aid agency after a given time, equal to the length of the loan. This assumption reflects the real behaviour of aid agencies which usually sell their share of capital to the private sector after the firm starts operating.

In the case of the subsidized loan, the expected yearly profit of the foreign investor is:

$$E\pi_c = [Er - ai_s - (1-a)i_m]K \tag{11.1}$$

whereas in the case of equity subscription it is:

$$E\pi_a = (Er - i_m)(1-\beta)K \tag{11.2}$$

where:

Er = expected yearly revenue from the investment,
K = overall equity of the firm,

a = share of equity held by the foreign investor financed with the subsidized loan,
i_s = subsidized interest rate,
i_m = market interest rate,
β = share of equity subscribed by the aid agency.

The foreign investor will be indifferent to the two options when expected profits are the same:

$$E\pi_c = E\pi_a$$

which can be rewritten as:

$$a(i_m - i_s) = \beta(i_m - Er) \qquad (11.3)$$

From (11.3) we can see that, whereas in the case of the subsidized loan the subsidy is independent of the revenues of the investment, this is not the case for the equity subscription. If $Er > i_m$, as $i_m > i_s$ by definition, the foreign investor will prefer the subsidized loan. In this case, the equity subscription of the aid agency implies a loss of profits for the private investor, even if, alternatively, he or she had to finance the whole equity subscription by borrowing at a market rate i_m.

On the other hand, equity subscription represents an implicit subsidy when $Er < i_m$ (that is, when expected revenues are less than the market interest rate); a subsidy which increases as far as Er decreases. Revenues inferior to the market interest rate are a likely outcome under specific circumstances. Consider, as an illustration, highly risky investments with a large variance in revenues or investments that become profitable after a lengthy period of time. From (11.3) it is possible to infer that for values of:

$$Er < i_m - (a/\beta)(i_m - i_s) \qquad (11.4)$$

the subsidy granted by equity subscription will be larger than for subsidized loans.

Now, why is equity subscription not considered to be distorting in the debate amongst donors? Because aid agencies could invest in equity on a pure market basis. In this case, the new firm in the developing country (whose capital is shared by the aid agency and the private foreign investor) is equivalent to a joint venture (JV) between private investors; that is, market signals are not distorted. This point is an introduction to the discussion in the next section, where the effective role played by aid agencies and particularly by Public Development Finance Corporations (PDFC) is examined.

3 PUBLIC DEVELOPMENT FINANCE CORPORATIONS: BETWEEN MARKET AND CO-OPERATION

The promotion of the private sector requires specific instruments, selection procedures and skills which differ from those employed in more traditional forms of aid intervention. For this reason, many aid agencies have found it more efficient to confine this activity to special institutions and they have founded PDFCs mainly on the lines of the International Finance Corporation (IFC) of the World Bank.

PDFCs are therefore institutions that try to operate in a peculiar balance between market and co-operation. Following the argument of the previous section, two points need to be examined. First, it is not clear whether PDFCs act on a pure market basis, as would follow from the argument that equity subscription is not distorting. Second, if this is the case, we need to examine whether this orientation is not in conflict with the co-operation objective of channelling additional flows of resources to LDCs. In other words, if PDFCs follow the market, they finance only investments with higher revenues and lower risks: that is to say, by following the market, PDFCs would go where private investments go by themselves.

Pressure on PDFCs to maintain a satisfactory level of profitability of their investments has been rising in the last few years. For example, both CDC and Proparco tend to subscribe an equity share only when expected profitability is high.[3]

At first sight IFC seems to be moving in the same direction. Some 46 per cent of the funds committed in 1988 were invested in countries with an income per capita between 2000 and 6000 dollars, but only 15 per cent in countries with an income per capita of less than 500 dollars. It is possible to identify a positive correlation between the IFC's investment flows and income per capita of the receiving country, which is particularly large for investments in equity.[4]

These results should, however, be interpreted cautiously. If most of IFC's investments are directed towards countries with a higher income per capita, this does not mean that the objective of promoting investments in more depressed areas is denied. Obviously, the majority of private investment flows are directed towards more prosperous countries. In this perspective, it is not surprising to find that the activity of the IFC is mainly concentrated in those countries. However, the subsidy is not determined by the volume of PDFCs' equity investments. As we can see from condition (11.4) of the previous section, risk coverage, and thus the subsidy, is higher the higher the share of equity β subscribed by the aid agency. The correlation between the share of equity β subscribed by the IFC in individual investments and income per capita of the receiving country is negative.

As equity subscription is the only subsidy granted by the IFC to private investors (loans are always at market rates), the evidence shows that the subsidy increases the more depressed is the receiving country, that is the less attractive are investment opportunities. In other words, the IFC seems to successfully reconcile market orientation and investment promotion by channelling the majority of its funds to more promising countries and granting, at the same time, a higher subsidy in less attractive countries.

As far as the objective of promoting foreign investments of SMEs is concerned, market orientation does not appear to be particularly effective. On the basis of the available evidence, financial incentives seem to be effective in compensating the higher risk of investing in LDCs, as perceived by SMEs. Unfortunately, figures on the distribution of PDFCs' commitments with respect to the size of the recipient firms are available only for German aid. However, the case of Germany is particularly meaningful. SMEs' investments in LDCs are promoted by DEG and KFW. DEG only grants loans at a market rate: in 1984 only 10 per cent of the projects financed (3 per cent of total invested resources) was undertaken by firms with sales of less than ten million marks, although the promotion of SMEs' investments is one of the major objectives of the programme. On the other hand, the 'technology programme' of the KFW grants subsidized loans to promote the transfer of technology by SMEs. The risk is further reduced because, if the investment does not yield the expected revenues, the firm is released from the obligation of repaying its debt. Between 1984 and 1987, 78 loans were granted for a total amount of 106 million marks. The projects financed in 1988 have led to the creation of 5467 new jobs in LDCs.[5]

Also, the case of JAIDO in Japan is extremely interesting in this context. JAIDO was founded as a joint venture between OECF and 100 private large enterprises to promote investments of SMEs in LDCs through equity subscription. JAIDO will soon become a private institution as OECF will sell its share of capital to the private sector.

In this case, we have risk sharing within the private sector: more experienced large enterprises take upon themselves part of the risk of the smaller ones. This solution is very much geared to the Japanese model of foreign investments, where large enterprises act as the front runners for smaller firms that invest subsequently in order to create a system of Japanese subcontracting in the host country.

4 CONCLUSIONS

The impact of financial incentives on the promotion of foreign investments is rather controversial: it is not easy to find the balance between market and development objectives. If aid agencies and, more specifically, PDFCs intervene only on the basis of market signals, they are ineffective in promoting development objectives, that is in channelling resources that do not go to the LDCs on a mere market basis.

Both objectives can be achieved by using extremely selective procedures that allow for subsidies only when market imperfections or development objectives justify their use. On the other hand, PDFCs can invest part of their resources on a market basis in order to reach a satisfactory level of profitability in their overall investments.

The ability of PDFCs to be sufficiently selective is essential. Their existence is justifiable on the basis of a subtle balance between the two sets of objectives they face. Pursuing only one of them would undermine their very nature. In this perspective, PDFCs seem more effective in promoting foreign investments to LDCs than direct government intervention, as is the case for Italy. Direct government intervention does not have the variety of instruments which are available to PDFCs. It is therefore likely to be biased.

GLOSSARY

CCCE = Caisse Centrale de Coopération Economique, France
CDC = Commonwealth Development Corporation, United Kingdom
DEG = Deutsche Investitions und Entwicklungsgesellschaft, Germany
IFC = International Finance Corporation, World Bank
KFW = Kredit für Wiederaufbau, Germany
MIGA = Multilateral Investments Guarantee Agency, World Bank
OECF = Overseas Fund for Economic Co-operation, Japan
OPIC = Overseas Private Investment Corporation, USA
SACE = Società di Assicurazione per il Commercio Estero, Italy

NOTES

1. This chapter is based on the findings which emerged in a research project co-ordinated by the author for the Centro Studi Luca d'Agliano in Turin (Barba Navaretti, Perosino and Zanalda, 1991) and partially financed by the Directorate General for Development Co-operation of the Italian Ministry of Foreign Affairs. The part of the project on the role of aid agencies in promoting foreign investments, to which this note is related, has greatly benefited from the background material prepared by Giancarlo Perasso, Anna Maria Corazza and Francesco Daveri.
2. OECD, 1990.
3. Gourdain Mitsotaki (1986); Barba Navaretti, Perosino and Zanalda (1991).
4. The evidence on the IFC is based on Perasso (1990).
5. Gourdain Mitsotaki (1986).

REFERENCES

BARBA NAVARETTI, G., G. PEROSINO and G. ZANALDA (1991) 'Investimenti con Ripartizione di Controllo nei Paesi in Via di Sviluppo: Trasferimento di Capacita' e Ruolo degli Organismi di Cooperazione', Centro Studi Luca d'Agliano, Turin.

GOURDAIN MITSOTAKI, A. (1986) *Public Development Finance Corporations. Their Role in the New Forms of Investment in Developing Countries*, Paris: OECD Development Centre.

OECD, (1990) *Promoting Private Enterprise in Developing Countries*, Paris: Development Assistance Committee.

PERASSO, G. (1990) 'Aiuto Estero allo Sviluppo: Problemi e Prospettive alla Luce della Creazione di Capacita' Imprenditoriali nei PVS', Turin: Centro Studi Luca d'Agliano, background paper.

12 The Theory and Policy of Structural Adjustment: A Note

Marco Missaglia

1 INTRODUCTION

The criticisms made regarding structural adjustment policies are mainly based on theoretical grounds but on concrete issues. Emphasis is placed, in particular, on the social costs associated with deflationary measures, without however doubting their effectiveness in stabilizing the economy: that is, their capacity to bring inflation under control and to improve the foreign balance of payments. The World Bank itself recognizes these social drawbacks but it insists on the need to implement stabilization programmes which are based on traditional orthodox economic thought.[1] Hence it is reasonable to presume that in the next few years international agencies will try to deal with the continuing imbalances in the developing world, balance of payment problems, inflationary pressures and internal financial problems, by making use of customary instruments of political economy such as: devaluation, limits on the money supply and liberalization of goods and capital movement. In this paper I shall try to show how economic theory can explain why policies of structural adjustment have failed and why many poor countries went through economic crises in the 1980s. To this end I shall refer to structuralist-based models with an emphasis on demand and where wages are present both as cost factors and, of course, as elements of demand. I shall also refer to models from the neoclassical tradition, in which the use of a standard production function is by itself enough to move the emphasis of the analysis towards the 'supply side' as it is known.[2]

Not only in structuralist economic theory, but perhaps surprisingly also in neoclassical theory, there are analytic categories able to point out the inefficiency, or at the very least, the insufficiency of traditional structural adjustment policies. This is the basic idea around which I will develop my brief and incomplete observations, which are presented in a 'literary' and non-mathematical style of language.

2 DEVALUATION: A STRUCTURALIST ANALYSIS

The devaluation of the exchange rate, or rather the increase in the price of foreign currencies in local monetary terms, often comes into stabilization programmes proposed and/or imposed by the World Bank and above all by the International Monetary Fund. Traditionally the objective of this devaluation of local currencies was to reduce the commercial deficit that is typical of many less developed countries (LDCs). Furthermore, it is held that, by increasing the local value of exports, and so stimulating the production of exportable goods, devaluation can create a general expansion effect. Is this scenario realistic? To this question, structuralist economic theory gives a negative response, basing itself on three 'basic ideas':

(a) Devaluation creates an increase in the general level of prices owing to the need to support the higher costs of intermediate import goods (it should be remembered that the structuralists almost always use a 'Kalecki' theory of prices, which states that every increase in variable costs will be reflected in the general level of prices as a result of the 'mark-up' rule). The resulting reduction in real wages will bring about a redistribution of income from the workers to capitalists and so cause, *ceteris paribus*, a fall in the aggregate demand.
(b) If, as often happens, the devaluation of the exchange rate is a result of an attempt to reduce the external deficit, then it is very probable that this, independently of any variations in real wages, will reduce the aggregate demand. Indeed the devaluation on the one hand allows exporters to make larger gains, while on the other it inflicts higher costs on importers. Given a current account deficit, the overall effect is depressive.
(c) The probability of a decrease in demand, as pointed out in point (b), will be greater if export elasticity is small, in respect to prices. Recent empirical studies have shown that in many cases this elasticity is small, and so in just as many cases, devaluation leads to stagflation.[3]

The recessive effects of devaluation, and especially the difficulties of managing an economy in which its effects are produced, can be easily visualized (see Figure 12.1). If B is the current account balance of the party concerned, we have:

$$B = B(G, E) \tag{12.1}$$

where G is the level of public spending and E is the exchange rate. Suppose that $dB/dG < 0$; an increase of public spending causes a worsening of B, $dB/dE > 0$, the devaluation improves commercial performances (this is a standard hypothesis which we could see come true at least in the medium term). If the aggregate production, X, depends on public spending and the exchange rate, we have;

$$X = X(G, E) \tag{12.2}$$

with $dX/dG > 0$ and given a hypothesis of recessive devaluation, $dX/dE < 0$.

In Figure 12.1, the $X = X_0$ and the $B = B_0$ lines are the locus of constant value of aggregate production and of current account balance. The line $C = C_0$ represents an improvement in the commercial balance. It can be seen that in this case the shapers of political economy should compensate the recessive effects of devaluation with an expansive fiscal policy, increasing the level of public spending. In reality, orthodox stabilization programmes usually call for a reduction of this spending, which can only make further recession. On the other hand, 'to increase the financial deficit when the balance of trade is worrying would, *prima facie*, seem to be a risky move'.[4]

This example gives an idea of the difficulty of management of economic policies in a 'stagnationist' economy,[5] in which the theoretical bases of orthodox policies are reversed: not only does devaluation

Figure 12.1 The effects of devaluation

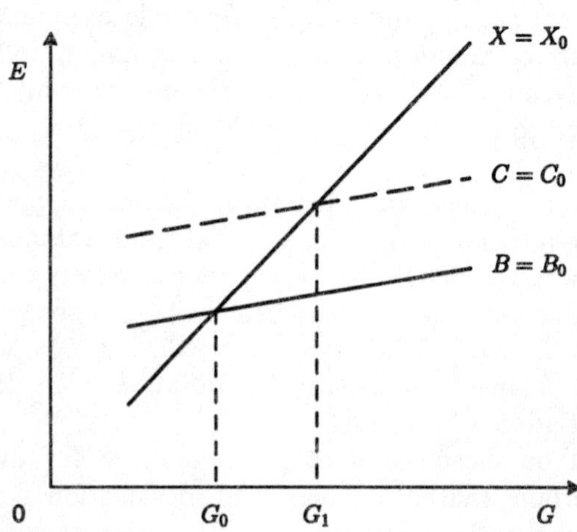

become a recessive policy, but also – and symmetrically[6] – the increase of money wages would favour an increase of production and of employment.

The structuralist conclusion depends crucially on the three 'basic ideas' mentioned above. They in turn rest upon a theoretical support which can be generically defined as Keynesian, where the emphasis is placed on demand and on the relationship between the distribution of income and the level of economic activity.

We can therefore propose a theoretical and politically important line of questioning: apart from structuralist theory, do there exist any other analytical categories which can explain the possible stagnationist effects of devaluation? More specifically; does orthodox economic theory provide us with a consistently valid intellectual justification for orthodox policies? Or do these policies depend upon 'excessively' ideological concepts?

3 DEVALUATION: A NEOCLASSICAL POINT OF VIEW

In order to answer the questions which have been raised in the previous section, I shall refer to a model presented by Islam in 1984.[7] The model is typically neoclassical; there is a production function which allows complete substitution between inputs, a supply function is derived from the production function with the usual procedure of profit maximization. Finally the model presents an aggregate demand function, with real balances – or rather the relationship between money supply and the general price level – in place of real wages. Islam showed that devaluation might lead both to inflation and to recession. Given the framework of neoclassical economy, the 'main ideas' which lead to this conclusion, are the following:

(a) Devaluation produces negative effects on the supply of goods destined for the internal market ('non traded goods'). Indeed according to neoclassical production theory, supply is inversely correlated to the cost of production, which increases following a depreciation of the local currency: the cost of imported intermediate goods and money wages increase, because of some type of indexation. Thus devaluation produces an inflationary pressure.

(b) The effect on the demand of goods destined for the internal market is uncertain. Indeed, on one hand, devaluation produces an increase in income in the export sector, and for this reason contributes

to the increase in demand for 'non traded goods'. On the other hand devaluation reduces the real value of monetary balances; therefore, the consumers are likely to save more in order to regain the real value of their money stock, M/P. However, there is another way by which devaluation reduces the demand of goods destined for the internal market: it increases the price of imported consumer goods (and in effect many developing countries import such goods). Indeed, this increase causes a reduction in the demand for local goods if, as is often the case in LDCs, there is a relatively low price flexibility of local goods in respect to imported goods, or in other terms, the income effect is relatively more important than the substitution effect.
(c) It is reasonable to think that the output of the export sector increases following devaluation, but it is equally necessary to remember that an increase in the cost of production (due to higher money wages and higher prices of imported intermediate goods) produces opposite effects.

Hence the stagnationist effects of devaluation can also be demonstrated by using typically neoclassical tools. A confirmation of this point can be found in an econometric research by Faini and de Melo (1990). The two authors, taking into consideration a sample of 83 LDCs, showed that the macroeconomic effects of the 'maxi-devaluation' from between 1982 and 1988, caused an average depreciation of the real exchange rate by 40%. Their results confirmed that in the short term the impact of devaluation on supply was clearly negative. The production of tradable goods (exports) increased, but this was a limited effect because of the short-term difficulties in shifting resources from production of non-tradable goods to tradable ones. Given the reduction in the supply of goods produced for the internal market, the overall effect of devaluation on the GNP was negative. Thus orthodox policies are not necessarily confirmed even by orthodox theory.

4 TRADE LIBERALIZATION

Commercial policies are perhaps the most 'structural' of the so-called structural adjustment policies: they are indeed designed to effect profoundly the structure of an economy in its long-term development.[8]

The supporters of 'free trade' take a basically Ricardian point of view; notwithstanding revisions and corrections modern 'laissez faire' theory is always based on the comparative advantages of specialization. The critics of 'free trade' base their arguments on the basic idea that a LDC must protect its infant industries from international competition, and indeed preserve their very existence. However, here I shall only investigate the implications of short period liberalization policies and their capacity to stabilize an economy.

Taylor has presented a 'fixed price/flexible price' model (a typical analytical instrument for structuralist macroeconomic theory) which shows the difficulties of liberalization policies, and their different effects.[9] He considers an economy in which the importation of certain crucial intermediate goods (transport, energy, communication networks and so on) are subject to a maximum level of duty, which, for example, is designed to favour an industrialization process based on import substitution. What will be the effects if the government allows the importation of more intermediate goods? The relative price of locally produced intermediate goods decreases because of rising competition from imported ones, and this stimulates both their domestic and external demand. However, the reduction of the relative price of the intermediate goods also implies a smaller value of the output for the national sector which produces them. If this leads to a considerable reduction of the physical output of these goods, then the liberalization policy will have a recessive effect.

However, we can see that orthodox theory does not always provide a watertight justification of the orthodox policy also in the case of trade liberalization. By taking into account the possible stagflationist effects of devaluation, Islam examines what other short-term policies could improve the current account balance. The perhaps surprising answer lies with measures that would normally be classified as distorting ones, because they modify market prices and introduce commercial barriers. Indeed, Islam's proposal consists of the imposition of additional taxes *ad valorem* on the importation of consumer goods foreseeing further subsidies for exports: taxes and subsidies must be such as to leave unchanged the relative price between exports and imports of consumer goods.

Islam's proposal amounts to a devaluation that does not regard the importation of intermediate goods. The idea is that, in order to reduce the demand of imported intermediate goods, one must use methods which do not produce recessive and inflationary consequences, as could be the case with devaluation. In Islam's case the cost of imported intermediate goods does not change, and the only mechanism which might reduce domestic output would be wage indexation: money wages would react to the increase in the price of imported consumer goods. Islam concludes that, if the imposition of taxes on imported consumer goods should be insufficient, given the limited reduction of output, in balancing foreign trade, then a certain degree of monetary restriction could be applied. However, the author believes that a 'tax-subsidy policy' should be enough to tackle current account difficulties. Therefore, contrary to devaluation, a 'tax-subsidy policy' does not increase the cost of imported intermediate goods, hence the volume of exports can grow more appreciably, as it is not negatively affected by the increase of that cost.

If we take into account the huge foreign debt of many LDCs, then the problems created by devaluation can be seen even more explicitly, because the debt burden obviously increases after a devaluation.

5 RESTRICTIVE MONETARY POLICY

Amongst the traditional structural adjustment policies, restrictive monetary policy is the one which provokes the greatest amount of disagreement between the neoclassical school and the structuralist school. This is due to the fact that the two schools adopt theories of inflation which are irreconcilable. The neoclassical/monetarist view is based on the proportionality between value of transactions and money supply. If the output is constant, at full employment level, then a reduction in the amount of money in circulation must be associated with a lower price level. Seen in this way, restrictive monetarism is a fundamental anti-inflation policy.

We now point out the basic elements of the structuralist theory of inflation; a theory which casts doubts on the real effectiveness of monetary policies in LDCs.[10]

(a) For the structuralists, the increase of the money supply is not the true cause of inflation, but only a necessary vehicle for it. They believe that money supply responds passively to other factors, which are the real cause of inflation.

(b) These 'other factors' are the true structural destabilizers and must be looked for in the real part of the economy. For example, inflation may be the result of the rigidity of the supply of consumer goods (usually agricultural ones), and this may be due to institutional and political factors, namely the existing property rights system. Inflation may be the result of class conflict, whenever workers and capitalists try to maintain real wages and profit margins at levels which conform to their own expectations: 'Inflation is a means by which capitalists try to hide class conflict'.[11]

(c) Restrictive monetarism, by leading to an increase in interest rates, negatively affects the cost of production. In LDCs firms are often forced to pay production factors in advance and therefore to run up debts with the banking system in order to finance circulating capital. In the great majority of cases higher financial costs lead to a reduction of activity which can – in theory – more than make up for the reduction of aggregate demand. If this were to happen it would result in additional inflationary pressures.

6 CONCLUSIONS

These short 'observations' try to bring together some of the theoretical reasons that are at the basis of the partial inefficiency of structural adjustment policies. It must be emphasized that orthodox theory should not be identified with othodox policy, perhaps – as we have seen – with the exception of restrictive monetarism. Of course alternative policies must be confronted with those advocated in structural adjustment programmes.

NOTES

1. See World Bank (1990) pp. 103–20.
2. For traditional structuralist models see Taylor (1983) and for the neoclassical line of thought see Islam (1984).
3. See for example Taylor (1988).
4. See Taylor (1990) p. 205..
5. For a comparison of the 'stagnationist' system and the 'exhilarationist' system, see Bhaduri and Marglin (1990)
6. The condition under which there is recessive devaluation is absolutely identical to that which would create expansionist effects of higher monetary salaries. It depends on the application of a Kalecki type of price theory, common to most structuralists.
7. See Islam (1984).
8. See Basu (1984), ch. 4.
9. See Taylor (1990), ch. 9.
10. For an analysis of the structuralist theory of inflation see, for example, Ros (1988).
11. See Taylor (1983), ch. 11.

REFERENCES

BASU, K. (1984) *The Less Developed Economy. A Critique of Contemporary Theory*, Oxford: Basic Blackwell.

BHADURI, A. and S. MARGLIN (1990) 'Unemployment and the real wage: the economic basis for contesting political ideology', *Cambridge Journal of Economics*, vol. 14.

FAINI, R. and J. DE MELO (1990) *Adjustment, investment and the real exchange rate in developing countries*, The World Bank, Country Economic Department, WPS 473.

ISLAM, S. (1984) 'Devaluation, stabilization policies and the developing countries', *Journal of Development Economics*, vol. 14.

ROS, J. (1988) *On Inertia, Social Conflict, and the Structuralist Analysis of Inflation*, Helsinki: WIDER.

TAYLOR, L. (1983) *Structuralist Macroeconomics*, New York: Basic Books.

TAYLOR, L. (1988) *Varieties of Stabilization Experience*, Oxford: Clarendon Press.

TAYLOR, L. (1990) 'Income Distribution, Inflation and Growth: Lectures on Structuralist Macroeconomic Theory', mimeo, MIT.

WORLD BANK (1990) *World Development Report*, Oxford: Oxford University Press.

Part IV

Development, Democracy and the New Economic Order

13 Recent International Developments and the North–South Dialogue

Youssef Boutros-Ghali[1]

1 INTRODUCTION

Ever since the North Atlantic countries (on both sides of the ocean) realized that there was life below the 40th parallel there has been a dialogue between the north and the south. This momentous event is estimated to have happened somewhere in the late 1960s to early 1970s. At first, the phenomenon appears to have been restricted to academics in the fields of political science and economics. It later appears to have spread to politicians who seem to have greatly contributed to obscuring the debate.

The central questions at the root of the debate were, and I believe still are, 'why is the South in the state it is in, is there anything we can do and, if there is, what and how?' I simplify greatly but I believe that this is the core of the arguments. The debate did get into serious issues of resource transfers from the North to the South, the New International Economic Order and so on. Nevertheless the dialogue, and I bring you a view from the south, the dialogue has remained academic. I cannot trace a single major change in the international economic order that can be attributed to the North–South dialogue. I also cannot picture the smooth functioning of international economic relations without somewhere in the background a North–South dialogue. Obviously something is being achieved; the problem is we in the South cannot figure out what.

Be that as it may, there have been recent developments in the world scene that bring back, with greater urgency the need for the expansion of the dialogue. These developments, if not addressed explicitly, will alter fundamentally the North–South relations in the world. Chronologically the first oil crisis of 1973–4 brought forth the issue of resource transfers, the second oil shock of the late 1970s served to strengthen the foundations of the problems laid down by the first shock. The debt crisis of the early 1980s signalled that a structural problem existed in the world economy that needed to be addressed with novel means and novel tools. The confusion of the mid-1980s in addressing the problem, rescheduling, debt forgiveness, the Baker Plan, its later incarnation the Brady Plan, all attempts to address a systemic issue within the existing system, furthered the debate but did not address the fundamental issues. Now the emergence of Eastern Europe among democratic, market-oriented nations, and its dire need for assistance, has further altered the world scene. So much so that a new look is in order and a new evaluation of where we are going is called for.

2 EAST–WEST DIRECTIONS FOR THE DIALOGUE OF THE 1990s

The last years of the 1980s have left us with a legacy that will shape international relations well into the next century. I will leave aside the changes in the world political scene, which are momentous,[2] and will instead concentrate on the expected resource flows that these changes will occasion and their impact on the South, the deep South, since now there has appeared on the world scene countries with some southern features without the southern location.

These countries, despite the admiration we feel for their success in emerging from decades of totalitarianism and paralysed economies, pose a threat to the tenuous world economic order as it stood until two years ago. The very features of these countries will affect North–South relations in ways that, if not analysed, and put in their proper perspectives, could relegate a significant portion of the South to perennial under-development.

The stylized facts of Eastern European economies point to systems that share, as mentioned, some of the features of the South, such as low standards of living, low per capita income, undeveloped potentialities, a weak export capacity and other ills of under-development. Admittedly these features, and those I will outline below, vary in degree between one country and the other. The hardships of Romania differ from those of Poland or former East Germany; all nevertheless remain on the same scale.

There are, however, fundamental differences from the third world, the South as we know it. The infrastructural base of these countries, again to varying degrees, is reasonably well developed. The labour force is relatively skilled, literacy rates are high and the industrial base, although antiquated, inefficient and incapable in its present state to cope with the rigours of international competitiveness, has nevertheless left an industrial structure, a state of mind in the workforce, a familiarity with industrialization. All these elements, despite the vagueness of some, are essential for a speedy, effective structural reform and economic development. Adequate financial resources, properly placed, will bear fruit in a relatively short time.

The differences with the South do not stop here. There is one basic feature in Eastern Europe that is absent in most of the debt-distressed third world, namely the possibility, if not the existence, of a social compact between the governing and the governed. The struggle to freedom, the long years of repression, the access to government, have generated in the peoples of Eastern Europe a willingness to accept austerity, and painful reforms as a final chapter of a long crusade. The Polish structural adjustment programme and its stabilization measures are witness to the willingness of the Polish people to bear harsh measures in the hope, indeed the knowledge, of a better future.[3]

Complementing this are factors that will reinforce the willingness of the people to enter into long-term social compacts with their governments. Chief among them is income distribution. Although no firm data appear available, it stands to reason that, after 40 years of egalitarian regimes, income distribution would be relatively even across social strata with the exception of a few top echelons in the local party structures. Economic reform – and again I simplify – does not have to deal with redistributing income from one resisting class to another envious one, rather it will have to generate additional resources relatively equally from all classes. No mean feat admittedly, but one with fewer social tensions, one would hope.

These intrinsic features are not the only characteristics that differentiate the 'New South' from the old. Others are uncomfortable to mention but nevertheless will play an important role in East–West financial relations. These are the undeniable affinities between the peoples of Eastern Europe and those of the West. The human physical features are similar, the languages are similar if not identical, the mentality, a hazy word admittedly, is similar, Eastern European peoples have natural constituencies in the West. Even the far away North American continent has important constituencies of Eastern European stock. It is easier to give to a brother than it is to a cousin.

These features, their combination at this juncture of international financial relations, will have two major consequences for the relations between North and South. The South in this case is below the 40th parallel. The first concerns us in this section and is centred around resource flows from the developed to the under-developed world. It is no secret that resource transfers to developing countries, barring some minor exceptions, have declined over the past decade. Official Development Assistance (ODA), multilateral assistance and commercial lending have all shown a declining trend. Optimism would push us towards hoping that the trend will stabilize or better yet will reverse itself in the near future. Nevertheless, the peoples of the developed world, their parliaments and their budgetary constraints make an increase in resource transfers to developing countries over present levels unlikely. Parliamentarians across the world such as the American Congress, the French National Assembly and so on will say, with good reason that charity begins at home. Indeed it does, especially if the home has just welcomed a new, close relative who is destitute, offers great potential for growth and will provide ready markets for exports of goods and service in a future that is not too distant. This leaves us with the rest of the developing countries receiving less of a commodity that, given their limited capacity for generating domestic savings, is essential not only for economic growth but also for structural reforms.

Despite assurances to the contrary, developing countries below the 40th parallel are bracing themselves for a gradual reduction in the financial flows that can be expected from the North. The Iron Curtain has fallen from across Europe, only to rise again on the southern shores of the Mediterranean.

3 MULTILATERALITY IN INTERNATIONAL FINANCIAL RELATIONS

The second development, that in conjunction with the first will greatly affect North–South relations, is the increased multilaterality of financial relations in the world of today. The 1980s with all their economic crises have brought a fundamental change in the relations between the North and the South. Development assistance and structural reforms are increasingly under the tutelage of the two Bretton Woods organizations, the World Bank and the International Monetary Fund. Moreover, 'it has been reported in the OECD Development Assistance Committee and elsewhere that bilateral aid agencies increasingly take macro-economic and structural policies of recipient countries into account in their aid decisions and that many agencies extend balance of payments assistance specifically in support of policy reform'.[4] Of course,

> decision making with regard to aid matters still remains a necessarily complex matter as it must balance the relative importance of historical ties, bilateral political relationships, commercial interests and long-term developmental and humanitarian concerns, as well as take account of the economic policy environment of the recipient country. Increasingly, nevertheless, bilateral donors will rely on the reports and recommendations of the World Bank and the IMF to make their evaluation of the adequacy of policy reforms in developing countries.[5]

This is a welcome development. Policy reform programmes have often floundered because of insufficient external financing, inappropriate financial flows or untimely disbursements in otherwise adequate resources. In addition, the existence of well-formulated, internally consistent stabilization and structural reform programmes provides optimal frameworks for the efficient use of external resources and their management.

This scheme of things has two basic flaws, however. It relies almost exclusively on the assessment of the two multilateral organizations – the IMF and the IBRD – of the adequacy, timeliness and content of policy reforms of developing countries and it will limit its methods of assistance to those that benefit from unanimous consent in the international financial community. The reliance on the almost exclusive assessment of the Bank and the Fund is not, in itself the issue. On the contrary it would provide an assessment that is technically correct, objective and uniform across all countries. It is this uniformity across countries that, in the light of the recent developments in Eastern Europe, could worsen the flaws in the conceptual frameworks on which the two organizations base their policy prescriptions.

I shall take the example of the recently enacted reform of the Polish economy. I take the Polish reform as representative of reform programmes that are appearing on the East-European scene these days. All measures in it denote an undeniable courage and determination to reshape the economic system along more efficient lines. All measures also rely on an essential ingredient for their implementation, namely the existence of a clearly defined social compact within the community. The Polish people would accept the austerity of today for a clearly defined improvement tomorrow, while believing that all strata of the population will be equally – or almost equally – affected. This is a core ingredient of the structural reform and stabilization programme of Poland. Real wage declines that were fought bitterly on the barricades of Gdansk several months ago are accepted magnified fourfold today. Despite its crucial importance, this critical mass of popular support is never explicitly mentioned, while without it none of the measures would be viable. It is this essential component that makes the East European paradigm of reform inadequate in most developing countries below the 40th parallel.

The necessity of a strong social compact in the community for the successful implementation of the reform measures in the programme is the very feature that is lacking in the rest of the developing world. This absence will cause reform programmes patterned along East European lines to fail as they will antagonize all strata of the population simultaneously. In the third world, such programmes do not have natural constituencies. Not at least in the short run, and the long run is mistrusted by all.

Yet the Polish reform programme is gradually becoming the paradigm of reform programmes proposed by the two Bretton Woods institutions. It is slowly becoming the measure against which other reform packages are judged. With time, the measures it comprises and their magnitudes will come to be essential components of the reform packages proposed by both the Bank and the Fund. As a result, negotiations between third-world governments will take longer, more programmes of the two institutions will fail, more stabilization measures will be judged inadequate and in the present world environment greater resources will be withheld pending 'better' measures. The declining trend in resource transfers to the third world will be compounded by creditor nations unwilling to commit the little that is available to support what multilateral institutions judge as insufficient reforms.

The second flaw in the increased multilaterality of international financial relations stems from the nature of the imbalances in a large number of third-world countries. As will be shown in the next section these imbalances spring essentially from, and are compounded by, a massive debt overhang burdening the balance of payments of all such countries. The nature of the external resources required to deal with such an overhang has to date eluded the international financial community. Admittedly, the broad features of the type of external assistance required are known to all. The Toronto summit of the G-7 countries in 1988, the Houston summit in 1990, attest to the fact that the international community is increasingly aware that the only lasting solution to the debt overhang of the third world lies in outright debt forgiveness on a fairly massive scale. Yet the solution is not widely adopted and faces a number of practical problems of which not least is the issue of moral hazard. The reaction of the Bretton Woods organizations and the world community has been, to date, to continue applying the orthodox solution of austerity and debt rescheduling. The latter merely postpones the problem while the former is unable, by itself to resolve it.

What is needed is a multilateral methodology for the assessment of the extent of debt forgiveness needed in each individual case, the distribution of the burden of this forgiveness among creditors and the assurances that forgiving the debts of one needy country will not create incentives for others, less needy, to force the same outcome. Clearly a multilateral framework is the best suited for resolving such issues. Paradoxically, it is the present multilateral aspect of international financial relations, requiring consensus among creditors with different legal, budgetary and financial constraints, that is the biggest obstacle in the path of a solution.

The case of the Egyptian economy is representative of the nature of the external imbalances typical of a number of third-world debt-distressed countries.

4 THE EGYPTIAN ECONOMY: A SOUTHERN VIEW[6]

A number of studies by international organizations and private individuals[7] go through elaborate projection exercises to prove that with the current debt service profile the balance of payments of Egypt is not viable. In these analyses financial viability is usually defined as the ability of the Egyptian economy to generate enough surplus foreign resources to service all its external obligations *as they stand at present*, without requiring any exceptional financing, that is rescheduling or concerted lending.[8] To reach such a goal, arguments are then developed, especially in the reports of international organizations, that, with a hefty dose of austerity accompanied by economic growth, however this may be achieved, and repeated reschedulings of current obligations for a number of years to come, financial viability could be restored to the Egyptian balance of payments.

The proposition presented here purports to prove, using much simpler arguments, that with the solutions presently at hand – annual rescheduling of current principal and interest obligations – any projections relying on the present debt service profile, however rearranged over time, are not viable. Viability here is defined as a solution that can stand being applied year after year for a relatively long period. Thus a minimum growth rate for the economy is subsumed in the analysis.

The problem, it is shown, lies more in the arithmetic of the projection of the debt service ratio for Egypt than with any inherent characteristics of the Egyptian economy. First, postulate that, given its existing macroeconomic structure, its population growth rate and its investments needs, the Egyptian economy cannot spare in the medium term more that some 20 per cent of its current account receipts for servicing existing, as of June 1988,[9] external debt. The proportion chosen is, almost, completely arbitrary and some may argue that the Egyptian economy can generate a greater 'surplus' with a better use of its resources. This is irrelevant and, as will appear below, misses the point.

Second, we will project total current account receipts at their maximal, bordering on the absurd, growth rates. More specifically, the structure of Egypt's current sources of foreign exchange shows a large relative share of low-growth or declining revenue sources, and a very small relative share of high-growth, high-potential sources of foreign exchange revenues. Thus between two-fifths and two-thirds of commodity exports are concentrated in crude oil and its products. Admittedly, both volume and price projections over the medium term for the commodity do not suggest very high rates of growth, if any at all. Workers' remittances, and the Suez Canal, while likely to maintain positive growth rates, cannot be expected to show growth rates greater than a few percentage points per year. We are left with the two remaining potentially dynamic elements in the current account: tourism and manufactured exports. Both these sources of foreign exchange can show high growth rates but their relative share in total foreign exchange receipts is, at present, small. A number of years of uninterrupted growth will need to pass before these two elements can lead the structure of exports of goods and services.

Despite this structure of foreign exchange revenues and its inherently low potential growth rate, we have assumed a maximal overall growth rate of some 10 per cent for all foreign exchange receipts. Thus, as projected, the foreign exchange receipts present the outer limit of expected receipts to the Egyptian economy. The proportion of these resources allocated for debt service payments is shown as curve A in Figure 13.1 below.

We will furthermore assume, unrealistically again, that the financing gap in the balance of payments over the coming medium term will be financed with non-debt-generating capital flows. In other words, the financing gaps of the coming years do not in the present projection generate any additional service burden in the balance of payments.

Finally, the present payments difficulties are reflected in the projection in the form of three consecutive reschedulings: a first rescheduling for the obligations of the second half of 1986/7 and those of 1987/8. A second rescheduling for the obligations of 1988/9 and a third for the obligations of 1989/90. The last year where debt service obligations exceed the foreign exchange available for debt service payments, 1990/1, is ignored. It is worth noting here that rescheduling, along the present terms offered by the Paris Club, has a snow-plough effect characteristic of solutions geared towards resolving short term cash flow problems. First, a rescheduling will postpone rescheduled obligations into a hump in the future (the years 91/2–96/7 in the graph), second it will increase the overall debt as interest obligations are capitalized through the rescheduling process, finally while the debt service burden is reduced during the consolidation period,[10] it is increased in subsequent years as moratorium interest is due on rescheduled amounts until their new maturities. Thus the original debt service profile (curve C in Figure 13.1) is restructured into curve B, which illustrates these features, the characteristic hump, the declining savings from rescheduling as their number increases and the increase in the overall debt service burden over the medium term.

The conclusion of this section is illustrated in Figure 13.1. Take the amended debt service profile (curve B): despite three reschedulings and despite the absence of any additional debt service due to new borrowing and despite unrealistically high growth rates in foreign exchange receipts, debt service payments remain above the payments capacity of the economy as defined by curve A.

At the confines of realism, Figure 13.1 illustrates the non-viability of the present debt service profile when compared to the present structure of foreign exchange receipts of the Egyptian economy. More strikingly, abstracting from the external debt payments profile of curve B, the country underlying the projections is for all intents and purposes a 'viable' country, enjoying adequate rates of growth, a healthy growth rate in exports of goods and services and domestic policies that

Figure 13.1 Debt service profiles, 1987–99

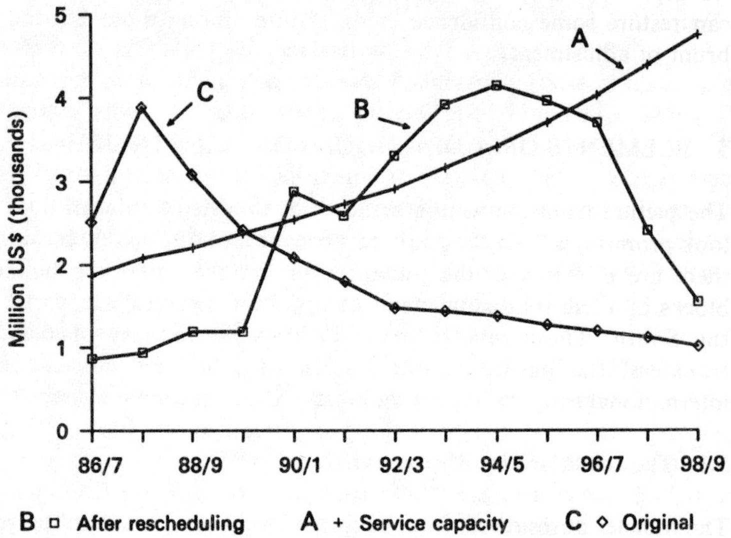

manage to attract some US$ 1–2 billion of foreign investment a year. Yet the arithmetic of the debt service profile of curve B affirms a non-viable system. Thus the problem lies in the magnitude of external debt rather than in the structure of the economy. A healthy Egyptian economy with the present debt structure would not be able to remain so without continued exceptional assistance for a period of indefinite length. Nothing short of outright debt forgiveness can restore viability to economies such as Egypt's.

This problem of 'systemic non-viability' is not particular to Egypt alone. It is representative of the majority of debt-distressed countries. It is very likely that the same exercise, with the same results, can be performed for Poland.

In the case of Egypt, the remedies offered to date have consisted in austerity programmes coupled with rescheduling exercises under the auspices of the Paris Club.[11] With negative growth rates in real GDP, prevailing since 1986, an average annual decline in real wages of some 8 per cent, high inflation and weak redistributive mechanisms for national income, greater austerity, or even continued austerity, is not viable in the medium term. In the absence of an explicit social compact, continued austerity cannot be made viable politically and socially unless it is seen to lead in the medium term to the resolution of the balance of payments constraint of the economy – unless, in other words, it is accompanied by some form of permanent debt relief that can restore some confidence in the future among those bearing the brunt of adjustment.

5 ELEMENTS OF A DIALOGUE FOR THE FUTURE

The picture from the southern shores of the Mediterranean does not look promising: from the heart of Africa it looks positively bleak. Yet there are elements in the present situation that offer the building-blocks of a fruitful dialogue and co-operation between the North and the South. These revolve around the conditionality of resource transfers, the nature of debt relief and the new modalities of international support, to mention just a few of the more salient issues.

5.1 The conditionality of resource transfers

The transfer of resources from developed to developing countries must be performed in an organized and orderly fashion. It is inevitable that, under such a scheme of transfer, there appears the need for the orderly monitoring of progress, and for the establishment of coherent frameworks for macroeconomic management in the recipient economies. Such requirements will necessitate that a set of performance criteria, monitoring benchmarks and indicators be established; more specifically, that there be a framework of mutual conditionality between creditors and debtors. There can be no disagreement on such principles. It is also recognized that the Bretton Woods institutions of today could, with proper guidance, play a central role in this respect.

Nevertheless,

> the principal responsibility for designing and implementing structural adjustment programs must remain with the national authorities of debtor countries. These countries must be satisfied that these programs represent the appropriate course of action for ensuring the sustained growth of their economies and command the political and social support necessary for the adjustment process.[12]

The present structure of conditionality, with its monitoring and performance criteria, by the two Bretton Woods institutions, is not geared to *short-term monitoring* of economic growth, its sources and problems, issues of employment generation, social equity and income distribution. These issues become important when medium-term strategies of reform consist, as is the case at present, of a series of short-term stabilization plans. Instead, the present conditionality framework, at least where the IMF is concerned, will track very accurately any excesses in demand, with little room for monitoring shortfalls in supply, declines in employment or any deterioration in the standards of living of the poor.

What has come to be known as 'adjustment fatigue' among developing countries stems in part from a crisis of confidence, on the part of these countries, in the effectiveness of internationally sponsored stabilization programmes. They have serious misgivings about the ability of these programmes to provide the needed structural changes in their economies, in a politically and socially stable environment.

A reformulation of the monitoring criteria to be geared towards tracking economic expansion, employment generation, and real income distribution in the short run, in addition to spending contraction, would restore, over time, some confidence in the measures advocated when concerted international assistance is provided. Establishing criteria for the short-term monitoring of such variables will alter the policies advocated in a way that will better serve economic development in the third world, while preserving a greater degree of social and political stability during transitional periods of adjustment.

Such a new basis for conditionality, to be effective, will have to be developed jointly between debtors and creditors within an appropriate multilateral framework. It should lead to tangible changes in the way stabilization programmes are formulated, implemented and monitored. This task should be initiated at the earliest opportunity as it will affect the programmes supported by the international community, and therefore the extent to which debtor countries will be able to benefit from the present framework for the resolution of the third-world debt problem.

The two Bretton Woods institutions have not remained insensitive to the mixed results of their prescriptions. The Fund began, a number of years ago, to be concerned about the short-term effects of its conditionality on economic growth, employment and broader social issues. The concern has surfaced in a few recent arrangements with African and Latin American countries. The Bank is also introducing a social dimension to its structural adjustment programmes. These measures, while important, do not address fully such problems nor will they resolve them. The issue at hand is the absence of significant constituencies supporting the reforms advocated by the two institutions. This is compounded by the often near-impossibility of a strong social compact between governing and governed that will bridge the short-term austerity inherent in these reforms.

What is needed is a multilateral framework, where both developed and developing nations can rework the conditionality attached to multilateral assistance. Both sides should co-operate in a redrafting of the conceptual framework that is, and should be, at the base of multilateral support of stabilization and structural reform. Conditionality should be geared towards addressing in quantifiable, monitorable fashion issues such as short-term growth, employment generation, income distribution and other such issues that will create a domestic constituency for reform.

5.2 Debt relief and the nature of international financial assistance

A second area of debate should revolve around the type of external assistance provided to countries implementing structural adjustment programmes. Like Egypt, such countries can benefit from their structural adjustments only if debt relief that will eliminate the debt overhang burdening them is forthcoming. Admittedly, issues of implementation, continued leverage and moral hazard will need to be addressed – no mean task, but one that is urgent.

5.3 New modalities of international support

A third area of debate should centre upon the mode of intervention of multilateral institutions in the third world. The financial problems of world economy in the late twentieth century can no longer be resolved along nationalistic lines. The time has come for regional coalitions for the resolution of problems such as the debt crisis, under-development, free trade and so on. Developing countries, however, lack the means, the co-ordination and the necessary complementarity to initiate such regional coalitions for development, for the resolution of their debt problems or for their structural reforms. Domestic problems pose too great a burden on them to leave much time or energy to address issues in a regional context. It befalls multilateral institutions to pave the way, among developing countries, for regional integration and the regional resolution of national problems. The present framework of relations between developing countries and institutions such as the Bank and the Fund encourage micronationalism, a framework that will doom countries in the African continent, for example. Financial resources should be geared explicitly towards regional programmes of reform, regional projects, regional integration and programmes of regional stabilization.

At first blush the term 'regional' may convey the impression of a large and unwieldy number of countries engaged in complicated multilateral negotiations. 'Regional' should be understood to start with as little as two countries with obvious economic affinities such as Egypt and Sudan, Brazil and Argentina, BCEAO[13] countries and so on.

6 A POSTSCRIPT: THE GULF CRISIS

The Gulf crisis, with all its suffering, turmoil and instability, appears to have been the catalyst, on the economic front, that could precipitate the formulation of novel means of dealing with third-world economic distress. The United States has forgiven Egypt's military debts to it, Arab countries have also forgiven bilateral debt owed to them. The remainder of the international community has pledged in an unusual meeting of the Paris Club (November 1990) to consider medium-term viability of the balance of payments when discussing debt relief for Egypt. Novel tools will be devised to address the issue of permanent debt relief. Despite strenuous affirmations that such unusual means and attitudes are based principally on political considerations, the principle has been established, the precedent if implemented has been set and the post-crisis consciousness will most likely crystallize such steps into an acceptable, repeatable format. Poland's name, in conjunction with Egypt's, has been heard in some corridors of the French Ministry of Finance.

NOTES

1. The views expressed in this paper are the author's; they do not commit any of the institutions to which the author may be affiliated.
2. The Gulf crisis occurred after the bulk of this paper was written. It is addressed briefly below.
3. See Lipton and Sachs (1990a, 1990b) and Balcerowicz (1989).
4. International Monetary Fund (1989).

5. International Monetary Fund (1989).
6. Taken from Boutros-Ghali (1989).
7. See various country reports by the International Monetary Fund and the World Bank and more recently Kheir-el-Din (1989).
8. Concerted lending is typically forced lending and consists in new money provided by commercial banks at the insistence (coercion) of international organizations such as the International Monetary Fund and the World Bank.
9. This date was chosen because it follows immediately the end of the consolidation period of the first, and only, rescheduling that Egypt has undertaken. it is worth mentioning that the forgiveness of US military debt and the forgiveness of all official Arab government debts, effected in the third quarter of 1990 and amounting to a combined relief of some 13 billion US dollars, do not alter the results of the analysis presented.
10. Defined as the period during which all rescheduled obligations fall due and are therefore not paid. See Boutros-Ghali (1987).
11. All indications are that this is expected to change, given the drastic changes in the balance of international relations engendered by the Gulf crisis. Until the application of a new approach, however, we can only assume that existing solutions will continue to be applied.
12. International Monetary Fund (1989).
13. Banque Centrale des Etats d'Afrique Occidentale, the French Franc zone of West Africa.

REFERENCES

BALCEROWICZ, L.(1989) 'Polish Economic Reform 1981–1988, an Overview', *Economic Studies*, no. 1, Economic Commission for Europe, ADECO.

BOUTROS-GHALI, Y. (1987) 'The Paris Club: Principles and Practice', unpublished manuscript, Cairo University.

BOUTROS-GHALI, Y. (1989) 'Egypt's External Debt Problems: Elements of a Solution', *Working Papers in Economics*, Center for Economic and Financial Research and Studies, Faculty of Economic and Political Science, Cairo University.

INTERNATIONAL MONETARY FUND (1989) *World Economic Outlook*, October, Washington, DC.

KHEIR-EL-DIN, H. (1988) 'Towards Managing Egypt's External Debt', *Working Papers in Economics*, Center for Economic and Financial Research and Studies, Cairo University, September.

LIPTON, D. and J. SACHS (1990a) 'Creating a Market Economy in Eastern Europe, the Case of Poland', draft paper for presentation at the Brookings Panel on Economic Activity, 5–6 April.

LIPTON, D. and J. SACHS (1990b) 'Poland's Economic Reform', *Foreign Affairs*.

14 International Debt and the New World Order

Giovanni Goria

1 INTRODUCTION

The proposition that international debt is the most serious problem now posed for world economic policy is both unsound and double-edged. Unsound, because the real problem is the creation of a new economic world order, above all to provide a suitable solid base for growth in the countries which are now worse off; double-edged because a cure administered by means of an all-out, over-rigorous enforcement of the rules of the market would not afford (if it did not actually undermine) any prospect for overall development in the debtor countries.

What is needed instead (today more urgently than ever) is to come directly to grips with the problem of growth in developing countries and, within this framework, to find fair and realistic solutions, not least to the international debt problem. Accordingly, the problem has to be posed in far more general terms. The twentieth century has seen, at times, the fierce clash of two divergent political and economic systems: the present system in the free industrialized nations, politically democratic and pluralist and economically market-oriented; and the one which has held sway in the Communist countries, politically authoritarian and centralist, and economically based on state planning.

Even on the admission of the relevant powers that be, the second system has totally failed to achieve its goals and is now in the process of being rejected, or at the very least being reformed from top to bottom, in particular in the countries which have experienced it. Moreover, in this day and age, there is no conceivable 'third way'.

The situation which has been brought about does not entitle the 'winning' system to indulge in any form of triumphalism, but rather places it before an even greater responsibility. Since the democratic, pluralist, market-economy system is the only real alternative, it must draw on its own resources in order to overcome the intolerable inequalities and injustices still lurking within it. Above all, they must not be thought endemic to the system: this would dash the hope of a freer and more just world which has inspired, and is still inspiring, millions of men and women in their search for truth and a life of charity.

If conquering inequalities and injustices in each and every country is the prime task of national politicians, conquering the inequalities and injustices still evident between poor and rich countries is a matter for all nations together, even if the greater responsibility falls to the latter category as they have more resources and greater capacity.

It is up to the free western societies to promote a new world economic order in which every people may, with dignity, assume its place in contributing to the prosperity of all, while guaranteeing its own prosperity.

2 TRADE LIBERALIZATION

A new world order is now possible (as well as necessary and urgent), and the key lies in the liberalization of international trade, in particular trade from developing countries towards the industrialized ones. The conclusion that trade liberalization is the key to building a more effective, and more just world order is underpinned by a combination of theoretical considerations and practical analysis. As far as theory is concerned, it is correct to say that free trade is the means of enabling each citizen of the world to seek out what he needs, and of ensuring it is of the highest possible quality and obtainable at the lowest possible price. If the free movement of goods and services is shackled, only those who produce them and provide them can have the best: the rest must make do with, and pay for, second-best.

As far as analysis is concerned, it is accurate to put huge figures on the flow of resources which could be channelled to the developing countries if the industrialized nations were only persuaded to forgo protectionist barriers. To measure the size of this phenomenon, it is useful to consider the data provided in 1985 by the World Bank; the products of the developing countries subjected to obstacles other than tariffs for imports into the industrialized nations, and considered as a share of all non-energy imports of the industrialized countries, resulted as follows: EEC 21.8 per cent, Japan 10.5 per cent, the United States 12.9 per cent. The same 'protectionist' shares for imports from other industrialized nations were 10.5 per cent, 9.5 per cent and 3.4 per cent, respectively. This means that the protectionism of the industrialized countries is stronger towards poor nations than the other rich ones.

A significant example of the meaning of the liberalization in the international trade, where the growth of the developing countries is concerned, is that of Puerto Rico. An important factor in the case of Puerto Rico is the fact that the products of this island can be sold in the United States without tariffs; this, together with an abundance of labour and cheap but high productivity, was the reason for Puerto Rico's expansion.

To continue this analysis, one might refer to the statements of the EEC Executive Commission:

> A system of free multilateral trade without protectionism is essential for sustainable development. In spite of generalized and regional regimes of preferential tariffs, the industrialized countries keep tariffs for exports, which are very important for developing countries, particularly for agricultural products, textiles, shoes and assembled products. (SEC (90) 228, 12 February 1990)

> Only with the guarantee of the sure and effective access to the market of the industrialized countries and of the developing ones, would it be definitively possible to give a determinant boost to make those economies free, modern, varied and able to integrate themselves in the world economy.' (SEC (89) 1086, 7 July 1989)

> The industrialized countries should contain and eliminate protectionist measures which are quite expensive and act as a brake on the necessary insertion of the developing countries in the world economy. (Document of the EC services examined by Council on 20 December 1989)

> In what concerns agriculture, the amount of support to production in many industrialized countries is such as to act as a brake upon effective and fair redistribution of this sector in the world and particularly in the countries with intermediate revenue and full of natural resources. (Document of EC services, as above).

What must be absolutely clear from the outset is that liberalization cannot apply to 'some' markets only. At least as far as the industrialized nations are concerned, it must apply to them all in the same way and at the same time. This implies not only a strong need for improved international consultations, but also the possibility for individual governments to 'cover themselves' with multilateral decisions, thereby placing themselves in a better position to withstand the inevitable opposing pressures that face each individual country.

Some points must be stressed:

(a) Liberalization of trade would be of substantial benefit to the people of the rich countries who would spend much less on their consumption, for instance of agricultural produce, if they were to buy it from developing countries.[1]

(b) For the developing countries, the benefits would, in relative terms, be even greater because, once assured of a return on the produce they sell, they would see phenomenal growth in their income.

(c) The developing countries would use the new resources primarily to obtain industrial manufactures and services supplied by countries which could provide them under the best conditions, and this would keep up the buoyancy of economic activity in the industrialized nations while preserving international economic stability.

(d) Higher growth rates in developing countries would produce a knock-on effect for the industrialized economies, thus leading to a higher degree of development than would have existed had there been no liberalization of trade.

(e) Because of their faster growth rates, the developing countries would be able to shoulder the burden of such international debt as might result from any measures taken in the international financial sphere.

The debt problem consequently arises once again, but this time placed within an overall vision of a better world economic order in which every person is truly in a position – just as he wished to be – to take advantage of the opportunities which present themselves, contributing with dignity to the prosperity of all.

A further effect is to overcome the absurd opposition between the development of the rich countries and that of the poor countries. For too long it has been mistakenly supposed by a lot of people that, to satisfy the needs of the developing countries, it was necessary to slow down or freeze growth in the rich countries. This premise is unambiguously false: only if there is vigorous growth in the rich countries do the growth prospects of developing countries become credible. To give a brief idea of the order of magnitude involved, it is perhaps useful to recall that the Baker Plan,[2] and others that followed it, were based among other things on 5 per cent annual growth in the indebted countries, a figure presumed to be possibly subject to 'at least' 3 per cent growth in the rich countries and annual expansion of 'at least' 5 per cent in the volume of world trade.

Before probing more deeply into the subject of international debt in its proper context, it is necessary to return to the question of liberalization of the market in order to understand it fully, not least in relation to the objective difficulties posed. Of these difficulties, the most fundamental is finding other sectors in which to redeploy the people who have been employed in producing goods for export to the developing countries.

This applies first and foremost to a considerable number of agricultural workers, although the problem is also likely to arise in the case of steel, certain branches of the textile industry and of leather goods, ship-building and many other smaller sectors. Opposition to this is not only understandable but legitimate as well.

However, as far as the specific case of agriculture is concerned, one factor to be borne in mind is the age structure and the resulting likelihood of a high degree of 'natural wastage' in the labour force: the other sectors stand to benefit from the substantial boost (see above) which the new world economic order is likely to give to all economies, including those of the industrialized nations. If the developing countries are to find new markets, there will have to be a new investment drive in order to strengthen their production structures, thereby setting in motion a genuine development 'multiplier'. For the industrialized nations a one per cent rise in economic growth, brought about by expanding international trade, means approximately one million new jobs a year, over and above those which would be created in the absence of the booster effect. The management of the process of trade liberalization entails bold and far-sighted political choices, and it is precisely these that are most needed today.

3 INTERNATIONAL CO-OPERATION AND THE CUTTING OF MILITARY EXPENDITURES

A better world economic order would also stand to gain very considerably if the rich countries were to step up their policies of international co-operation with the developing countries. It is useful to remember that many developing countries do not produce enough foodstuffs, not only because the relative prices discourage farmers, but also largely because of great structural problems.

If it is to develop in a desirable manner, the overall situation accordingly demands a very substantial increase in the resources available for international co-operation. At the present time, however, an increase on that scale is impossible unless (and this is another goal with immensely far-reaching implications) further steps are taken down the road to detente and to disarmament. In this way, vast resources, which could be used for international co-operation, could be recouped on at least two fronts: military spending and cuts in nuclear arsenals.

Military spending is 'public spending' in a narrow sense: the possibility of redirecting it towards other goals is desirable and feasible, and the amounts involved could be truly astonishing. To think in a more concrete way about this question, someone who can be considered an expert for his intelligence, knowledge and freedom of judgement about this matter, Robert McNamara, believes it possible for the United States, in the period 1991–5, to reduce military expenses by $400 billion. In similar terms in Europe, in the Soviet bloc and in the developing countries (which on their own spend each year more than $200 billion), the total reduction, and consequently the quantity of resources which in the following five years could be used for the expansion of the poorest regions in the world, would be more than $1300 billion, of which about $650 billion would come from rich western countries. To assess these figures more effectively, it should be remembered that rich western countries would have assigned (without any new policies) to the expansion of developing countries in the next five years no more than $250 billion. Thus the total amount available for international co-operation could be more than tripled.

With regard to the use of these resources, it is useful to remember that in contrast to a per capita wealth of about $14 000 a year in the European Community (about $20 000 in the USA), China, India, Sub-Sahara Africa and Southern Asia show figures of a little more than $350 and that today more than a billion people live in total poverty – 20 per cent of the world's population.

In practice, cuts in nuclear arsenals can be brought about only by 'burning out' the war-heads in power-stations or converting agents of warfare into fuel for civil uses. There is no reason why the monetary proceeds of such conversion should not – and every reason why they should – be used to aid the less wealthy countries, thus fulfilling the prophesy which has it that 'armouries shall be emptied and barns filled' and, what is more, to increase the resources available for international co-operation.

To think about the scientific truth of this hypothesis it is useful to consider the initiative taken in November 1989 by Professor Eduard Ameldy (Scientists and Technologists for the Ethics of Development).[3] There is also a political truth in this hypothesis. A reference to this can be found in the Treaty of Nuclear Non-proliferation of 1970, which among other things stated the principle that advantages of peaceful use of nuclear technology, including any by-products that the countries with military nuclear power could obtain from the development of nuclear explosive devices, should be available for pacific aims on the part of all parties to the treaty, whether or not they had a nuclear capacity.

As for the economic aspects of this proposal, it is useful to remember that the Treaty on Intermediate Nuclear Forces (INF) of 8 November 1987 has demonstrated the possibility of a significant reduction in nuclear weapons of the two super-powers. What is more, the recent American–Soviet summits have stressed the common aim of a greater reduction in nuclear capacity.

It is not easy to assess the quantity of recovered resources, but taking the hypothesis of a progressive dismantling of a few tens of thousands of missile-heads from the 58 000 which exist and so (as is stressed by the *Studi Sociali* review of July–August 1989) making available about 1000 tons of uranium and 200 tons of plutonium, this estimation would permit the following forecast: with this new availability it would be possible to provide maintenance for 30 years of about 50 one-thousand megawatt reactors, saving each time about 300 000 000 tons of coal. The money evaluation is quite difficult, but according to authoritative sources, it could be more than $350 billion.[4]

4 POSSIBLE SOLUTIONS OF THE DEBT CRISIS

As already mentioned, in a better world economic order, international debt could appear in a different light from the present and so be of greater use for balanced use of economies as a whole. For a clearer grasp of the problem, a distinction has to be drawn between two principal categories of international debt: (1) the debt owed by the poorest countries (so poor that they have never been of interest to the big banks) to richer countries; and (2) the debt owed by moderately wealthy countries to the international financial system.

In the case of the first category, what is needed is not to write off the debts, and in this way restrict the opportunities for the countries concerned to draw on new credit – as they will have to do – but rather to re-schedule them over the very long term at basically nominal rates of interest. In view of the 'public' nature of the creditors, the operation will not be feasible unless concerted planning takes place at an international level, avoiding bilateral arrangements which would not resolve the problem as a whole, but merely add to the injustice of the situation.

As far as the second category is concerned, it is essential to bring about a solution involving:

- the debtor countries, which have generally been guilty of squandering the resources obtained on loan and of unlawfully building up vast hard currency reserves outside their territory;
- the international financial community, which has been guilty of acting in an unpardonably irresponsible way;
- the rich countries which have been guilty of failing to act promptly by organizing effective international consultations along at least similar lines to those eventually set in motion when the problem burst onto the scene in terrifying proportions.

There are various formulas for stabilizing the situation and so for rephasing payment dates over a reasonable period, with, as part of that process, charges being brought into line with the actual capacity of the debtor countries to pay back what they owe (which is basically determined by trends on the commodity and agricultural markets).

For instance, the debt could be left to stand at its present amount (a burden for the debtor countries); the financial community would waive a substantial proportion of its returns (a burden for the financial community); and the industrialized nations could compensate the financial community by means of tax measures (a burden for the rich countries).

The above proposals amount to a co-ordinated scheme of measures aimed at:

(1) maintaining the debt by phasing repayment of the principal over a reasonable period;

(2) calculating an approximate interest charge to be paid by the debtor countries, index-linking it to the prices of the commodities and agricultural produce of greatest importance to the same debtor countries;
(3) reducing the return accruing to the creditors by setting it to a fixed level in time;
(4) compensating the creditors through tax channels for a reasonable portion of the charge borne by them, which would be a consequence of return reduction; and
(5) introducing an adjusting mechanism to balance the ratio between a variable charge (payable by the debtor countries) and a fixed return (accruing to the creditors).

Any losses which might be occasioned could be charged to international co-operation, just as any surpluses could be released for measures to aid the weakest countries.

The trickiest part of the theory set out above appears to be point (2). However, it should be borne in mind that the proposal is in no way new. As Paolo Baffi, late Governor of the Bank of Italy, observed some years ago, Lindbeck proposed that the existing debt should be converted into a consolidated debt which, as far as interest payments were concerned, would be held over to run concurrently with new loans and would yield a lower interest rate than market rates or be index-linked to the export prices achieved by the debtor countries.[5] A somewhat similar proposal was put forward in 1977 by Carli and Tarantelli when they suggested that public authorities should provide the necessary funding by taking up securities that were index-linked to the growth rate in developing countries.

As for point (3), it must not be forgotten that the banks have been gradually showing a more pronounced willingness to reduce the returns on their credit: in Mexico's case the creditor banks recently agreed to make a substantial cut (about a third) in the interest rate payable on approximately half of the credit, and, with regard to a further 40 per cent, opted to reduce the nominal value of the debt by 35 per cent, equivalent to an even bigger interest-rate cut. However, breaking the link between a substantial proportion of international debt and current interest rates would also have another consequence, this time of particular benefit to the industrialized nations: it would 'free' the monetary policies of those countries (and in particular of the United States) from the weight which inevitably fell on them on account of their indirect impact on the situation in the developing countries and the latters' capacity to pay back their international debt. The value of this new 'freedom' is admittedly impossible to measure, but it is correct to suppose it to be truly significant.

There are of course some difficulties in realizing such a hypothesis and it is no use ignoring them. The idea of some sort of huge 'clearing house' between the fixed interest rate promised to creditors and a changeable one due to debtors could give rise to a possible burden. This is not easily quantified and can rightly cause negative reactions. The analysis of each single case has been partially left aside and this inhibits a real 'philosophy'. Banks need 'fiscal incentives', and for this several national 'systems' would have to be changed, probably causing a protest by national parliaments. But these difficulties should at the same time offer a new concrete solution. No 'formula' used to tackle international debt and no new and better world economic order will propose a solution for developing countries if all this does not go together with financial and economic restructuring. The internal policies of the developing countries should thus be totally changed.

Beyond the technical/political solutions, however, there remains the fundamental truth that the problem of international debt, viewed in isolation, appears difficult if not impossible to solve; viewed in the context of a better world economic order it takes on profoundly different and, to some extent, less fearful connotations.

NOTES

1. The amount of savings is difficult to quantify but, in case of a definitive liberalization of the market, it should be an substantial amount.
2. International debt management plan proposed some years ago by James Baker, at that time US Secretary of the Treasury.
3. See Proceedings of the Study Seminar, 'Nuclear disarmament, Energy for an industrial strategy, Development of the world', Roma, Libera Università Internazionale degli Studi Sociali, 29 November 1989.
4. See Study Seminar: report by Professor Mario Silvestri.
5. See Paolo Baffi, 'L'indebitamento esterno dei Paesi in Via di Sviluppo, situazione e prospettive', Roma, Palazzo Giustiniani, 26 February 1986.

15 International Democracy and Economic Development

Guido Montani

1 THE WORLD ECONOMY AFTER THE COLD WAR: WHICH DEVELOPMENT MODEL?

The international political equilibriums arising from the Second World War have imparted, for better or worse, a specific path of development to the economic forces of the two opposing camps. In the West, in the vast area from the Atlantic to the Pacific brought together under the leadership of the United States, the principle of economic liberalism has prevailed. In the East, the principle of a centrally planned economy asserted itself, which, as far as international trade is concerned, was translated into the socialist division of labour organized under careful Soviet oversight. The third world – in the specific sense of non-industrialized world – has been kept at the margins of this process. The logic of the Cold War has excluded any third party not able to put across its arguments by means of adequate power. During this historic phase the world economy has therefore developed along bloc lines: even though the integration of the world market continued to move forward, as is particularly apparent in the financial and productive sectors (with the multinational companies), the tendency of the super-powers has been to favour trade and growth within each area of influence. The world economy as a whole has thus developed without interruption, but with strong differences in the three worlds. While there has been strong growth in the Atlantic and Pacific areas, the area of real socialism has not been able to keep up with the economic–social progress made by the western system. At the same time a veritable abyss has opened up between the industrialized world and the poor countries of the South.

With perestroika in the USSR and the beginning of detente between the super-powers an entirely new phase has begun in international politics. The Cold War has ended. Everyone agrees that we have entered into the after-Yalta age. Yet the great changes in history rarely occur without new contradictions arising and possible regressive phases taking place. In fact few commentators will risk making predictions regarding the main features which might characterize the world's politics and economy during the coming historical cycle. There are certainly good reasons for this extreme caution. The USSR must face three formidable challenges – the democratization of its political system; the transition from a planned to a market economy, and the transformation of the union into a true federation – and there has as yet been no sign of consistent success along any of these three fronts. If at the international level the gradual retreat of the USSR from its role as a super-power has, on the one hand, allowed a substantial reduction of armaments in Europe and the democratization of Eastern Europe, on the other it has left the United States with enormous room for manoeuvring as a military super-power, which could, if unwisely exploited, exacerbate relations with the South. In fact the situation looms whereby a United States world supremacy – a unipolar political system – might replace the traditional bipolarism of the Cold War, not so much because of a greater economic–political power for the United States but because of a relative retreat by its antagonists.

Nevertheless, the above gives a simplified picture of things, since it ignores the emergence of new political actors on the international scene. Japan and the European Community, for example, by now represent two redoubtable competitors of the US economy, even if their military potential is obviously not comparable to that of a super-power. Some commentators, such as H. Kissinger or the historian P. Kennedy,[1] speak in fact of the emergence of a multipolar world in the economic field, which will coexist with a bipolar military balance in decline. The important leading poles of the 'pentarchy' of the new multipolar world would be the United States, the USSR, China, Japan and the European Community. The two super-powers, however, would still maintain for a long time to come a nuclear deterrent monopoly that is clearly superior to that of all other nations of the world, which could provide them with certain strategic advantages, even if nuclear arms cannot easily be used in regional conflicts. In particular, the United States would have to manage a long phase of relative decline, as occurred with Great Britain at the beginning of the century, though this would still be a 'relative' decline, since its productive, technological and military potential would, if well administered, allow it to maintain its pre-eminent role.

This viewpoint, put forward by the theorists of political realism, is certainly that which best describes the contemporary world, and it must be admitted that very probably we will have to deal with this type of international equilibrium for many years, if not decades. But it is also true that, at the same time that perestroika asserted itself and the first disarmament negotiations were successfully concluded, the image of a 'new era in world politics' appeared on the international scene, which the extraordinary events of 1989 almost made tangible. Perhaps this does not signify a chimera or a utopia, but a new way of facing the increasingly more complex and dramatic questions of international politics. Everyone recognizes that interdependence extends to the most fundamental aspects of human coexistence. The economy is a world-wide one; the ecologic system is world-wide; the information and scientific systems are world-wide; and, of course, the political system is world-wide. In short, the survival of mankind itself by now depends on its ability to act like a community of destiny, in which no shred of humanity must be excluded from the search for solutions to common problems. However, a political community, in the modern age, can arise and develop only on the basis of democratic principles. The intuition contained in the idea of a 'new era' in world politics consists therefore in the adoption of the democratic method not only for resolving political disputes within nations, but also between nations. This is not a miracle-like method. It is only a method that in principle proposes to exclude violence from politics. It is thus a choice in favour of political pluralism in domestic politics and of peaceful co-operation in international disputes, since in a world of sovereign states the alternative to peaceful co-operation can only be to turn, as a last resort, to the barbarous and inhuman instrument of war.

This political project, which we might call 'democratic pacifism', and which corresponds in outline to the 'new thought' put forward by Gorbachev as the basis of his international perestroika, also includes, even though an explicit debate in this regard has not yet been opened, the kernel of a new growth model for the world economy. If it is true that ours is an age of growing interdependence, it then becomes absurd to continue to base economic relations on protectionism, monetary nationalism, and on the arms race. The new model of growth must be based, on the contrary, on disarmament, international economic integration, and on solidarity towards the poorest peoples. And we must also recognize that the Soviet Union has to a large extent already moved in this direction. The Soviet government has in fact interrupted the arms race with the United States and has urged the completion of the disarmament process in Europe that began with the Helsinki Accords in 1975. In addition, the USSR has often declared its intention to become part of the main international institutions for economic co-operation, such as the GATT and the IMF.

We should observe at this point that the new model of 'democratic pacifism' in international relations is opposed in principle to the old model adopted by the cultural tradition of political realism, which we can for brevity's sake call the 'balance of power', since it posits that the world should be governed during the coming political cycle by a multipolar system, eventually including within itself a bipolar subsystem in the military area. The juxtaposition of these two ideas regarding international relations is justified by the fact that, while the model of political realism does not at all exclude recourse to war as a way of solving international controversies, and thus also justifies a growth model in which interdependence – when national self-sufficiency is not possible – is directed to the maximization of one's own power, thereby excluding policies aimed at solidarity with regard to the development of the poorest peoples, the democratic pacifism model encourages economic integration, is in favour of solidarity toward development, and thus to equality among peoples, and rejects war in principle as a means for the resolution of international controversies.

We should now look at the potential, as well as the limits, of the new prospects regarding international politics and economic development. But before doing so we should dwell upon the significance of the end of the Cold War, because the post-war period, characterized by the bipolar equilibrium between the USSR and the United States, also represented an era in which two important models of international relations and development were put to the test: the liberal model of the West and the socialist model of the East. Many today admit that the socialist model has failed, while there is not the same agreement on the fact that the liberal model as well risks the same fate. And yet, as far as the realization of the objectives of international co-operation is concerned, the liberal model is not that far from failing. For this reason it can be useful to discuss at length the way in which the international economic system was organized during the Cold War era and the reasons that have led the bipolar world to its slow, though irreversible, decline.

2 THE CRISIS OF INTERNATIONAL SOCIALISM

With the beginning of perestroika and the fall of the East European communist regimes, the statement that the system of centralized planning has failed was received as an undisputed truth. Nevertheless, there still remains the problem of knowing whether this failure involves socialist thought as a whole. In fact, while Gorbachev and the Soviet leaders that support perestroika are willing to admit that the system of centralized planning can no longer meet the development needs of the Soviet economy and that the market must be given ample room, they are not at all willing to admit that the socialist system has failed and has no future prospects. Perestroika means simply that a certain historical experience regarding the carrying out of socialism has failed. Other ways may be tried, as for example joining socialism with the market.

There is nevertheless a second direction in which the critical scope of perestroika must be extended: that is, the attempt at organizing an international socialist economy. It is easy today to observe that the Comecon experiment – that is, the socialist common market – is on the way out. But this is not enough. We must take note of the reasons that led to its creation and of its intrinsic limits that appeared right from the start, since these appear as errors deeply rooted in the idea of international socialism, and which are still largely present in the current debate on the construction of the new international economic order. The famous Brandt Report, for example, which attempts to formulate a vast range of 'recommendations' to the rich countries for helping the poor countries to develop, proposes carrying out international solidarity without ever questioning the existing 'world balance of power', thus without ever trying to change the 'governing' structures of the world economy. As a result, despite the fact that a unanimous chorus sang the praises of the plan for its strong humanitarian values, we must recognize that after many years it has not succeeded in eliminating or reducing the income gap between rich and poor countries.

To get to the root of the problem it would perhaps be useful to re-examine the circumstances that led to the more advanced attempt at planning the international economy and to its failure. The Comecon was founded by Stalin in 1949, after the Second World War, as a response to the Marshall Plan by the United States, which had even attracted the attention of several East European countries. But in order to understand its structure and limits we must briefly mention the position occupied by the USSR in international politics during that historical period.

The Bolshevik Revolution enabled Lenin's party to overthrow the old autocratic regime, but, as is well known, there was no precise development plan for the Soviet economy and for the realization of communism. In fact the years immediately preceding and following the death of Lenin represented a period of intense and lively debate regarding the prospects for industrialization. For the first time in the history of mankind the problem of a rational plan for gradually improving the standard of living of an entire population was confronted, with the country moving from a mainly agricultural economy to a modern industrial one. Until then men had endured the blind forces of the market. The moment had arrived to bring these under the control of the plan, in which the collective will can reveal itself and prevail over the economic system, with all its determinations which individuals have no choice but to bear passively. This represented a grandiose challenge to which all the new intellectual energies involved in the revolutionary effort sought to provide an answer. Even today we must view that debate as a fundamental stage in the history of economic thought, since from its outcome a great project of accelerated development by means of the five-year plans emerged. And in fact the 'Soviet model of industrialization' has inspired similar development plans in many other countries, in particular in the third world, once colonial domination had ended.

In presenting the terms of that debate, its international aspects are often omitted. Yet its outcome depended not only on domestic development needs but, in a much more important way, on the European and world situation in which the first experiment in collectivist planning was carried out. Lenin viewed the Bolshevik Revolution as the first episode of a world revolution, which would be quick in coming, thanks in part to the efforts Lenin himself immediately made, by founding the Third International, to 'export' the revolution. However, when the choices regarding the development prospects for the Soviet economy had to be decided on, the idea of extending the revolution to Europe was already fading away. Only Trotsky held firm to the prospect of a world revolution, even after his exile. Bukharin, his main adversary, had instead adopted a much more pragmatic vision of international relations and of the role of the USSR. According to Bukharin, development had to be carried out at 'a snail's pace', relying above all on the strength of agriculture in the Soviet economy and on the taxation of agricultural profits to facilitate accumulation in the industrial sector. The exportation of primary products would then have allowed for the importation of machines and equipment from the more advanced European countries, such as Germany, thereby making the accumulation process easier. Bukharin's plan would thus have had to be accompanied by detente (or 'stabilisation' in Bukharin's terminology) on the international scene, allowing the USSR to count on the possibility of stable and lasting trade with the other industrialized countries. Even the Trotskyist left – whose economic proposals were drawn up by Preobrazhensky – pointed to the possibility of help from the other more developed European countries, though within a different international political context from that assumed by Bukharin. The idea was that sooner or later other revolutionary hotbeds would have arisen outside the USSR. For Preobrazhensky it was necessary to aim for a 'primitive socialist accumulation', by exploiting all the available resources in a rapid development process for heavy industry on a large scale, in order to obtain the advantages of an integrated development project among several sectors. The resources were to be obtained through a squeeze on prices and private agricultural incomes with respect to prices for manufactured goods, whose factories had already become state property. The agricultural surplus was to serve for industrial accumulation. In this way the urban proletariat would have gradually improved its life style while also supplying an outlet for the production of consumer goods, once the critical phase of development of heavy industry had passed, during which everyone would necessarily have to make heavy sacrifices. A development spread out over time, as Bukharin sought, would have favoured the farming class, while an accelerated development would have strengthened the Soviet proletariat and thus the prospects for a world revolution. In this regard, Trotsky continued to think and maintain that without the help of the proletariat of the economically more advanced countries the Soviet industrialization plan would fail, since, in the age of the formation of a world economy, development was no longer possible within the narrow national borders. The outbreak of the First World War had in fact been caused by the extension of capitalism on a world scale and by the need of the bourgeois governments to find international outlets through imperialism. The national state – said Trotsky as early as 1914 – represented 'an unbearable obstacle to the development of the productive forces'.

Nevertheless in 1924, shortly after Lenin's death, the theories of the Bolshevik right and left were subjected to the criticism of a new point of view, that of Stalin's 'construction of socialism in a single country'. At first this position passed almost unnoticed. But in the following years it gained increasingly more consensus, finally becoming the keystone of the success of the initial five-year plans that allowed the

USSR a very rapid industrialization, its victorious participation in the Second World War and, at the end of the conflict, the assumption of new international responsibilities as a world super-power alongside the United States. According to Stalin, Trotsky's position was based on an uncertain premise: that the Soviet revolution would spread to Europe. 'What do we do,' Stalin asked himself, 'if the world revolution is forced to arrive with a delay? Will there still be some ray of hope for our revolution?' Trotsky evidently could not answer these questions without betraying his internationalist vision. In fact, solidarity among the international proletariat was missing because of a scission between communist parties, which supported the Soviet experiment, and social-democratic parties, which instead pointed towards the possibility of gaining power in the context of the existing democratic regimes. The Soviet proletariat, if it wished to continue to hold power, had only one choice: to aim for the autonomous development of the Soviet economy. History showed that several countries – the 'second comers' – which had attempted to catch up the pioneers of industrialization, such as Great Britain, had succeeded in their aim. 'We know,' wrote Stalin at the time, 'that already by the beginning of the 20th century Germany and Japan had made such a strong leap forward that the former managed to overtake France and began to replace England on the world market, while the latter was leaving Russia in her tracks.'[2] The USSR's size with regard to population and resources was such as to allow her to successfully attempt the experiment of the 'creation of socialism in a single country'. However, the fundamental features of this plan could not accommodate the way indicated by Bukharin, that of development at 'a snail's pace'. In fact the international situation did not allow the USSR to point toward the long term and the peaceful co-operation of the other European powers. The Versailles Treaty had left open deep wounds and all signs pointed toward the beginning of a new conflict rather than a situation of detente. For this reason the USSR not only had to 'do it herself' but also had to aim for an accelerated development, in order to eliminate as soon as possible the gap that still existed with the other great political and economic powers on the continent. Stalin therefore accepted the economic proposals of the left, though he inserted them within a new political context, that of nationalism. One may certainly debate – as will be done for a long time – whether the determination and ferocity shown by Stalin in carrying out the initial five-year plans were truly necessary. But this is only a question of more or less. There appears to be no doubt, on the other hand, that the way of the 'accelerated' construction of socialism in a single country was the only feasible one for the USSR in that particular international context.

After the victory against Nazism, the USSR was able to assume the role of super-power alongside the United States. Europe, reduced to a battlefield, was subdivided into two large hegemonic areas, separated by an increasingly more impenetrable iron curtain. An important event in these first years of the Cold War was the American proposal for a large aid plan for the reconstruction and development of the European economy. The Marshall Plan was launched in 1947 and the American offer was made both to western European countries and Eastern European ones, even if the conditions laid down for their inclusion would have clearly imposed the abandonment of the communist regime. 'The real aim of the Marshall Plan,' said Stalin at the time, was to 'create a western bloc and to isolate the Soviet Union . . . by means of loans . . . that could not be had without important limitations on the political and economic independence of the recipients.'[3] In fact Czechoslovakia tried to accept the American offer, but was immediately stopped, together with all the other European countries belonging to the Soviet area of influence. As a response to the American attempt to organize European reconstruction *Pravda*, on 29 January 1949, published a plan of economic co-operation among socialist countries. The Comecon thus came into being. This nevertheless, at least until Stalin's death, meant nothing other than an impediment to co-operation with the western economies. No common plan was ever drafted to organize a socialist economy on an international scale. Each European country, no matter how small (Albania, for example) had in fact to undertake the strategy of the construction of socialism in a single country. During the Stalinist years the Comecon represented the absurd summation of national economies closed to reciprocal trade movements, except for the priveleged relations that each of these had to have with its powerful protector.

It was only during the fifties and sixties, as the successes of the Common Market became increasingly more evident, that the attempt was made to achieve an effective 'socialist international division of labour'. This attempt was in part successful, though its limits were clear. This in effect involved co-ordinating the various national plans through intergovernmental agreements. These agreements were bilateral in nature and common instruments of integration were not undertaken. The idea of a convertible ruble never became reality. Unlike the European Community, in which only European countries took part, not their Atlantic ally, the USSR also belonged to the

Comecon, thereby creating a 'fundamental disequilibrium' which the East European countries could only hope to resist through the principle of the defence of national sovereignty. For this reason, even when it was decided to move to more advanced forms of integration with the Complex Programme of 1971, it was clearly affirmed that 'socialist economic integration does not involve the creation of any supranational body'.

For this reason, when the objective of inserting the Soviet economy into the world economy explicitly appeared among the aims of perestroika, it became clear that the Comecon's days were numbered. The system of centralized planning was not able to ensure the same efficiency as the market economies had, not only because it could not carry out any 'economic calculations' in the absence of a market, but also because of the lack of international integration among the planned economies. An effective system of planning for the international economy would naturally require the existence of a supranational body (like Gosplan) with sufficient powers for organizing production in the different national territories. As can easily be seen, this would represent an enormous power, since assigning the various types and shares of production would automatically represent a distribution of wealth in the territory, so that the wealth of every nation would depend on the decisions made by the hypothetical international Gosplan. The resistance put up by the East European countries to the creation of 'supranational institutions' within the framework of Comecon is therefore perfectly understandable. But equally understandable is the impossibility of carrying out, by means of intergovernmental co-operation, an effective socialist international division of labour: if within each state, every region, province and city wished sovereignly to decide on its plan, accepting only to barter on the outside the surplus for all goods that arose with respect to domestic needs, then the result in terms of efficiency would probably be as catastrophic as that achieved by the Comecon. Productive efficiency implies a confrontation between various productive units, that is, competition. The larger the market the greater the efficiency. The method of national planning by nature leads instead to closed productive systems. A productive area is arbitrarily isolated from the rest of the world. The factory becomes very similar to a barracks. It functions only so long as the feelings of duty and loyalty towards the political authorities remain high. But everything comes apart when these sentiments are missing.

The ultimate cause of the failure of international socialism is the lack of democracy. Perestroika brought the democratization of the

Soviet system onto the agenda. This is not only a question of a need for political pluralism and liberty. It is also the precondition for a radical reform of the productive system, since a market is impossible if not accompanied by the liberty (which in economics includes the risk of lost earnings or the hope of extraordinary income) of each individual to choose his own employment. At the international level perestroika, understood in its more radical sense, involves the achievement of international democracy. Economic interdependence and solidarity between different nations can only develop with the consensus of the peoples – that is, through the creation of democratic supranational institutions. In today's world, where it no longer makes sense to discriminate between international trade and intraregional trade, the lack of a solution to the problem of a democratic governing of the international economy represents the main obstacle to economic development. The Comecon's failure does not therefore also signify socialism's failure. What has failed is simply the attempt to achieve international socialism without international democracy.

3 THE CRISIS OF INTERNATIONAL LIBERALISM

The years of frantic economic nationalism that preceded the Second World War represented the negative model of the new international order that the United States, together with its allies, prepared to build at the end of hostilities. Everyone saw the need to organize economic interdependence on the basis of permanent and common institutions, in order not to repeat the mistakes of the past. But there arose the difficult problem of who would be able to lead this effort at refounding the international order. The old hegemonic power, Great Britain, had begun to show signs of inexorable decline, such as the gradual withdrawal of the pound as reserve currency. At Bretton Woods the confrontation between the worn-out European power and the rising American super-power was thus inevitable. Diplomatic summits of this type are naturally won by the country that has the necessary means for exercising power. The United States in those years possessed a productive capacity approaching half of the world's industrial production. There was no other conceivable alternative leadership. As a result everyone accepted an international monetary system based on the dollar as reserve currency and on a fixed exchange-rate system, controlled by common monetary institutions, such as the IMF. It is worthwhile mentioning in this regard, since the problem is still very much alive today, that Keynes's proposals for the reform of the international monetary system, precisely since they reflected the point of view of a weak country, put more emphasis on the need for a collective management of the system, through the creation of a world currency, the Bancor, and a more balanced division of the rights and duties of the participating countries.

The American empire grew in a very short period of time, firmly spreading its roots in all those parts of the world where there was the problem of 'containing' the Soviet empire. The Cold War certainly explains in part the success of the American expansion in Europe and in other important areas of the world. However, to the political factor we must add the correct intuition to organize the international economy on the basis of free-trade principles. The advantage for the USA was clear. Great Britain did no differently in the nineteenth century, when it made itself the champion of the doctrine of the open market, secure in its superior competitive capacity, especially in the manufacturing sector, where it preceded all the other countries with its industrial revolution. The USA, thanks to its enormous productive potential which had emerged unscathed from the Second World War, could count on a similar comparative advantage. The European allies, victors and losers, were interested instead in facing their very serious reconstruction problems, not only being able to count on American aid but also on mutual collaboration. And the framework for this common understanding could only be guaranteed, during the Cold War years, by the strongest, American, ally.

The result of this complex process was the creation of a vast Atlantic and Pacific free-trade area. The success was impressive. During the 1950s and 1960s the world economy grew at rates unheard of during the classic gold standard years, which were nonetheless happy ones. Today many economists look back at this period with nostalgia as the 'golden age' of the international economy. And in fact we can trace back to this period the beginning of the phase of profound productive changes, which in the jargon of Eastern planners was called the 'scientific and technological revolution', and in the West is more generally known as the 'post-industrial economy'. This involved the introduction of automated production methods on a large scale, which led to a rapid growth in labour productivity, with consequent radical changes in the structure of society. In fact, there was a constant growth in gross product (and thus in welfare) in the most advanced countries, even in the presence of a reduction in the working-class population in industry, while there was a notable expansion in the service sector, both private and public services. These economic successes probably caused the gradual erosion of consensus in the USSR for the old leadership group, which was united in defence of the bureaucratic and centralist planning methods. Even in the 1960s, Khrushchev could support the doctrine of an 'overtaking' at an indefinite moment in the future. Yet by the 1970s, in particular in East Europe, where the successes of the European Community could be seen from close at hand, opinions were moving in the opposite direction: the planned economies inexorably lost ground against the more dynamic market economies. The truth could no longer be concealed. In the scientific and technological age, where important advancements in development take place not only in the large enterprises, but perhaps to an even greater extent in the small ones, in the absence of individual initiative economic development will inevitably remain imprisoned within the narrow confines traced by the bureaucrats of the plans.

Despite this outstanding success the western economic system suffered from a fundamental imbalance, whose negative effects were slowly revealed over the decades, and which had already caused, and will continue to do so to an ever greater extent, very serious breakdowns in the international economy. We are talking of the monetary problem. No market, especially in a modern-day economy which is highly interdependent in the productive and financial sectors, can function for long without monetary stability. And we must recognize that today the dollar is no longer a currency that offers guarantees of stability, as a true international currency should. This situation began to be discussed from the end of the 1950s. The economist Robert Triffin observed that the system of the gold-exchange standard based on the dollar would, sooner or later, cause an untenable situation for the reserve currency country.[4] The state of the world economy had changed markedly over the preceding 15 years. Japan and western Europe had growth rates that were much higher that those in the United States. In addition, the international exchange of goods, services and capital grew at such high rates that one could hold that trade was the real 'engine' of development. But to finance this growing trade volume dollars were needed, which could only be used by the western countries if the US balance of payments was in deficit, since the reserves in gold, which could have represented an alternative to the dollar, were growing at too low a rate with respect to currency needs. Of course it was not difficult for the United States to create a deficit in its own balance of payments and the corresponding international liquidity, but in the long term this imbalance would have undermined the trust of the financial market in the dollar's convertibility into gold.

Triffin's dilemma exactly described a structural difficulty of the international monetary system. In fact, during those years US gold reserves were gradually being transferred to the vaults of the European central banks and the real capacity of the United States to satisfy a sudden request for convertibility was beginning to be questioned. France, during de Gaulle's presidency, for example, openly contested the United States' 'exorbitant privilege' in acquiring foreign products by simply printing paper money, unlike all the other nations of the monetary system, who had to redress any deficits in their balance of payments through domestic spending cuts. A crisis was put off only by the fact that the countries who had excess dollars often refrained from asking for the conversion of their credit into gold, since they could get higher interest rates by re-utilizing their dollars in the United States itself. But in this way, as the French economist Jaques Rueff observed, 'the gold-exchange standard has succeeded in achieving the amazing revolution of conceding to those countries possessing a currency having international prestige the marvellous secret of a painless deficit, which allows one to give without taking, to make loans without borrowing, and to buy without paying'.[5]

Economic processes often reveal their effects completely only in the long term. Moreover, in the international economy these effects present themselves as spurious phenomena, in the sense that political and economic causes cannot easily be separated, unlike those which take place within states. It was thus that the crisis of the dollar became particularly acute only after the Vietnam crisis, when the United States was forced to spend heavily for defence. Toward the end of the 1960s, speculative phenomena in Europe followed one upon another owing to the economic agents' lack of trust in the stability of exchange rates, and on 15 August 1971, the American government finally declared the dollar's inconvertibility into gold. The era of fixed exchange rates begun at Bretton Woods had ended. The world economy had by then said good-bye to its period of prosperity. Shortly thereafter a continuous succession of oil crises and high inflation rates were added to the shock caused by the fluctuating exchange rates. International trade underwent a drastic reduction and the most important industrialized countries were forced to create a type of directorate – the so-called

G-7 – for the world economy, in the attempt to govern the most important international tensions together. However, the problems did not stop mounting. The third-world debt crisis is nothing other than another facet of the international monetary crisis, since at its roots lies the strong increase in interest rates that the US monetary authorities were forced to adopt in order to attract capital into the United States. In this way a situation was created which is the exact opposite of a healthy monetary system: capital flees from the poor countries to be used in the rich ones. Robert Triffin has rightly denounced this unhealthy mechanism of regressive distribution of international wealth as a *World Monetary Scandal.*

We can thus state that by the beginning of the 1990s a highly-integrated world market exists, but that there no longer exists an international currency that enjoys the full trust of economic agents. The present international monetary system consists of an immense house of cards that may cave in at the first breath of wind. The stock market crisis in 1987 was a warning sign. The attempt by the G-7 to give a unified direction to the world economy is only a palliative. It represents a defensive situation growing out of the weakness of the US economy, which seeks the collaboration of its European allies and Japan. The western governments, in fact, are not yet willing to recognize the new reality. The economic weight of the United States is today only 20% of the world total, while at the productive and commercial levels it is now often put on the ropes by the more dynamic economies of Japan and the European Community. The truth is therefore that the United States is now only a regional power in the economic field, while it continues to exercise the responsibilities of a world super-power in the military field. Moreover, in a situation in which the USSR must concentrate above all on its domestic problems, the United States runs the risk of taking on even greater world responsibilites than it can effectively manage.

International liberalism is thus in crisis. It has prospered in the immediate post-war period thanks to the natural US leadership. But today this leadership has vanished, and all the most important institutions of the international economy must be reshaped from top to bottom. The market cannot operate without rules and without a stable currency. Modern international liberalism has developed, from Adam Smith's time, under the protective wing of a hegemonic power. But is this model still practicable? Or has the time not come to attempt the way of international democracy, that is, a responsible participation of all peoples in the governing of the world market?

4 WAR AND ECONOMIC DEVELOPMENT

In the history of economic and political thought, it is only in this century that a correlation between war and economic development has emerged with a certain importance. For example, in classical economists we find considerations on finances in times of war and peace, but no important theories are put forward on the effects which industrial development would have on foreign policy, except for the obvious considerations, for example those made by Adam Smith, that the more advanced nations can rely on much more powerful military equipment than the 'uncivilized' peoples. In the liberal and democratic tradition of the first half of the nineteenth century there instead appears the conviction that there is a negative correlation between war and economic development. For Benjamin Constant 'war comes before commerce. The former represents an uncivilized impulse, the latter a civilized calculation. It is clear that the more the commercial tendency dominates the more the bellicose spirit must weaken.'[6] In Great Britain the free-trader Richard Cobden expressed himself in a similar way. The aspirations of nations for international trade are opposed to war. War can, at the most, represent the interests of sovereigns and the aristocracy. The remedy for the belligerence of the aristocratic regimes is representative government. The democratic solution at home guarantees a peaceful international order as well.

Socialist ideology, which developed in a period when the equilibria of post-Napoleonic Europe were changing as a result of Italian and German unification, began to show greater preoccupation with the growing militarism which, nevertheless, would have been defeated once socialism had been achieved at home. In 1878, Engels wrote in the *Antidühring* that 'militarism carries in itself the seeds of its own ruin', since the competition among states forces them to use more and more resources for military expenditures, until the working masses finally revolt and achieve socialism, 'and this means,' Engels concludes, 'blowing up militarism from the inside and, with it, all the permanent armies'.[7]

Until this point we can therefore state that no necessary correlation can as yet be seen between economic development and military policy. It is only towards the end of the century, when the race among the European powers for the colonization of those regions of Africa and Asia which were still free was heightened, that there appears the suspicion of a necessary link between the capitalist order, the process of accumulation and expansionist foreign policy. The first to formulate this hypothesis is the English liberal Hobson, who explained the race for colonial conquests by the need to find outlets for a productive system threatened by permanent under-consumption, due to the low salary levels. However, the most interesting theoretical debate took place within the socialist tradition. Very well known are the contributions of Rosa Luxemburg, Kautsky and Lenin, whose formula of imperialism as the ultimate phase of capitalism took hold over the entire socialist movement until recent times. During the Vietnam war, for example, two Marxist economists, Baran and Sweezy, published a study which attempted to update Lenin's theory,[8] based on the classical theory of competition, in order to take into account the operation of an economy dominated by the great trusts and by monopolistic capital. For Baran and Sweezy as well, the phenomena of imperialism and militarism were ultimately explained by the inability of the capitalist system fully to absorb its surplus product.

Today the Marxian theory of imperialism has almost been entirely abandoned by the political forces active on the international scene. This result is not of course due to the success of the scientific criticism of those who hold that the theory of imperialism is unable adequately to explain the international rivalry among the socialist states themselves, or the inexistence of armed conflicts within a state area with different degrees of capitalistic development. In politics, different points of view continue to resist tenaciously, even when effectively confuted by scientific criticism, because of their important practical implications. As far as the theory in question is concerned, since the cause of war is attributed to the capitalist system and the establishment of socialism in all countries is indicated as the remedy, it is clear why this was passionately defended, during the Cold War years, by those political forces arrayed in defence of the Eastern socialist bloc, even if it was necessary to use convoluted intellectual reasoning to justify the limited sovereignty of the East European countries with respect to the USSR, or the Sino-Russian conflict.

In order to better understand why today, after the beginning of East-West detente, the economic theory of imperialism has once and for all been discredited we must therefore refer to the new world situation. If we examine international relations as a whole and in all their complexity – thus East–West, North–South and South–South relations – we see that there no longer exists a positive correlation between armaments, imperialism and economic development. In fact, the opposite is now becoming true: that those wishing to aim for development must also aim for the transformation of the war-type economy into a peace-type economy. This represents an important feature of the 'new model of development' that is increasingly grabbing the attention of governments and peoples.

4.1 East–West relations

Detente between the United States and the USSR has not come about for purely economic reasons, though these are not at all extraneous to the process. The bipolar system of governing the world that characterized the Cold War era was based on the equilibrium of terror, that is, on a stock of nuclear armaments that, if utilized, could have placed in danger the very survival of the power that unleashed the conflict. The race for supremacy between the two military blocs imposed a continual accumulation of armaments on the super-powers, until it became clear that war could no longer be considered the continuation of politics by other means. War simply means planetary catastrophe, that is, the disappearance of civilization itself, as Einstein in fact had already warned at the beginning of the nuclear age. If we add to this the enormous amounts that the United States (by the 'star wars' project) and the USSR had to spend on armaments, thereby taking away important resources for civilian uses, then the change of course, called for by Gorbachev, and quickly taken up by Reagan, becomes understandable.

The attempt by the USSR to democratize its political system, to move from a planned economy to a market one, and to fully participate in the world market has come up against serious difficulties. The United States is finding it equally difficult to manage its left-over military responsibilities, which has led to a financial burden out of proportion to the size of its economy. However a return to the Cold War is unthinkable. The folly of a headlong race towards the accumulation of nuclear arms has been recognized by world public opinion as part of a past which can no longer return. Crises in international detente are possible, but the re-forming of the old opposing military blocs is unthinkable. On the horizon of North–North relations has appeared the hope of a new age of peaceful co-operation, which revolves around the project for a Common European Home, that is, a large open space from Vladivostok to San Francisco. For now this remains only a hope. But even hopes, when they concern peoples, have political value, since the degree of interdependence attained by modern society is so high that the governments which desire to work to smother the expectations of a peaceful world, in order to return to the icy ideological frontiers of the past, will have to openly oppose themselves to public opinion, which by now is able to make its voice heard even in the eastern countries.

4.2 North–South relations

Third-world claims for a new international economic order have followed on one another for decades now without the beginning of a true North–South dialogue. The gap in wealth between rich and poor is growing instead of being eliminated by effective co-operation plans for development. During the Cold War era this break between North and South was accompanied by a foreign policy based on political, economic and military support for those third world regimes siding with one or the other of the blocs. There thus was created a tragic trade network at whose extremes were found, on the one hand, the arms producers protected by obliging and hypocritical governments (since with their right hand they took from the poor countries what they gave in 'development aid' with their left) and, on the other, the autocratic governments of the third world that strengthened their power behind the shield of well-armed armies, that protected them both with regard to their own subjects as well as their neighbouring rivals. The result of this shameful international order has been the birth in the third world of regional microimperialisms that, while not able to promote any real progress, can threaten world equilibrium.

The Gulf war, where a coalition of western countries led by the United States opposed Iraq, was the tragic outcome of the old international order based on the balance of armaments. There are some lessons to be drawn from this dramatic event that probably marks a turning point in North–South relations. The first is that the illusion that peaceful relations between North and South can be maintained on the basis of old or new military equilibriums should now be abandoned for good. Any equilibrium is deceptive in regions undergoing rapid change, with strong differences in their supply of natural resources and wealth, and inhabited by peoples who have been humiliated for centuries by colonialist exploitation. For these peoples power and arms are synonymous, and those countries that obtain these will sooner or later want to use them. Second, the North has undergone the bitter experience that, when a conflict breaks out, the paltry amount of development aid reluctantly conceded to the poor countries, is immediately multiplied by a tenfold coefficient because of the necessary military expenditures, without considering the suffering and the enormous waste of human life that can never be compensated. Third, the third-world countries themselves must realize that the massive commitment of financial and human resources for arms has little to do with economic and social development plans, where the priority lies in civilian infrastructure spending, such as schools, hospitals, roads and so on. Co-operation for development will thus be ineffective until these countries free themselves from the constraints imposed by the military equilibriums, since economic development is inseparable from cultural, political and economic integration among different civilizations.

In conclusion, the detente between the super-powers allows us to glimpse the possibility of a new era of peace in North–North relations. But it is not right to exclude the earth's damned from the banquet, by putting up a new iron curtain between the two hemispheres. The same prospects for peace and prosperity must also involve the South. This represents a specific responsibility of the rich countries. Detente between the rich and poor means that the North must agree to take on the development problems of the South. Without this effort the cost of a failed dialogue will grow higher and higher each year, since entire continents will not passively accept, and forever, a situation of marginalization and misery.

4.3 South–South relations

The theory of imperialism is completely silent on the possibility of hegemonic attempts arising among the third world countries. And yet experience has shown that armed conflicts between under-developed countries are possible and increasingly more frequent. Large countries, such as China and India, have already undertaken hegemonic policies against bordering states, and even smaller-sized countries, such as African ones, are certainly not above this kind of temptation. In these cases it is not only a question of denouncing the waste of resources with respect to possible alternative uses. The problem is a more serious one. Governments that base their power on military forces are forced to aim at an autarkic economic development (when possible), or one dependent on military supplies from some rich country. In the best of cases, when the country is particularly rich financially (as in the Middle East) this dependence is manifested only with regard to the sellers of arms. The mirage of microimperialism thus makes one lose sight of all the advantages that could accrue from development plans integrated among several complementary economic regions. The situation is particularly serious for Africa, where extreme state fragmentation makes it practically impossible to carry out successfully any 'national' development plan.

It seems that we are correct in saying that, at the threshold of the twenty-first century, the world is forced to consider the problem of the transition from a war-type to a peace-type economy. The need for a new model of development does not, however, only come out in the area of wasteful military spending. All of mankind must also face the threat of ecological catastrophe, which requires a great effort in industrial reorganization on a planetary scale. International co-operation is no longer a choice which governments might or might not make. It is a necessity, which nevertheless comes up against the inability of present international institutions to respond to the new challenges, in order to allow for an effective democratic planning for the transition phase. We must innovate. But we do not start from scratch. Silently, and almost unbeknown to the theorists of economic development, an experiment has been promoted in Europe which can provide us with useful indications for facing the more complex problems of the development of the world economy.

5 THE EUROPEAN MODEL

Within the context of the present international equilibrium the European Community occupies an important position in the economic field: in fact, as we have said, many commentators, drawing inspiration from the doctrine of political realism, believe it legitimate to speak of international polycentrism. In fact it has been the economic success of the European Community, together with that of Japan, that has gradually made the United States resume the rank of a regional power. After the fall of the Berlin wall, the desire of East European countries to join the Community as soon as possible was clearly evident. If we add to this the negotiations under way between the EC and the countries of the European Free Trade Association (EFTA), we can see how pre-eminent the role of the Community will become in world economic policy. We are talking of an area with a population more than double that of the United States, with a per capita income only slightly lower (in some countries, such as West Germany, it is in fact greater), and with more promising growth prospects, once the initial difficult problems regarding the transition to a market economy in the Eastern countries are overcome.

We can try to enclose the reasons for Europe's success in a simple formula, even if, as usual, any attempt at schematizing an historical process inevitably simplifies, and sometimes distorts, reality. However economic analysis cannot do without the formulation of models and typologies. In this case, we can thus put forward a hypothesis according to which the reasons for this European success are found in the formula: economic integration *plus* European democracy. Let us now try briefly to justify this statement.

In the first years of post-war reconstruction, among the European political class the idea persistently circulated that without the creation of a European federation the European national states would have succeeded in repairing the damages caused by the tragic conflict only by means of unprecedented sacrifices. Yet no concrete initiative was put forth until the Americans unblocked the situation with their Marshall Plan proposal. This forced the Europeans to collaborate in the common management of the aid, and it was in this context that the political episode that was decisive for the future of Europe matured: Franco-German reconciliation. It was this sentiment of a refound cultural and civil unity among peoples of different nationalities that made it possible to propose, and have accepted by the governments and by public opinion, the first common European institutions, such as the European Coal and Steel Community (ECSC) and the European Payments Union (EPU), which played a decisive role in making possible the convertibility of the European currencies. These first attempts at unification went so far forward that it was only owing to French opposition that, in 1954, the project for a European political community, with its own defence, a government and a directly elected parliament, fell through.

It was on the basis of these first successes – and failures – along the way toward European unification that, in 1957, the Rome Treaty was signed for the creation of a European Common Market (ECM) among the six countries of 'little' Europe. This immediately turned out to be a decisive step forward, even if in practice it meant nothing other than a customs union, since during the first phase it was principally meant to eliminate the tariff barriers among the six, while keeping alive a common external tariff (which caused a very strong reaction from the United States). But the possibility of being able to operate in a continental market favourably influenced the expectations of European industry, which quickly adapted the size of its plants to the larger economic areas, thereby breaking out of the tight clothes that several decades of protectionist policies had forced on it. There thus began to be talk of a German miracle, an Italian miracle and so on. The Europe of the six grew at rates even double those of the United States and of countries, such as Great Britain, that were not wise enough to take part in the project.

During those years of rapid growth the economists who studied the problem of European integration attempted to explain the phenomenon mainly in terms of trade creation and economies of scale.[9] Of course, these explanations are satisfactory to the extent that they take into consideration the pure positive advantages of European integration. But this approach completely ignores bringing into account the costs of the failed integration. In other words, it is more correct, in a global approach, to take into consideration the fact that, if the European states had not managed to find the way towards peace and an increasingly deeper co-operation, the years following the Second World War would not have differed, in terms of relative welfare, from the years that followed the disasters of the First World War. In fact the European governments would have been forced to undertake protectionist policies and to spend considerable amounts on arms. In short, the entire economic process would have been carried out in a hostile political environment, with strict currency controls at the borders and high tariff barriers. The technology of the 1950s was not much different from that preceding the Second World War, but in a situation of strong economic nationalism it would have been very difficult to move in the succeeding phase to a modern post-industrial economy based on electronics, automation and a high standard of social services. To have some idea of the destiny that would have awaited Europe in these conditions we need only compare the different levels of affluence existing today in East Europe and the European Community, at the moment of the removal of the Berlin wall. This is not only a question of the wonders of the market, on the one hand, and the defects of planning, on the other. The productivity of labour in a closed national economy of the size of a European country like France or Czechoslovakia – not to mention Albania or Denmark – would never have attained the levels that permit us today to speak of 'the affluent society'.

The heart of the process of economic integration lies in monetary unification. Without a single currency there is no common market. Yet when the Common Market was created the Rome Treaty completely ignored the monetary aspects. This is perfectly understandable. The introduction of the monetary aspects in the Treaty would have obliged the governments to consider the problem of the transference of national monetary sovereignty to a European monetary authority. But this necessity did not present itself. In those years one could reasonably count on the assumption of the maintenance of stable exchange rates among the various national currencies. Thanks to the success of the EPU the goal of convertibility had been reached. Moreover, the Bretton Woods agreements guaranteed stable exchange rates between the European currencies and the dollar, so that it could even be said that in effect the European currency was the dollar. For example, when the Common Agricultural Policy was introduced, European prices for agricultural products were expressed in dollars (one dollar was equal to the European unit of account that was used in Community accounting).

The real difficulties only came out during the 1970s. In 1971 the dollar's inconvertibility was declared and the era of fluctuating exchange rates began. In 1973 the crisis of oil and raw materials upset the international market and opened a recessionary phase for all the western economies. The Common Market went into crisis. For the first time intracommunity trade underwent a marked slow-down, and at times a decline, owing to the return of protectionist practices among the member countries. The 'beggar my neighbour' policy lasted, however, only a few years. The integration of the European economy had solid foundations by then, and public opinion began to grow aware of the need for a relaunching of the process of unification. It was thus that, in 1979, the European Monetary System (EMS) was launched, with the aim of guaranteeing an 'area of monetary stability' in an international economy increasingly hit by monetary, financial and commercial crises. The EMS was a success, as in the following decade there was a strong recovery in the competitive capacity of the European economy with respect to Japan and the United States. In the psychology of the economic agents, Eurosclerosis had given way to Euro-optimism.

The EMS experience, though a positive one, still revealed obvious limitations. An exchange-rate agreement does not mean that in reality monetary stability will be maintained in the area in question. And in fact, since inflation rates remained different from one country to the next, parity adjustments had to be adopted on several occasions. For this reason, the idea of a central European bank, even if not approved, was immediately brought up for discussion, as well as that of the creation of a single Community currency. The day of reckoning came with the decision, in 1985, to relaunch the Common Market (under the new name of 'single market') by 1992 and, subsequently, after the fall of the Berlin wall, with German unification, which brought up the dramatic alternatives of a German Europe or a European Germany. The European Community was truly at a crossroads. Any progress towards economic integration was frustrated by the impossibility of fully taking advantage of the continental size of the market in the absence of a single currency. In addition, German unification threw a hegemonic shadow over Europe that, if it had taken concrete form, could have upset the entire Community construction, which was still based on the fragile pedestal of intergovernmental co-operation. The facts showed these worries to be unfounded. In public opinion the feeling of belonging to the European Community showed itself as already prevailing over that of left-over nationalism. German unity was completed during 1990, but at the same time the project for a single currency and a central European bank beginning in 1994 was launched.

It must be observed that the process of economic integration could develop, with its inevitable crises, during the second half of the century on the basis of a twofold push. French–German reconciliation represented the political precondition for the entire process, and the ECSC became its symbol. This initial Community institution not only took on an immediate economic objective – the common management of the (then strategic) resources of coal and steel – but also a clear-cut political aim: the European federation, which was indicated to be the arrival point of the process. Without this explicit goal it would have been very difficult, during the crises which occurred during the 1950s (after the fall of the European Defence Community) and 1970s, to raise the necessary solidarity among European countries in order to refuse a return to the national scale concept of economics and politics.

In fact at a certain point in the process economic integration would certainly have marked time, faced with the difficulty of moving toward the construction of a European single market if the political reform of the Community had not been put on the agenda. At the beginning, during the 1950s and 1960s, there was only a negative integration, in the sense that the drive towards development came mainly from the removal of domestic customs barriers. But subsequently this situation passed over to the carrying out of true common policies (agricultural, industrial, ecological, to name a few) at whose epicentre is the monetary instrument. Economic–monetary union is the coherent answer to the need to undertake common policies, but this is not possible without a common European government. According to the idea of the modern social state a similar set of decisions cannot be entrusted to purely technical bodies. For this reason the push for the realization of a European democracy has grown during the last few decades. In 1979 the European Parliament was elected by universal suffrage, and it put forward the first reform proposals of the Rome Treaty (Spinelli Project, 1984) in order to transform the Commission into a true responsible government before the Parliament. After an initial failure, the project was taken up again during the relaunching of the economic–monetary union in 1989–90. This debate is still under way. But, even if the nationalistic forces opposed to European unification are still very active, we can foresee that it will be very difficult to create a central bank without conceding the necessary powers of control over the economy to the Community's democratic institutions (the European Parliament); powers that the national authorities for economic policy have in any event by now lost.

Before concluding it would be as well to point out a decisive characteristic of the Community model. The federalist approach allows us to conceive of a process of integration in the form of concentric circles, in which a central nucleus of countries can represent the hub for the co-operation and association of other countries, until the practical conditions are ripe for their complete membership. This is thus an essentially anti-imperialist model of integration. The history of Community relations is rather significant. Several Mediterranean countries, such as Spain, Greece and Portugal, were able to join the Community of the six as soon as they had rid themselves of their dictatorial regimes, and after a brief transition period, in order not to expose their industries too suddenly to competition from the Community ones. This same process is getting under way for the East European countries. Furthermore, even with regard to the third world the Community, with the Lomé Convention, has shown that it has placed the North–South dialogue on non-hegemonic institutional bases. This represents the first multilateral co-operation agreement for development whose management is entrusted to a joint assembly made up of European, African, Caribbean and Pacific countries.

The Community is not a perfect model of integration, for the simple reason that it has not yet been able to institute an effective democratic mechanism for the governing of the economy. Nevertheless, it surely represents the most advanced model of international democracy, from which lessons can be drawn for facing the dramatic problems regarding the development of the contemporary world economy.

6 THE WORLD TOWARDS A NEW MODEL OF DEVELOPMENT

No matter how open the European model of economic integration is to new members, we must recognize that Europe is not the entire world; that is, at the world level problems will come up which are not only on a larger scale, but which are also qualitatively different from those the European Community has faced. Of course, in all the continents processes of regional integration are under way. Latin America has tried several times to undertake projects similar to the European common market. In recent years there has begun to be talk of an economic union between the United States, Canada and Mexico, going even so far as to consider a free-trade area from Alaska to the Tierra del Fuego. In Asia there are continental-sized states such as China and India (which already has a federal structure). In addition, the Association of South-East Asian Nations (ASEAN) might be induced to follow the example of the EC, by strengthening its political institutions. Similar movements of regional or subregional integration can be seen in Africa (such as the Economic Community of West-African States, ECOWAS) as well as in the Middle East, where, despite the region's precarious equilibrium, the Arab League has taken on the difficult objective of the unity of the Arab nations. Nevertheless, the problem of the governing of the world economy as a whole remains fundamental, since after the events which have ended the Cold War phase the world is asking itself about its future. What role will the two super-powers have? Will new economic–military poles arise which are able to take on responsibilities similar to those of the United States and the USSR? In other words, is the present polycentric equilibrium, which until now has manifested itself only in the economic field, destined to become a politico-military equilibrium among five or more world super-powers?

The theory of political realism does not permit us to give sure answers, or even answers which are more likely than others. It is true that in the past we have witnessed significant changes in the international equilibrium, as occurred during this century when the European state system was replaced by the world bipolar system. But the present situation does not have the same features. The tendency to form new world super-powers is not in fact inescapable. To the degree that new super-powers emerge alongside the two traditional ones, by now in decline, the world could relive a phase of international tensions very similar to those that characterized the beginning of the Cold War, even if the greater interdependence and the ever-present threat of the use of nuclear arms would recommend a much more prudent management of the inevitably opposing interests to all states. On the contrary, the consensus that the new phase of detente between the United States and the USSR has aroused in all continents is a sign of how permeated world public opinion now is by 'democratic pacifism'. A system of international relations based on an equilibrium between super-powers, and thus on the possibility of the outbreak of nuclear conflicts, would not only be radically in contrast with the development needs of the modern economy, but would also leave little hope for third world development. This would in fact be a strongly reactionary system, since the constant search for power, or the maintenance of an already-achieved equilibrium between a few large world poles, would tend to exclude any process of change whose outcome might be a greater equality among peoples. In short, international political realism – whose conceptual core is nothing but a set of analytical concepts for understanding political events – is often used to justify the existing power equilibriums by those political forces that, consciously or unconsciously, exclude the emancipation of the third world and the overcoming of power politics from their conceptual horizon.

In the contemporary world, on the contrary, it is perhaps more 'realistic' (in the same sense in which during the French Revolution it was realistic to take the side of the critics of the *ancien régime*) to pursue a project that has the fundamental objectives of international democracy and the equality of all peoples on its agenda. In any event, it is not a case here of making predictions, but of indicating those lines of action which are more practicable than others, on the basis of the degree of development of the world economy and international political relations. So, if the analysis we have undertaken has some foundation, there are two structural features that should condition any future international economic policy: an ever-increasing degree of economic integration on a world scale and an increasingly unpropitious effect of military spending on the development capacities of both the industrialized and under-developed countries. The conservative use of the doctrine of political realism, even while taking into account these circumstances, directs thought and action towards the maintenance of national sovereignty, guaranteed by one's own arms and currency. The European example shows, on the other hand, that the construction of a supranational community of states (an international state) is possible in which the independence of each state gradually becomes co-ordinated with the legitimate need for independence of the other state units. The greatest contemporary tragedies, including the supreme one of war, occur precisely because of the failure to recognize the need to democratically organize the interdependence between various political communities. In an increasingly more cosmopolitan world, the defence to the bitter end of the nineteenth-century principle of the closed national state represents the main obstacle to social–economic development. The modern economy – unlike the ancient (based on slavery) and mediaeval ones (based on serfdom) – is based on the principle of free and creative work, which can occur to a greater extent the vaster and more competitive is the market in which a certain productive activity is carried on. For this reason, the tendency towards an increasingly strong integration of the world market is in itself a factor of dynamism and development.

Thus, in the new era of international politics the way of democratic pacifism is practicable and necessary, in order to spare humanity further suffering and disasters and to allow all peoples to participate in a global development project. Of course, democratic pacifism has fallen into disrepute in the past, owing to its naive and primitive formulation (such as Constant's). It should thus be stated that, in order not to commit the same errors of liberal and socialist internationalism, today's renewed democratic pacifism has to be supported by suitable international institutions, which are provided with limited but real powers. To this end the model of integration already experimented with by the European Community can point the way, if we take several important differences into account. While the European Community has been able to initiate its unification experiment on the basis of a common feeling of reconciliation among peoples who had already acquired democratic liberties, these preconditions are either missing or exist to a small degree on the world scene. East–West detente undoubtedly represents the condition for a new policy of co-operation among the most important industrialized countries, which will surely have positive repercussions as well on North–South relations. But we must keep in mind that for a long period, at the world level, age-old, sometimes centuries-old, rivalries between different civilizations will have to be overcome.

For this reason the United Nations (UN), the organization in which until now all the peoples of the world have agreed to talk, when this has been possible, is the only institutional framework in which it seems possible to develop a serious policy of cultural integration and economic–political co-operation. Naturally the UN suffers from all the defects of an institution that arose during a phase of incipient Cold War, where all the main levers of control were monopolized by the victorious powers. Now that the Cold War is over and the construction of a new international order is on the agenda, the main objective of the forces of renewal should consist of the democratic reform of the UN. History teaches us that equality does not exist right from the start, but is the fruit of a struggle between individuals who enjoy the same rights. Yet at the world level there is still no constitutional pact, such as exists in all democratic regimes, which would make the struggle for equality effective. For this reason the peoples – individually and collectively, as the expression of an emerging common world citizenship – must draw up the new rules of international democracy, with the awareness that it will not be possible to construct, as in the already-existing states, a systematic and organic legal system by means of a single provision, as can occur within a state already in existence. The new world of international democracy can only spring from a long and difficult process of trial and error. It is nevertheless true that, from this perspective, the UN will, at the same time, have to become more and more the propelling centre for reform and the government of international relations.

Let us now consider the three most important areas of intervention on which actions for the renewal of world politics should concentrate.

6.1 Collective security

Detente between the super-powers and the beginning of the disarmament process will not become a permanent feature of international relations until the UN assumes effective powers for monitoring and guaranteeing that states will not go beyond the agreed-upon arms levels. No state should exceed the agreed-upon minimum threshold according to the doctrine of the defensive defence. Moreover, since tensions in North–South relations will continue for a very long time, the UN should be made able to carry out an autonomous international policing role (consider for instance the Middle East case), thereby assuring that states or coalitions of states are not induced to use their own military means to resolve local controversies. Finally, the UN must carry out an increasingly active role in the control and repression of arms sales.

6.2 Stability and development of the world economy

Ever since the dollar ceased to be able to carry out its function as international currency there has been insistent talk of a new Bretton Woods. The need to restore a system of stable exchange rates at the world level is clear to all. But we cannot ignore the fact that the strength of the dollar was based on the leadership capacity of the American economy over the western world. An international monetary system cannot be built on sand. Some solid foundations are indispensable. For this reason, it is unlikely that a serious reform can be started until the European Community is able to use its own money for international payments and until the USSR succeeds in making the ruble convertible. If these conditions should take place, then it will become possible, as occurred with the EMS, to reform the present-day IMF at the world level in order to permit it to issue its own monetary unit (similar to the current special drawing rights – SDRs) based on a basket composed of dollars, the European currency, yen, rubles, and any other currency that feels it can play a reserve currency role.

In the second place, the UN must be able to begin to undertake an autonomous role in promoting third world economic development. To this end its capacity to regulate international credit (no longer subject to influence by individual countries) becomes essential, as well as the possession of its own budget resources. Concrete proposals in this regard already exist (such as those contained in the Law of the Sea). But it is clear that any step forward in this direction is not possible without a political reform of the decision-making system (no taxation without representation).

6.3 Ecological restructuring of the world economy

Ever since the ecological problem took on a world dimension it has become clear that without the possibility of enforcing respect of international standards (that is, without an international legislation) no country has any interest in 'virtuous' behaviour in ecological matters. In fact, the 'polluter pays principle' cannot be applied without an authority having law enforcement powers: the individual country, on the other hand, has an opposing interest to the extent that the introduction of environmental technologies is more costly than retaining the traditional polluting technologies.

But that is not the only question. The UN has already promoted a fertile debate on the prospects of a sustainable development, whose end is to not compromise, by irrationally exploiting the existing environmental resources, the welfare of future generations. It is necessary not only to co-ordinate several policies which states already intend to undertake, but also to promote completely new development prospects. Let us consider the attempts of the third world to industrialize. If these countries are successful in imitating the production and consumption models of the rich countries, then very soon world growth will become even more 'unsustainable'. Consider in fact how much air pollution will increase if all the planet's inhabitants had a per capita consumption of automobiles, oil, electrical appliances, residences and so on, similar to that of present-day affluent societies. But can the modern world give up oil, automobiles and the rest? And what are the alternative technologies? What is needed is a radical reform which must involve all countries, however small and backward. Only an intense debate within the UN and the assumption of its precise responsibilities in the area of scientific research, the exploitation of natural resources, industrial policies and so on will permit the necessary change of course to be made in the world production system.

Before concluding, it should be made clear that the development of common policies cannot initially involve all the planet's states. As occurred within the European Community, the development of common policies will require the UN to be reformed at the same time in order to guarantee a greater participation and an effective power of control of all peoples in its governing. It is of course not possible here, nor necessary, to point out the specific reforms that it will be necessary to introduce in order to turn the UN into a true planetary 'common home'. It is nevertheless natural to expect that at first only those peoples who have already affirmed the values of democracy and of the respect of the rights of man within their own states will fully participate in the world government, while those states which still deny the fundamental political rights to their citizens should be excluded. But it is also to be hoped, and expected, that the world democratic revolution, to the extent to which the UN begins to exist as a new subject in international politics, will spread more and more quickly thanks to the support of all the individuals and peoples who consider the value of a common world citizenship as prevailing over the cultural, religious and racial prejudices on which the dictators base their power.

NOTES

1. Among the numerous works by H. Kissinger see, for example, *Observations. Selected Speeches and Essays, 1982–84* (Boston, Mass.: Little, Brown, 1985); and by P. Kennedy, *The Rise and Fall of the Great Powers. Economic Change and Military Conflict from 1500 to 2000* (London: Unwin-Hyman, 1988), in particular the Epilogue; in addition, on the theory of political realism in international relations cf. Kenneth N. Waltz, *Theory of International Politics* (New York: Newbery Award Records, 1979).
2. J. Stalin, 'The October Revolution and the Tactic of the Russian Communists', *Pravda*, 20 December 1924.
3. The citation is taken from the volume *Il Piano Marshall e l'Europa* (edited by Elena Aga Rossi) (Roma: Istituto della Enciclopedia Italiana, 1983) p. 37.
4. R. Triffin, *Gold and the Dollar Crisis. The Future of Convertibility* (New Haven, Conn.: Yale University Press, 1960).
5. J. Rueff, 'Le problème monétaire de l'Occident', in *L'âge de l'inflation* (Paris: Payot, 1963) p. 134.
6. B. Constant, *De l'Esprit de Conquête*, 1813.
7. F. Engels, *Antidühring*, Part II, ch. III, in *Karl Marx Frederick Engels, Collected Works*, vol. 25 (London: Lawrence & Wishart, 1987).
8. P. Baran and P. Sweezy, *Monopoly Capital, An Essay on the American Economic and Social Order* (New York: Monthly Review Press, 1966).
9. For a survey of the theories of economic integration during those years see Bela Balassa, *The Theory of Economic Integration* (London: George Allen & Unwin, 1961).

Conclusions: Thoughts on the Future

Gianni Vaggi

1 ECONOMIC THEORY AND THE DEVELOPMENT CRISIS OF THE 1980s: TOWARDS 2000 AND BEYOND

Development theory has learnt a lot from the economic events of the last decade. There are still controversial issues between the orthodox neoclassical approach and heterodox views, such as the 'structuralist' approach. However, on several questions a common understanding has been reached, or at least the area of disagreement has been greatly diminished (see, for instance, Taylor, 1988, ch. 5); let us briefly recall some of them here.

(a) Sound domestic policies are now widely recognized as a key feature of any development strategy. Fiscal discipline, and above all the implementation of an acceptable system of income tax collection – a fundamental requisite of structural adjustment programmes – is no longer under dispute. Good 'governance' and the avoidance of corruption and of pharaonic projects, that is to say 'white elephants', are unanimously regarded as essential elements of sustainable growth.
(b) The limits of stabilization and adjustment programmes which have characterized more than a decade of economic policy in LDCs are now clear. Devaluation has not always produced the expected results in terms of GDP growth. Faini and de Melo have shown from a sample of 83 countries that real exchange-rate depreciation which was designed to shift resources from non-tradable to tradable activities has generally reduced domestic absorption and above all investment, thus producing contractionary economic effects (see Faini and de Melo, 1990, pp. 13–16, 21; see also Faini et al. 1989).
(c) Debt relief and debt forgiveness cannot by themselves produce higher growth, but the removal of the 'debt overhang' is a necessary, though in itself not sufficient step to promote a favourable external

environment for developing countries. New lending by commercial banks and direct foreign investments will take place only if the international community is convinced that a country will not go bankrupt and that it will be likely to enjoy a period of economic growth. Free profit repatriation is an important component of the optimistic atmosphere but the decisive element is the explicit support of international organizations and of rich countries. A powerful trustee, who possibly endorses the new and old foreign commitments of an indebted country is the best 'collateral' to restore confidence and trade opportunities.

The Mexican case fits well into this paradigm. In 1989, the United States clearly showed by proposing the Brady Plan that it was not going to allow its southern neighbour to go bankrupt. Extremely favourable reschedulings of maturing debts cut net payments to creditors by four billion dollars a year from 1989 to 1994, and the new bonds were endorsed by the United States. This new climate produced some repatriation of previous capital flights (see Van Wijnbergen 1991), and all these events helped to reduce both the foreign financing gap and domestic interest rates. The confidence crisis in the Mexican economy seems to have been largely overcome and direct investments by American firms have been flowing south from the Texan border. Moreover the products of these border-line factories have been granted admission to the American market. These are important elements explaining the present (1992) Mexican miracle, with the exception of real wages that from 1982 to 1991 went down by 40 per cent. In the second half of the 1980s Mexico implemented some classical economic adjustment measures: liberalization, deregulation and privatisation. Notwithstanding all these actions, no economic recovery would have been possible without the possibility of reaping some of the benefits of the proximity to a large and rich market. (The role of effective demand and of large markets in economic growth had already been underlined by Adam Smith more than two centuries ago.)

(d) An outward oriented development strategy has always been supposed to produce good economic performances in contrast to an inward oriented attitude (see World Bank 1987, pp. 83–4). Outward orientation is often confused with export promotion and with commitment to '*laissez-faire*', while inward-oriented countries should be those which follow an import-substitution strategy. Thus the antithesis between outward and inward oriented policies is often considered as the same thing as that between the state and the market.

Nowadays it is clear that economic success by means of export-led growth does not necessarily mean the repudiation of planning and of direct state intervention. Many myths about the economic miracles of South Korea and Taiwan have been reinterpreted; in both countries the state played a robust and decisive role. Public enterprises were widely used, credit was channelled to specific sectors, the terms of trade between industry and agriculture were set according to political decisions, some sectors and national firms were heavily protected from foreign competition and so on (see Wade, 1991; Leipziger and Petri, 1986).

Recently a new classification of countries has been introduced which highlights the make-up of their exports (see, for instance, International Monetary Fund, 1990, pp. 106–7). According to their predominant exports developing countries are basically divided into three major groups: commodity exporters, which export mainly primary products and raw materials; fuel exporters; and manufacturing exporters. In the latter group we find the countries with the highest growth rates during the last 20 years – the four Asian NICs plus Israel, Thailand, Turkey and so on. The countries in this group have also been the most successful in adapting to the external macroeconomic shocks of the 1970s and 1980s (see Faini and de Melo, 1990, pp. 3, 19).

Classification according to predominant exports also reflects the production structure of a country. The ability to produce and to sell manufactures on international markets, preferably different types of manufactured products, is an important indication that a development process has been triggered; the country is already in a phase of *démarrage*. Such a diversified production structure is usually characterized by a significant degree of horizontal and vertical integration. Moreover, an economy characterized by diversified manufacturing exports is also likely to be able to innovate productive processes and to produce new goods. The capacity to generate technical progress indicates that a self-sustaining growth path has been achieved and that the economy can react to domestic and foreign shocks.

Looking at the recent success stories of the East Asian NICs, and at the earlier experience of Japan, the real problem does not seem to be that of whether a country must promote exports or substitute imports, but rather *when* the economy has achieved a degree of horizontal and vertical integration sufficient to successfully enter the game of international competition. From this point of view the opposition between outward- and inward-oriented policies loses much of its importance. The often berated view of development as a sequence of 'phases', one of which is likely to be characterized by import substitution, also needs fresh reconsideration.

2 SUSTAINABLE DEVELOPMENT AND INTERNATIONAL TRADE

Economic theory and above all recent experiences indicate some of the prerequisites for LDCs to start economic growth. The growth experiences of South Korea and Taiwan may not be easy to replicate, nevertheless development will probably occur for some third-world countries. Of course there is the problem related to the possibility of many LDCs simultaneously following an export-led growth strategy. By looking at the experience of the four Asian NICs it seems clear that some other economies must reduce their shares in world demand (see International Monetary Fund, 1990, p. 27). The increasing competition from developing countries' manufactures may influence the output of high-income economies. It is possible that some LDCs could experience a 'regressive' economic process, because of their inability to sustain competition on the international markets for manufacturing.

Moreover, the final outcome – a friendly society – may be different from what was expected. Some countries may not develop at all, others may develop, but with 'undesirable' economic, social and political attributes. All these themes are on the agenda of development economics and ask for a reconsideration of the 'grand issues' of long-term development and structural change (see Stern, 1989, pp. 614ff).

We wish to draw attention to two issues which are at the core of any sustainable development process in the coming century: *North–South trade relationships* and the *time element*, that is to say, the time required for an improvement of the social and economic conditions in developing countries. These are not new problems, but perhaps all the implications for high-income economies of providing satisfactory solutions to both problems have not yet been fully examined. The last two sections of this conclusion are intended to stimulate further investigations on these two issues.

3 NORTH–SOUTH TRADE

In the third world, economic growth can only result from a *comprehensive strategy* made up of three major elements: debt forgiveness, sound domestic policies and a favourable external environment. We have already examined both domestic policies and debt forgiveness; let us also bear in mind that a substantial cancellation of old debts is particularly necessary in the short to medium term in order to ease the debt burden on the people of severely indebted countries. Debt forgiveness is the only measure which can have an mmediate positive impact on the living standards of these people. Unfortunately debt cancellation may be less effective in the long-term; apart from the fact of removing the 'debt overhang', debt forgiveness by itself does not guarantee that developing countries are freed from the danger of falling into a debt trap.

In order to achieve long-term economic growth there must be a favourable external environment, which includes at least two conditions: (1) stability of international financial and commodity markets, thus avoiding sudden changes in real rates of interest; and (2) trade liberalization, in the sense of ensuring that LDCs products have access to the rich markets of OECD countries, where 'potential' demand is also 'effective' demand. Let us examine condition (1) first. Terms of trade may turn against commodity producers, which will then suffer from a shortage of foreign currency which will subsequently be a binding constraint on economic growth. Algeria and Nigeria are typical cases of countries whose debt indicators and macroeconomic aggregates dramatically worsened in the second half of the 1980s, because of the slump in the price of oil.

As for condition (2), many LDCs which are primary commodity producers suffer badly because of protectionist agricultural policies of rich countries, and in particular of the EC. However, manufacturing exporters are also badly hit because rich countries continue to protect their domestic markets. Bangladesh, a country with more than 110 million people and with a GNP per capita of 170 dollars in 1988, is an example of the damage done by protectionist policies of high-income countries. During the 1980s the development of a textile industry had been constrained because of the quota restrictions set on its exports to high-income countries under the Multifibre Arrangement (MFA) (see World Bank, 1990, p. 123). It has been calculated that a removal of bilateral MFA quotas and tariffs on textiles and apparel in high-income countries would result in a 38 per cent increase in the value of production of this industry for Bangladesh and the figure becomes almost 80 per cent for Brazil (see Trela and Whalley 1990, p. 1191).

It is worth remembering that OECD countries, with a population of roughly 765 million people, account for 75 per cent of the world GNP; an unequivocal measure of the ability to buy and of the capability to pay of high-income countries as opposed to that of the remaining 4700 million people. The elimination of tariffs and non-tariff barriers would produce more than 100 per cent increase in North–South trade and above all it would result in a manyfold increase in the volume of net exports of agricultural commodities and of non-mechanical manufactures of the South to the North (see Markusen and Wigle, 1990, pp. 1212–14). Moreover, this trade liberalization would pass on its beneficial effects also in terms of a larger South–South trade (see section 1 above).

The size of the market, how much it matters, is again evident. 'Supply' conditions are certainly extremely important in favouring economic development, but without major changes in North–South trade relationships sound domestic policies could not deliver the desired economic effects.

4 THE TIME CONSTRAINT

The second consideration we want to put forward does not concern the hoped-for outcome of the development process, but rather its timing, and also the nature and the quality of the process itself. Can we be sure that the road to economic welfare will not be either too slow, or too chaotic, or too costly for those people involved?

Sustainable development is not only a sensible use of natural resources, nor can it be described simply as being a self-reliant and self-propelling economy. Sustainable development is also a process which during its unfolding also improves the human condition. Therefore, the time profile and the features of the process itself are relevant. This is not only for obvious humanitarian reasons, but also because in our 'global village', where the media openly reveals large differences in the human condition, the outcome of the process may vary greatly, depending on the path which is followed. A development process itself may not be sustainable, or tolerable, if it consists only of promises for future generations and of sacrifices for the present one.

We know the present situation of the global economy, we also have some medium-term forecasts; during the last decade of the twentieth century economic growth is expected to take place in all world regions. But in most LDCs the growth rates are not likely to attain the high values of the 1960s and 1970s. The gap between rich and poor countries will persist and it may even increase.

The year 1989 has brought major political changes to Eastern European countries, implicitly regarded as the 'second world', whose economic systems are now facing a phase of transition towards full integration in the world economy. This, however, implies a new and large demand pressure on official aid and on commercial credit on international financial markets, which did not exist in the 1970s and 1980s.

If we add demographic considerations, the short- and medium-term picture looks even less encouraging. In many African countries population increases by as much as 3 or 4 per cent annually, which means a doubling time of one generation, or even less. Birth rates will probably decrease, but this takes time. Do we have this time? Probably we have, but we had better not wait until the twenty-first century.

The late 1980s and early 1990s have seen increasing awareness among scholars and international organizations that the process of transition now taking place in eastern economies and the economic recovery of many developing countries cannot be left to market forces alone. Here too the traditional antagonism between market mechanisms and state intervention should leave room for more fruitful considerations.

Nowadays social safety nets are seen as a necessary prerequisite to alleviate the shocks of economic changes in Eastern Europe and to mitigate the harsh living conditions which accompany structuctural adjustment programmes. Safety nets operate as a buffer mechanism and also include interventions on the market machine, which includes the labour market (see World Bank, 1991b, p.1; Fischer and Gelb, 1990, pp. 14–15); they also consider an active role for the state in supporting the poorest (see World Bank, 1990, pp. 90–1).

In 1759 Adam Smith wrote (Smith, 1759, p. 9):

> How selfish soever man may be supposed, there are evidently some principles in his nature, which interest him in the fortune of others, and render their happiness necessary to him, though he derives nothing from it except the pleasure of seeing it. Of this kind is pity or compassion, the emotion which we feel for the misery of others.

It may be that social safety nets are a modern substitute for eighteenth-century 'universal benevolence' (ibid., p. 235), and for that compassionate disposition which was supposed to be in-built in human nature, and which would temper both self-interest and the rude effects of the market.

In order to achieve sustainable development, during the next decades North–South economic relationships need to be governed. In the coming years both domestic policies and international economic conditions must guarantee not only '"a market-friendly" approach to development' (World Bank, 1991a, p. 1), but above all a *people-friendly* development process. This must be the primary concern of rich countries and of international organizations. We have both the resources and the technical knowledge to make this more a possibility than a hope. However, the successful achievement of a 'human-face' development path in the second and third worlds depends largely on a timely intervention by high-income countries and on the amplitude and quality of the assistance they will provide.

REFERENCES

FAINI, R., J. DE MELO, A. SENHADJI-SEMLALI and J. STANTON (1989) 'Growth-Oriented Adjustment Programs: A Statistical Analysis', *Luca d'Agliano Development Studies Working Papers*, no. 14, September.

FAINI, R. and J. DE MELO (1990) 'Adjustment, Investment and the Real Exchange Rate in Developing Countries', *The World Bank PRE Working Papers Series*, no. 473, August.

FISCHER, S. and A. GELB (1990) 'Issues in Socialist Economy Reforms', mimeo, November.

INTERNATIONAL MONETARY FUND (1990) *World Economic Outlook*, October.

LEIPZIGER, D. and P. PETRI (1986) 'Korean Incentive Policies Towards Industry and Agriculture', paper presented at the VIIIth World Congress of the International Economic Association, Delhi, December.

MARKUSEN, J. R. and R. M. WIGLE (1990) 'Explaining the Volume of North–South Trade, *The Economic Journal*, vol. 100, no. 403, December.

SMITH, A. (1759) *The Theory of Moral Sentiments*, D. D. Raphael and A. L. Macfie (eds), Oxford: Clarendon Press, 1976.

STERN, N. (1989) 'The Economics of Development: A Survey', *The Economic Journal*, vol. 99, no. 397, September.

TAYLOR, L. (1988) *Varieties of Stabilization Experience*, Oxford: Clarendon Press.

TRELA, I. and J. WHALLEY (1990) 'Global Effects of Developed Country Trade Restrictions on Textiles and Apparel', *The Economic Journal*, vol. 100, no. 403, December.

WADE, R. (1991) *Governing the Market: Economic Theory and the Role of Government in East Asian Industrialisation*, Princeton: Princeton University Press.

VAN WIJNBERGEN, S. (1991) 'Mexico and the Brady Plan', *Economic Policy*, April.

WORLD BANK (1987) *World Development Report 1987*, Oxford: Oxford University Press.

WORLD BANK (1990) *World Development Report 1990*, Oxford: Oxford University Press.

WORLD BANK (1991a) *World Development Report 1991*, Oxford: Oxford University Press.

WORLD BANK (1991b) *World Bank News*, vol. X, no. 23, June 6.

Index